P9-DBI-241

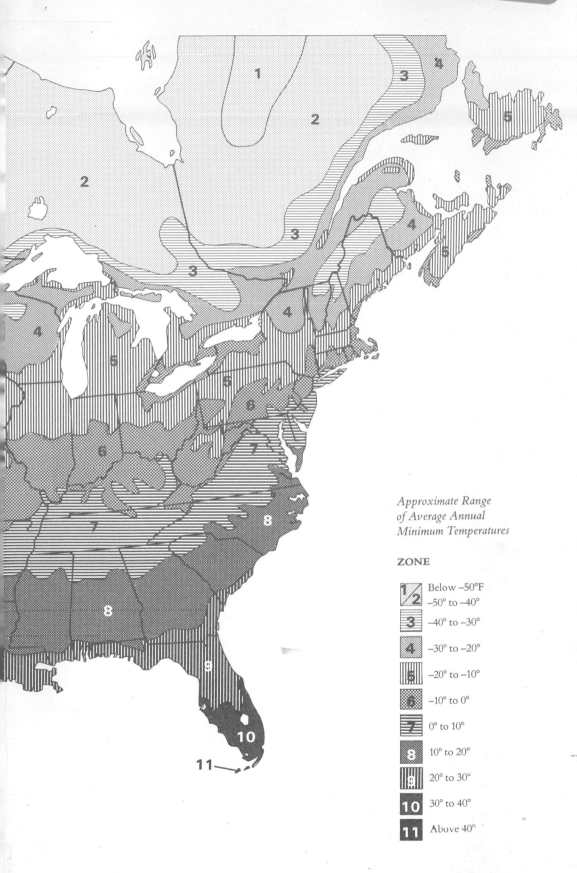

Approximate Range
of Average Annual
Minimum Temperatures

ZONE

1 / 2	Below −50°F
	−50° to −40°
3	−40° to −30°
4	−30° to −20°
5	−20° to −10°
6	−10° to 0°
7	0° to 10°
8	10° to 20°
9	20° to 30°
10	30° to 40°
11	Above 40°

IN MEMORY OF:

Floyd Carter
Marcile Clay
Byron McCoy

PRESENTED BY:

Van Wert Men's
Garden Club

THE

PLANT CARE

MANUAL

BRUMBACK LIBRARY
The plant care manual :
Buczacki, Stefan T.   635.9 BUC
NF   c1

3 3045 00032 6542

931969 $26.00
635.9   Buczacki, Stefan T
BUC   The plant care
                    manual

THE BRUMBACK LIBRARY
OF VAN WERT COUNTY
VAN WERT, OHIO

GAYLORD

THE
PLANT CARE
MANUAL

BY
STEFAN BUCZACKI

The Essential

Guide to Caring

for and

Rejuvenating

Over 300

Garden Plants

635.9
Buc

CROWN PUBLISHERS, INC.
NEW YORK

Where measurements are given for plants, the height is given first, followed by the spread.

Copyright © 1992 by Stefan Buczacki
Copyright © 1992 design and layout by
Conran Octopus Limited

All rights reserved. No part of this book
may be reproduced or transmitted in any
form or by any means, electronic or
mechanical, including photocopying,
recording, or by any information storage and
retrieval system, without permission in
writing from the publisher.

Published by Crown Publishers, Inc., 201
East 50th Street, New York, New York
10022. Member of the Crown Publishing
Group.
Random House, Inc. New York, Toronto,
London, Sydney, Auckland
Originally published in Great Britain by
Conran Octopus Ltd. in 1992.
CROWN is a trademark of Crown
Publishers, Inc.
Manufactured in Great Britain

**Library of Congress Cataloging-in-
Publication Data**

Buczacki, S. T.
    The plant care manual : the essential
guide to caring for and rejuvenating over
300 garden plants / by Stefan Buczacki. —
1st American ed.
        p.   cm.
    Includes index.
    "Originally published in Great Britain
by Conran Octopus Ltd. in 1992"—T.p.
verso.
    1. Plants, Ornamental.   I. Title.
SB407.B83   1993   92–34230
635.9—dc20   CIP
            ISBN 0–517–59283–5
            10 9 8 7 6 5 4 3 2 1
            First American Edition

Americanization:
Marjorie Dietz
with *Valerie Buckingham*
and *Beverley LeBlanc*

Illustrators:
Liz Pepperell (Plant portraits)
Vanessa Luff (Techniques)
Kay Schuckhart (Cover design)

CONTENTS

Introduction

This book is a guide to looking after the plants in your garden, and its principal purpose is to ensure that you obtain the most from them by feeding, watering, pruning, and otherwise caring for them in the best possible way. Because problems often arise as a result of mistakes in the choice of plants for particular locations, I have also provided some information on the requirements of certain varieties and guidance on how to plant them. Each chapter deals with a different category of plants – shrubs, climbers, herbaceous perennials, and so on – and discusses the care and treatment relevant to each group. Sometimes my advice may differ from that given in other gardening books, but my recommendations are based on personal experience and the procedures I suggest are those that I have found most successful. In the few instances where I discuss plants that I have not grown myself, I have taken the advice of fellow gardeners whose opinions I respect.

To cater for gardens over as wide a geographical area as possible, I generally refer in my recommendations to seasons rather than individual months. For gardeners in Britain and Western Europe, I interpret winter as December to February, spring as March to May, summer as June to August, and fall as September to November. The seasons are similar in the USA and Canada but the climates and weather may differ.

In discussing specific plants, I begin in every case with their site and soil requirements because inappropriate conditions are so often the cause of problems. The characteristics of all soils are defined by their texture and their structure. There is little you can do to alter the texture, which results from the relative proportions of sand, silt, and clay particles present. A high percentage of minute clay particles makes for a "heavy" soil, which is slow to warm up in spring but then retains heat well. It is rich in nutrients but poorly aerated, so root penetration is difficult and slow. Because of the close compaction of the clay particles, a heavy soil is poorly drained and may even become water-logged at certain times of the year. By contrast, a "light" soil has a high proportion of large sand particles and drains easily, thus losing both water and nutrients (by inference,

plants will require feeding more frequently); it warms up quickly in spring so growth may start early, but it cools down quickly, too, meaning that the growing season may be short.

If you cannot alter fundamentally the texture of the soil, you can, however, do a great deal to change its structure, which results from its "pore and crumb" composition. A well-structured soil consists of the right balance between pores, for aeration and drainage, and solid matter, the crumbs, containing nutrients. The extent to which soil particles bind together to form crumbs with pore spaces in between depends on the presence of the natural glue-like substances contained in organic matter. Paradoxically, therefore, both a heavy, waterlogged clay and a light free draining sand will be improved by the addition of organic material.

Watering and feeding are crucially important; very few plants will give of their best without the addition of some fertilizer to supplement that naturally available in the soil. I have, however, tried to keep matters as simple as possible, and I don't expect your garden shed to house a complete range of different blends of fertilizer to suit the individual requirements of every plant. Most of my recommendations can be satisfied with the following products: a balanced, general purpose fertilizer such as Gardentone or Plantone (organic) or 5–10–5 (commercial), bonemeal, a proprietary rose fertilizer, and a soluble or liquid fertilizer with a high potash content. For a few plants growing on alkaline soils, a fertilizer containing sequestered iron will help to control leaf yellowing (chlorosis).

I am a great believer in mulching, which I consider to be one of the most important of all gardening tasks. An organic mulch applied once or preferably twice each year will serve the dual roles of keeping the soil moist and of suppressing weed growth. And the best source of organic mulching material is the compost bin. Composting is an essential part of good gardening practice, and it also provides a means of recycling most garden and household waste. A compost shredder will render even woody material suitable for composting.

The scope of *The Plant Care Manual* is confined to medium- and long-term plants, some of which, like trees and shrubs, retain an above-ground woody framework, whereas others die down to a rootstock or some underground storage organ such as a bulb, corm, tuber, or rhizome. Trees and shrubs will often require pruning, and correct pruning technique is usually the key to their success as garden plants. I have therefore devoted a substantial part of the book to this aspect of plant care, and a good set of pruning tools should be high on your list of garden equipment. It makes sense to buy the best-quality pruners you can afford (preferably both the anvil variety for hard, woody material, and the scissor or by-pass type for softer stems), loppers, and a curved pruning saw.

But with the best will and the best management in the world, things sometimes go wrong. Pruning may be inadequate, pests and diseases may strike, or you may simply have inherited problems in taking over a garden whose plants have been neglected. This is where my troubleshooting advice may help because in many – perhaps in most – cases plants can be rejuvenated and rescued; you need to know what to do, how drastic your treatment can be, and when it should be undertaken. Pest and disease problems could fill a book on their own, but it is useful to be able to recognize the really common ones and know how to respond. Even though no husbandry will eliminate every problem, a well-fed, well-watered plant growing in optimum conditions will be the most likely to recover.

In most of the chapters I have given brief descriptions of the best ways to propagate the plants discussed. This is partly because I believe this is one of the most satisfying aspects of plant care, but also because in many cases rejuvenation (either on a regular basis or as a way of troubleshooting) can be achieved by way of cuttings, division, or seeds.

Detailed information on plant propagation is available elsewhere, but the methods that I have advocated require no specialized equipment. Softwood, semi-ripe, and hardwood cuttings simply take advantage of the growth stages through which plant stems pass in the course of a year. Softwood cuttings are generally taken early in the growing season, semi-ripe as the tissues begin to toughen and the stems become springy, and hardwood (from shrubs or trees) generally when the plant is dormant in winter. Any cutting bearing leaves must be kept in a moist atmosphere (such as a covered propagator or closed frame) to minimize moisture loss until it has formed roots.

Softwood and semi-ripe cuttings should usually be cut to a length of 4–6in./10–15cm., the cut being made just below a nodal point (where leaves emerge). The lowest few leaves should be pulled off and then, once the cuttings have formed roots, they should be potted on, the plants hardened off, and left in their pots for at least a year before they are planted out in the garden. There is a good deal of mythology attached to the taking of semi-ripe cuttings with a "heel" of old wood at the base, but for none of the subjects described in this book have I found that it makes any difference.

Leafless, hardwood cuttings of deciduous plants can be placed in a shaded spot in the open garden; they are generally the easiest type to take successfully although the slowest to root, sometimes requiring as much as eighteen months. Hardwood cuttings can be longer than other types, up to 8–10in./20–30cm.

A few plants are propagated by root cuttings. These are taken in winter when the plant is dormant, since they necessitate digging it up first. Short pieces of healthy root should be pushed vertically to their full length into pots of compost and incubated in the usual way.

Other means of propagation include layering, useful for evergreens, such as rhododendrons, shrubs and climbers that are otherwise difficult to root. It consists of anchoring into the soil a low-hanging branch while it is still attached to the parent plant. Division is a simple technique applicable only to nonwoody plants. It is best done in fall or spring, and comprises lifting an old-established plant clump with a fork and separating it into sections. The clump should be split into several pieces and only those vigorous parts from the periphery of the old clump retained.

Relatively few of the plants in this book are readily propagated by seed. With those for which it is recommended, sowing into a soil-based mixture in pots in spring in either a cold greenhouse or a cold frame will usually yield satisfactory results, although germination may sometimes be slow and erratic.

For every entry I have indicated approximate growth rates and ultimate sizes. Clearly, such factors vary from site to site but I have tried to give information based on more or less ideal growing conditions, the conditions, in fact, in which each type of plant *should* be grown. Hardiness Zones indicate zones where plants do best. (See Map on endpapers.)

COMMON PLANT PROBLEMS

This is a simple guide to the recognition and treatment of the commonest and most important plant pest and disease problems. There are, of course, thousands of others but only those listed here are likely to give rise to any real concern – and then only in a minority of cases. I have listed all these under the relevant plant entries, together with a brief indication of their commonest symptoms and, where appropriate, their treatment. This chart should always be read in conjunction with the plant entries since some of the problems are specific to certain types of plant. It can be extremely frustrating trying to match the symptoms of a particular disease to something seen on a plant on which the problem doesn't occur.

In many instances, a problem can be kept in check by following simple procedures of garden husbandry or hygiene, but for certain pests and diseases a chemical spray is the only realistic answer. I haven't hesitated, therefore, in suggesting the use of chemicals that are officially approved for use in gardens, but I do stress that they must always be applied strictly in accordance with the manufacturer's directions.

PROBLEM	RECOGNITION	TREATMENT
Adelgids	Woolly, white sap-sucking insects on needles and shoots, especially hemlock.	Spray with diazinon insecticide or SunSpray Ultra-Fine oil or a horticultural oil in spring and summer.
Aphids	Infestation of green, black, gray or brownish sap-sucking insects.	Spray with any contact insecticide.
Bacterial canker	Gum oozes from bark; branches die back.	If symptoms persist, fell the tree.
Beetles, Japanese	Metallic red-brown beetles attack leaves and flowers.	Hand-pick; or spray with carbaryl.
Birds	Buds removed, flower petals torn, fruit removed.	Use appropriate scarers/repellents or netting – remember all birds are legally protected.
Black spot	More or less circular dark brown or black spots, often with accompanying leaf yellowing.	Spray with proprietary fungicide; a specific fungicide-insecticide mixture will also control aphids and other pests.
Bulb, corm, tuber, and rhizome rots	Plants fail to flower or grow feebly; underground storage structure may be soft and moldy.	Destroy affected plants.
Canker	More or less rounded, sunken lesion on bark, usually with die-back of shoot beyond the lesion.	No treatment possible but badly diseased branches should be cut off.

PROBLEM	RECOGNITION	TREATMENT
Caterpillars, tent, gypsy moth	Foliage partially eaten or destroyed.	Spray with carbaryl. Destroy tent caterpillar nests at night.
Curculio, plum	Larvae feed on young fruit, making T-shaped punctures.	Destroy fallen fruit. Spray with carbaryl at petal-drop; repeat twice.
Codling moth	Fruit damaged inside along the core; a maggot often present within.	Use proprietary apple maggot traps or spray with carbaryl.
Coral spot	Tiny pinkish spots on bark, often with some die-back of the shoot.	Cut out and destroy affected parts.
Die-back	Shoot dies from tip down-ward, the tissue death gradually extending into previously healthy parts.	Cut out affected parts.
Earwig	Beetle-like insects eat foliage, flowers.	Spray or dust with carbaryl.
Eelworm (nematodes)	Vague symptoms but plants develop in stunted form, often in groups.	Grow plants on a different area of soil or fumigate soil. Dimethoate may help affected phlox.
Fireblight	Blossom dies and foliage appears damaged as if scorched by fire.	Destroy affected plants.
Flea beetle	Leaves close to soil level perforated with masses of tiny holes.	Dust proprietary soil insecticide around plants.
Fruit rots	Fruits decay, either when still on the plant or shortly after picking. Mold growth may be present.	No treatment possible.
Fungal leaf spots	Large or small, regular or irregular lesions on leaves, often displaying some concentric patterning.	With few exceptions (see Black spot), no treatment is necessary.
Gall	Irregular warty growth on stems or leaves.	Cut out and destroy affected parts.

Common Plant Problems

PROBLEM	RECOGNITION	TREATMENT
Gray mold	Fluffy gray mold associated with tissue decay and sometimes with die-back of shoots.	Spray with systemic fungicide or sulphur; destroy badly affected parts.
Honey fungus	Plant shows die-back and poor growth; toadstools and black strands may be present at stem base.	Seek specialist diagnosis before felling suspect trees.
Leaf attacking insects	Pieces eaten from leaves, either at center or margins; no slime trails present.	No treatment necessary. If severe, consult County Extension Specialist.
Leaf-blister mite	Small, irregular dark brown blisters.	Collect and destroy affected leaves.
Leaf miner	Wavy tunnels visible *inside* leaf tissues.	Collect and destroy affected leaves.
Mildew	Dusty white covering on leaves, buds, flowers, or other parts.	Spray with systemic fungicide or sulphur.
Narcissus fly	Flowers fail to form; tunneling, often with maggots present, in bulbs.	Destroy affected plants.
Nut weevil	Small holes in nuts with contents destroyed.	No treatment possible.
Peach leaf curl	Leaves distorted and at first covered with dusty white covering, later turning red.	Spray with copper-containing fungicide as leaves open and again as they drop.
Pear midge	Young fruitlets drop prematurely and contain tiny yellowish maggots.	Collect and destroy affected fruits.
Plum fruit moth	See Codling moth.	
Red spider mite	Foliage turns brown or bronze, usually accompanied by fine cobwebbing within which are masses of minute brownish mites.	Forcibly hose leaves; if infestation is severe and persistent destroy affected plants. Systemics (dimethoate) or SunSpray Ultra-Fine oil may help.
Root decay fungi	See Honey fungus.	

Common Plant Problems

PROBLEM	RECOGNITION	TREATMENT
Rust	Leaves and sometimes other parts have tiny black or brightly colored dusty lesions.	Spray with proprietary fungicide, such as propiconazole, sold specifically for rust control.
Sawfly	Leaves stripped; caterpillar-like insects may be present.	If insects are present, spray with contact insecticide.
Scab	Crusty lesions on fruit, leaves and/or stems.	Spray with benomyl in spring and then three times fortnightly.
Scale insects	Tiny, limpet-like sap-sucking insects accompanied by sticky honeydew.	Spray with systemic insecticide, or SunSpray Ultra-Fine oil.
Silver leaf	Foliage turns silvery and branches die back.	Cut off dead branches and wait to see if tree recovers; if not, fell and destroy it.
Slugs	Leaves and other tissues eaten; slime trails present.	Use proprietary slug pellets or other proven remedy.
Snails	See Slugs.	
Thrips	Surface of flowers and/or leaves minutely speckled.	Insecticidal soap, carbaryl, diazinon.
Tulip fire	Plants distorted, yellowish leaf spots, buds badly formed.	Destroy affected plants.
Water lily beetle	Furrows and small holes in upper leaf surfaces.	Wash off beetles with hose.
Whitefly	Tiny, white, moth-like insects, often accompanied by sticky honeydew.	Spray weekly with contact insecticide.
Wood decay fungi	Bracket-like fungal growth on stem.	No treatment possible but be aware that the tree may be physically unsound.
Woolly aphid	White, woolly tufts with small insects within.	Spray with Volk oil wash in winter.
Virus	Numerous symptoms: the commonest are irregular leaf mottling and overall small size.	No treatment possible, but do not propagate from affected plants and destroy any that are badly affected.

SHRUBS

Principles of Care

I consider shrubs to be the most important plants in the modern garden. By selecting carefully from the vast number of deciduous and evergreen varieties available, it is possible to have attractive flowers, foliage, bark, buds, and overall shape all year round. There are appropriate varieties for almost any soil and site conditions, although, as with other types of permanent (perennial) plants, relatively few are suitable for growing in deep shade. And while shrubs in general are rather more adaptable than herbaceous perennials, the commonest reason for failure is that no account has been taken of soil preference.

It is true that many shrubs will give perfectly acceptable results for several years with almost no attention at all, but feeding during the early part of the season with a general-purpose or rose fertilizer (the former for foliage and the latter for flowering varieties) will bring clearly recognizable benefits. If you feed shrubs twice a year, in late spring and in summer, they will do even better, and I find it sad that many gardeners regard this as unnecessary; in my opinion, it brings enormous rewards for very little effort. The addition of a moisture-retaining and weed-suppressing organic mulch early in the spring will also be beneficial. The stout woody framework of both trees and shrubs often causes gardeners to overlook the fact that they require as much protection from competing weeds, especially when young, as do any other plants. And when shrubs are planted in lawns or long grass it is important to leave an area of bare soil approximately 3ft./1m. in diameter around the base, on which mulch and fertilizer can be applied. While a spring mulch is most important for moisture retentiveness, a mulch applied around the base of the plant in fall will give valuable frost protection.

Few shrubs require staking unless they are to be trained in standard form (see page 18). Evergreen kinds will generally benefit from a protective screen of burlap or similar material during the first winter after planting, but only in colder areas. A winter screen will also allow the more tender wall-trained shrubs to be grown in colder regions.

Many shrubs (see Table), with the few important exceptions of those intolerant of dry conditions, make excellent subjects for growing in containers; this method is especially suitable for tender kinds as it allows them to be moved into a sheltered spot in the winter. Large containers that cannot be moved can be insulated by packing around them pieces of expanded polystyrene or similar material during periods of severe frost. A general purpose mixture of two parts soil, one part peat moss and one part sand can be used for container-grown shrubs; for rhododendrons, azaleas, and camellias, however, an especially formulated acid (so-called ericaceous) mixture should be used instead. The overall care, including pruning, outlined for shrubs in the open garden is equally applicable to those grown in containers, but here it is especially important to feed twice during the summer, especially if a soilless synthetic mix, which lacks nutrients is used. Pay careful attention to watering and mulching. Do not allow the medium to dry out. With correct feeding and mulching, the medium need not be replaced, but re-potting may be necessary once or twice at, say, three-year intervals, until the plant reaches its mature size. Given this care, there is no reason why a shrub in a container shouldn't live a long life.

SHRUBS PARTICULARLY SUITABLE FOR GROWING IN CONTAINERS

Abutilon	Hebe
Buxus	Laurus
Calluna	Lavandula
Camellia	Potentilla
Choisya	Prunus (Portugal laurel)
Cotoneaster	Rhododendron (including azalea)
Erica	Rosmarinus
Euonymus	Skimmia
Fatsia	Thymus
Fuchsia	Dwarf conifers

SHRUBS PARTICULARLY SUITABLE FOR TRAINING AGAINST A WALL

Abutilon	Escallonia
Callistemon	Forsythia
Camellia	Fremontodendron
Ceanothus	Garrya
Chaenomeles	Jasminum
Cotoneaster	Magnolia
Cytisus (battandieri)	Pyracantha

Pruning cuts

THE CORRECT CUT To prune most effectively, cut the plant stem just above a bud that faces away from the center of the bush: about ¼in./5mm. away from it is sufficient. Slant the cut downwards at a gentle angle away from the bud.

PRUNING

Countless shrubs survive for many years in gardens without ever being pruned. This may be because the species or cultivar will grow and bloom without any need for pruning; indeed, in a few instances, pruning would be detrimental. But most plants are unable to fulfil their real potential without it. Pruning is simply the deliberate removal of parts of a plant in order that the remaining parts will benefit. This benefit may derive from a more appealing shape, from increased flower or leaf production, from better light and air penetration, or from diseased parts being cut away. The operation can take several forms and in order that you may make best use of advice regarding specific types of shrubs, I must clarify certain general pruning principles.

Shrubs are almost always pruned by removing parts of their shoots, a general term that includes all the woody growth, be it part of the main stem or the branches arising from the stem. Pruning cuts are always made just above a bud, usually an outward-facing bud (one positioned on the outer side of the plant); if there is no convenient bud, or pair of buds, cut back to just above the junction with the parent shoot. It is a general maxim that when you cut off the end of a shoot, the buds farther down the stem (whether flower buds or leaf buds) are stimulated. If you regularly cut away the shoot tips, a more attractively compact, bushy, or more floriferous plant will result. Within limits, the more severely you prune a sparse hedge, for example, the more it will thicken. In due course, however, the increased branching can produce a rather congested mass of growth, and it may be necessary to undertake some thinning out by cutting away a proportion of the shoots completely and allowing light and air to penetrate to the center of the plant.

The task of pruning flowering shrubs will be made simpler and more logical if it is related to the flowering habit and flowering time of the plant. Shrubs produce flowers from buds borne essentially in one of two ways, either on woody shoots that developed during the same season as the flowers, or on shoots that developed in the previous or earlier seasons. Most shrubs that flower on older wood do so before midsummer: the shoots and buds are ready to burst into life from the start of the season. On the other hand, most shrubs that flower on the current season's wood do so after midsummer: the plant must wait until the new crop of flower buds has had time to develop and mature. By waiting until after a shrub has flowered before pruning it you will ensure that you don't miss a season's blossoming.

Another general maxim is that shrubs flowering before midsummer should be pruned immediately after flowering is over, whereas those that flower later may either be pruned immediately or left until early in the following spring. The latter approach has the advantage in colder areas of leaving some additional frost protection on the plant in the form of the bare

Deadheading

REGULAR DEADHEADING Encourage most plants, and particularly repeat-flowering plants such as modern roses, to produce further flowers by regularly removing the dead heads. Cut the stem just above the first leaf that has a fat, healthy bud in its apex. This will then shoot to produce a new flower.

Principles of Care

Understanding a shrub

Last year's flowered stems

Rubbing stems that can cause damage and so admit decay organisms

Inward-facing growth that will overcrowd the plant

New shoots emerging from the base, to be encouraged by pruning out old wood

Extensive rootball drawing nutrients from the soil

ASSESSMENT Pruning increases the vigor and overall health of a shrub, by, in simple terms, reducing the proportion of stems and leaves serviced by the roots. The roots have less old growth to support, so can throw up fresh, new shoots that will flower well.

framework of shoots that will trap warm air. In general, too, shrubs that flower in the first half of the year require fairly light pruning (the shoots are cut back only a little), whereas those that flower later in the year usually require harder pruning (a rather greater proportion of each shoot is cut back).

While the specific method of pruning advocated for each type of shrub is described under the individual plant entries, there are a number of guidelines which apply to pruning in general that are worth stating here. Many flowering shrubs (roses in particular) benefit from being pruned on a three-year renewal cycle. This entails cutting back to soil level one third of the oldest shoots each year and ensures a constant supply of vigorous new growth.

I have mentioned the importance of cutting away any obviously diseased or damaged shoots, and this should be a routine procedure in spring, once the new leaves have begun to burst. It will then be evident which parts have been killed by winter frost and these should be pruned away, cutting into a few inches of the living shoot at the base. (A useful way to check the viability of shoots is to scratch the bark with your thumbnail. If the tissue beneath appears fresh and green, it is living; if it is pale green or brown, it is moribund; and if dark brown, it is dead.) The presence of disease in a shoot is often revealed by feeble leaf development and some colored fungal growth on the bark; the salmon pink pustules of the coral spot fungus (nectria canker) are among the commonest (see page 9).

Shrubs with variegated foliage are popular and attractive but many are apt to produce "reverted" shoots with leaves of a uniform green. These all-green shoots are more vigorous than the variegated ones and will gradually take over, and it is important to cut them out as soon as they appear.

Shrubs that are commonly grown against walls in a more or less two-dimensional shape (see pages 14, 83 and overleaf) should, of course, have any shoots pointing directly towards or directly away from the wall cut away. But they also benefit from spur-pruning (see overleaf), in which the side-shoots arising from the main framework are cut back to within about 4in./10cm. of their bases each year to produce short shoots termed "spurs". This

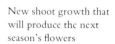
Light and hard pruning

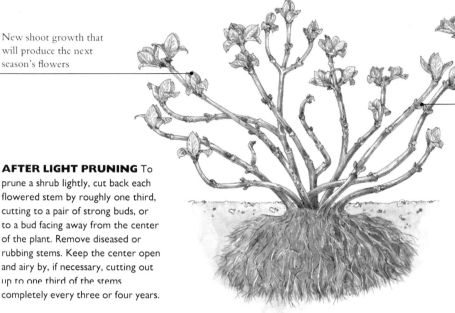

New shoot growth that will produce the next season's flowers

Buds further down the stems will now shoot into growth

AFTER LIGHT PRUNING To prune a shrub lightly, cut back each flowered stem by roughly one third, cutting to a pair of strong buds, or to a bud facing away from the center of the plant. Remove diseased or rubbing stems. Keep the center open and airy by, if necessary, cutting out up to one third of the stems completely every three or four years.

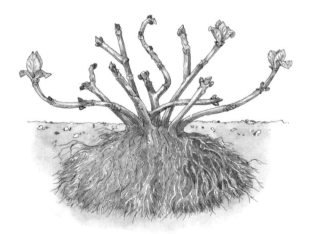

AFTER HARD PRUNING Cut back all the stems to buds as close to the base as possible. Vigorous new shoots arising from the base can be lightly cut back to a bud to stimulate further growth, or left alone. Where there are no buds near the base, or only very few, cut the stems back to the lowest strong bud, and cut out completely up to one third of the least healthy stems. Then feed and mulch the plant well to rejuvenate it and prompt new shoot growth.

operation helps to encourage the production of flowers in neat clusters rather than spaced along elongated branches, which may be acceptable for a free-standing plant but can look very untidy in a confined space against a wall.

On wall-trained shrubs, just as with climbers, growth in girth can result in ties cutting into the bark or soft tissue of the shoots, so all ties must be checked and re-tied annually.

Many gardening books include information on root pruning to reduce the vigor of large shrubs. This book doesn't, because I consider it a difficult operation likely in many species to lead to suckering. It is best left, in the rare instances where it is beneficial, to an expert; although I have given some information on the root pruning of trees which may be relevant (see page 196).

Principles of Care

Wall training shrubs

SPUR PRUNING This pruning method encourages flowers in neat clusters all along the stems. Every year at pruning time cut back all the side-shoots on the main stems to a bud that is within about 4in./10cm. of the base of the shoot.

Cut back the leader to stimulate growth on the left side

Train in a shoot horizontally to form a new arm

Spur prune side-shoots growing vertically

WALL TRAINING (*Pyracantha*) Prune wall-trained shrubs regularly to keep them in shape. In early spring remove any shoots facing directly into or away from the wall. Tie down horizontally the main arms, and spur prune all the side-shoots on them. Tie in the vertical leader, or stimulate growth further down by cutting it off at a bud.

Remove shoots growing into or away from the wall

TRAINING A STANDARD

There is one method of pruning that is applicable to a considerable number of shrub types and yet is not as widely recognized as it deserves to be. This is the training of a multi-stemmed shrub into a form with only a single stem. Such a plant is called a standard. The technique offers a most attractive alternative to buying a plant grafted onto the single stem of a different variety, and it achieves a similar result. Select a single, strong vertical shoot on a young plant, preferably one close to its center. Cut back the remaining shoots to soil level and tie the stem to a stake. Remove the side branches on the chosen shoot close to soil level. As the shoot elongates, tie it higher up the stake and continue to remove the side branches low down. Gradually, as the crown develops, remove side branches farther up the stem to create an attractive, well-shaped plant. Once it has reached the desired height, cut back the leading shoot to encourage further bushiness in the crown. The method is applicable to most multi-stemmed shrubs, but it is particularly successful for some of the willows, some cotoneasters, *Buddleia*, and most fuchsias.

When a shrub or climber is grown against a wall we take for granted that a permanent framework is left each year and pruning is restricted to the side-shoots. But a somewhat similar technique, analogous to training a standard, can be used with some freestanding shrubs such as *Buddleia davidii* and *Cotinus coggygria*. Instead of pruning them to the base, a framework of chosen size can be left, much as a single stem remains with the standard. Advice to prune to a point "above soil level" should then be interpreted as "above the framework".

Training a standard (*Buddleia alternifolia*)

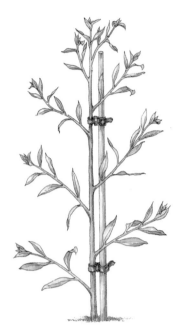 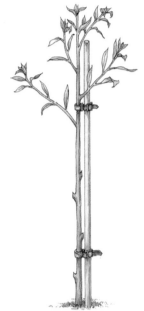 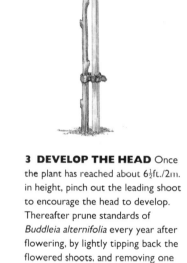

1 TRAIN THE PLANT VERTICALLY Select a strong stem on a young plant and remove all others. Stake the stem.

2 REMOVE SIDE-SHOOTS As the plant grows upward remove all the side-shoots on the lower part of the stem, and rub out the buds in the apices between shoots and stem. Leave the top 10in./25cm. of the plant untouched: this will form the head.

3 DEVELOP THE HEAD Once the plant has reached about 6½ft./2m. in height, pinch out the leading shoot to encourage the head to develop. Thereafter prune standards of *Buddleia alternifolia* every year after flowering, by lightly tipping back the flowered shoots, and removing one or two of the oldest shoots to encourage new growth. In the fall trim away any wayward shoots.

TROUBLESHOOTING

Any long-lived plant with a permanent above-ground structure runs the risk of developing problems through physical injury, disease, sheer neglect, or a combination of all three. Shrubs, tough as many of them may be, are no exception, and from time to time they present gardeners with problems regarding both diagnosis and treatment if they are to be given a new lease of life. In most instances, rejuvenation is perfectly possible and it is relatively rare that a plant must be discarded, but it is important to recognize the problem and to know both the correct remedy and the correct time of year at which to perform it.

The most common cause of problems is simple neglect: a plant in need of regular pruning has not been pruned; it has not been fed; or weeds or other plants have been allowed to grow too close and compete with it.

Frequently all three types of neglect go hand in hand, and the result is poor performance in the production of flowers or foliage, which is generally pale and small. It may also result in "legginess" – long, spindly shoots bare of leaves or flowers. It is surprising how often familiarity seems to breed a lack of awareness in gardeners regarding the condition of their own plants. Because they see a plant day after day they fail to appreciate that it could, in fact, be

Principles of Care

Troubleshooting: pruning

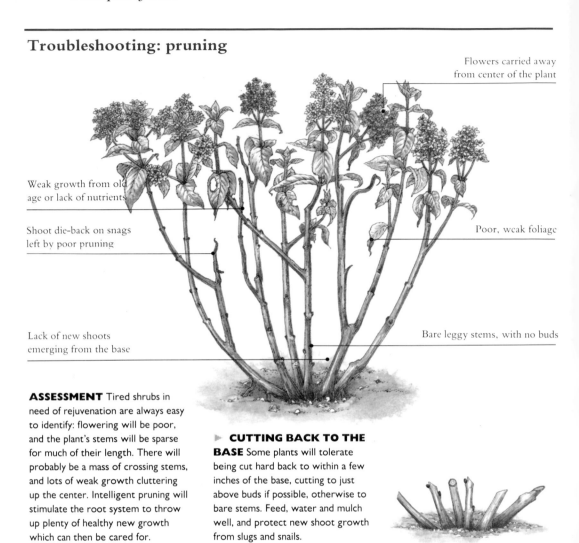

Flowers carried away from center of the plant

Weak growth from old age or lack of nutrients

Shoot die-back on snags left by poor pruning

Poor, weak foliage

Lack of new shoots emerging from the base

Bare leggy stems, with no buds

ASSESSMENT Tired shrubs in need of rejuvenation are always easy to identify: flowering will be poor, and the plant's stems will be sparse for much of their length. There will probably be a mass of crossing stems, and lots of weak growth cluttering up the center. Intelligent pruning will stimulate the root system to throw up plenty of healthy new growth which can then be cared for.

▶ **CUTTING BACK TO THE BASE** Some plants will tolerate being cut hard back to within a few inches of the base, cutting to just above buds if possible, otherwise to bare stems. Feed, water and mulch well, and protect new shoot growth from slugs and snails.

achieving far better results, and it is only when they come across the same species in another garden that they recognize the defect. A simple way to check a shrub's performance is to look at the shoot tips and see the amount of growth that has occurred in each season; if the amount of new growth is declining, especially on a plant only five or six years old, it is likely that something is amiss.

Frost damage, which is easy to recognize, takes the form of browning of the most vulnerable parts of a plant – the shoot tips, buds, and any newly opened or young leaves. Direct evidence of garden pests can generally be detected in traces of their activity – in leaves with holes or tattering, or small holes in woody tissues. Disease symptoms tend to be more nebulous,

but among the most common on above-ground parts are fairly regular spots or blotches on leaves, or colored, more or less powdery mold or pustules. Below-ground effects of fungal attack on roots are usually manifested by wilting or dying back from the tips of the shoots (since these are the parts farthest from the roots, they suffer first from an interrupted water supply). If you suspect disease on the roots, and particularly if the soil is waterlogged or poorly aerated, dig into the soil near the plant to allow inspection of parts of the root system. Blackening of the youngest and finest roots is a good indication of fungal decay.

While specific pest and disease problems may require specific remedies (see pages 8–11), a number of general first-aid procedures can be

Two-year rejuvenation of a shrub

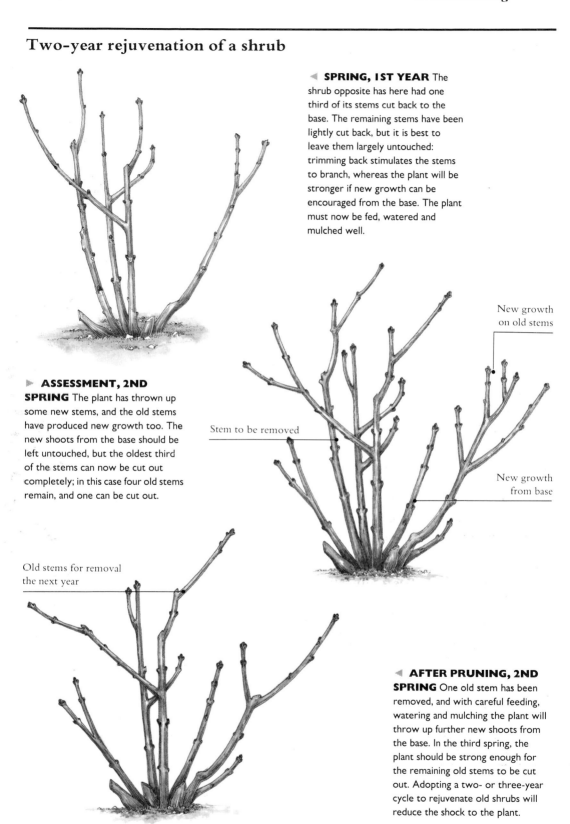

◄ **SPRING, 1ST YEAR** The shrub opposite has here had one third of its stems cut back to the base. The remaining stems have been lightly cut back, but it is best to leave them largely untouched: trimming back stimulates the stems to branch, whereas the plant will be stronger if new growth can be encouraged from the base. The plant must now be fed, watered and mulched well.

New growth on old stems

▶ **ASSESSMENT, 2ND SPRING** The plant has thrown up some new stems, and the old stems have produced new growth too. The new shoots from the base should be left untouched, but the oldest third of the stems can now be cut out completely; in this case four old stems remain, and one can be cut out.

Stem to be removed

New growth from base

Old stems for removal the next year

◄ **AFTER PRUNING, 2ND SPRING** One old stem has been removed, and with careful feeding, watering and mulching the plant will throw up further new shoots from the base. In the third spring, the plant should be strong enough for the remaining old stems to be cut out. Adopting a two- or three-year cycle to rejuvenate old shrubs will reduce the shock to the plant.

Principles of Care

Moving an established shrub

LIFTING AND REPLANTING
Prepare the new site by digging a large hole and incorporating plenty of organic matter. Thoroughly water the plant to be moved about an hour before lifting it, and if it is over about 6½ft./2m. tall cut it back by about half. Use a garden fork to lift the plant carefully, taking as much soil with it as possible and avoid tearing too many roots. Replant it in the new hole, and firm the soil in around it. Water and mulch well.

Make the new hole very large to accommodate the plant's roots

Incorporate plenty of organic matter in the new hole

Loosen the soil around the plant to minimize root damage

undertaken with any plant that is failing to thrive, and these are best carried out in spring. Weed growth or other competing vegetation should be cleared away over an area of approximately 3ft./1m. in diameter and the soil well forked over, a dressing of general-purpose fertilizer forked in, the whole well watered, and a mulch of organic matter applied over the surface. Remedial pruning should then be carried out unless I have indicated in the individual plant notes that a particular variety will not respond to it. With a few exceptions, pruning should be spread over two or even three years, each time cutting back half or one third of the branches to about 10cm./4in. above soil level. In a few cases (again, indicated in the individual entries), shrubs can be cut back completely to soil level in one operation.

If poor growth and performance are simply the consequence of the shrub having been planted in an inappropriate position, or if it is quite impossible to limit the plant's size in a confined space by pruning, moving it offers the best solution. While large shrubs can be moved, there is no simple rule-of-thumb method of

ensuring that a move will be successful. Magnolias, in particular, have a reputation for being difficult to re-establish once moved, but even they can be transplanted if the operation is done carefully and at the optimum time. In my experience, early spring, before growth has really recommenced, is the best time of year to move both deciduous and evergreen species. The essence of a successful move is to disturb the roots as little as possible, lifting the plant with a large ball of soil and ensuring that it is transferred and replanted without delay. Its new position must be carefully prepared with plenty of organic matter and a sprinkling of bonemeal first, and the plant watered very thoroughly for some time after the move until it is well established and growing strongly.

If poor growth is the result of the plant having been placed in inappropriate soil, the remedy may be more difficult as few gardens offer a range of soil types and it is as likely to fail in the new place as in the old. The only realistic option, if the plant is not too large, is to try growing it in a container filled with soil-based or synthetic soilless mixture.

HEDGES

HEDGES

A hedge is simply a group of shrubs (or occasionally trees), planted in a row and treated as a single entity. The plants must be placed close enough together to produce a continuous barrier with no gaps in five or six years or sooner depending on climate. Only certain shrub and tree species are suitable as hedging for they must be amenable to clipping and able to develop new shoots from fairly old wood.

SHRUBS FOR HEDGING

Berberis	*Ligustrum*
Buxus	*Lonicera nitida*
Cotoneaster	*Pittosporum*
Escallonia	*Prunus laurocerasus*
Euonymus japonica	*Pyracantha*
Forsythia	*Rhamnus* (deciduous)
Fuchsia	*Ribes*
Hippophaë	*Rosmarinus*
Lavandula	*Symphoricarpos*
Laurus nobilis	*Tamarix.*

TREES FOR HEDGING

Chamaecyparis/Cupressus/ × Cupressocyparis	
Crataegus	*Taxus*
Fagus	*Thuja*
Ilex	*Tsuga.*

HEDGE MANAGEMENT

Apart from a few species grown as flowering hedges, where the primary purpose is decorative rather than the creation of a barrier, there are certain fairly general rules about hedge maintenance. Gardeners differ widely in the way they manage hedging plants, but my practice is never to prune any new hedge until late in its first spring, at least one year after planting. Then, as an annual routine, I cut back one third (or two thirds on very vigorous types) of the leading shoot. This will encourage bushiness through the development of well-branched side-shoots. Once the lateral growth has begun to exceed the desired width, these side-shoots should be lightly trimmed, and when the leading shoots have reached the desired height, normal top and side trimming may begin, cutting back each year to the pre-selected level. Unless you have a very good eye, you will find sight lines of string attached to wooden stakes will make it easier to cut straight edges. It is nearly always impossible to clip a hedge as accurately as you can prune a freestanding shrub, and it is pointless to try to cut back to points just above buds. Indeed, it is a feature of the species that have proved themselves successful as hedging plants that their buds appear close together or are not prone to dying back from pruning cuts made between buds.

Bear in mind the general principle that pruning stimulates growth (see page 15): while a weak hedge can be improved by a hard trim,

Trimming a hedge

◀ **EVERGREEN HEDGE** Trim often to give a neat uniform appearance. If you don't trust your eye, establish a cutting line by pushing canes into the soil and tying string tautly around them. Trim the top flat, but slope the sides outward at the base – called a "batter". Light will then reach the base of the hedge and ensure even density.

▶ **ORNAMENTAL DECIDUOUS HEDGE** At the appropriate trimming time, give hedging shrubs such as forsythia a light all-over trim.

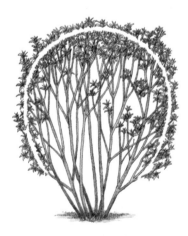

Hedges

Filling gaps in a hedge

▶ **ASSESSMENT** A hedge that is struggling to produce even, dense growth may need infilling with new plants. At an appropriate spot along the hedge, cut back the existing plants to make a gap in which you can work. With a sharp-edged spade or pruners, slice down through the existing roots to make a planting hole.

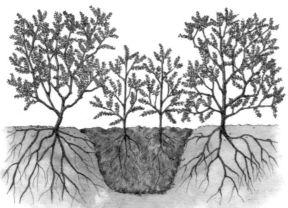

◀ **INFILLING WITH NEW PLANTS** Incorporate plenty of organic matter in the base of the planting hole, and fork it in well. If the soil is very heavy, work it well to loosen it and add grit to improve drainage. Plant in good container-grown specimens of new plants, planting two if the hole is big enough. Water and mulch well in the following growing seasons, and trim appropriately to give a dense hedge.

the less you prune the really vigorous hedging species, such as Lawson or Leyland cypress, the less pruning they require.

Details of the time and frequency of trimming are given under the individual entries for the hedging plants listed.

It is a curious fact that while most gardeners recognize the value of feeding and mulching freestanding shrubs, they very seldom do so for hedges. Yet, they too, certainly in the early stages, will develop better and more rapidly if they are similarly cared for.

HEDGE TROUBLESHOOTING

Hedges are as likely to be neglected and overgrown as other shrubs and can in many cases be similarly rejuvenated. Those that have grown too tall or too wide commonly present problems and it must be said that with most conifers, and certainly with cypresses, almost nothing can be done; they will not regenerate from old wood and if cut back there will be no new growth to cover the bare base. It is for this reason that I stress the importance of trimming gradually as the plant develops to encourage bushiness. I have no solution to offer the owner of a grossly overgrown coniferous hedge but to suggest that it should be removed and a fresh start made.

Those plants that I consider the best hedging species (most notably yew, beech and, to a lesser extent, box and hemlock) will, however, regenerate satisfactorily even when very overgrown. Irrespective of their present dimensions, cut back an overgrown hedge in spring to a height and width that is about halfway between the existing size and the desired size. Feed it well, and the following year cut it again to the size you want.

Gaps can sometimes be remedied by a combination of general cutting back and of wiring side branches across the gap (see opposite).

Troubleshooting: hedges

FILLING GAPS If the coverage of an evergreen is gappy or unsatisfactory, wiring can improve it substantially. At clipping time leave plenty of shoots around the gaps untrimmed. When the shoots are long enough, bend them down and wire them over the gap criss-cross fashion. Trim the ends lightly to stimulate growth, and feed the hedge well. The wires will quickly disappear into the foliage. The following season clip right over the repair as normal.

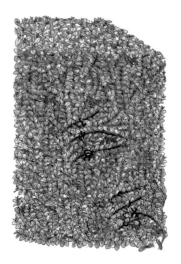

GAPS AT THE BASE Hedges that have become bare and leggy at the base are a common sight. At clipping time leave plenty of shoots low down on the hedge untrimmed, and let them elongate significantly. When they are long enough, pull them down and fix them securely, either pegging them into the ground or wiring them to the hedge stems. Trim the shoots with pruners until dense growth has been restored, then clip the hedge as normal.

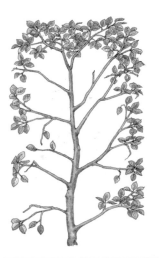

COMPLETE REJUVENATION Some hedges, particularly beech, become sparse and weak growing, or completely overgrown. If the plant is one that can be cut back very hard, it may be possible to rejuvenate the hedge by cutting it hard back on one side, right to the main stem. Feed, water and mulch well. In the following year if the hedge is recovering strongly, or in the year after that if recovery is sluggish, cut the other side back similarly.

Abutilon × suntense

Abutilon

A fairly large genus with species that range in habit from annuals to trees. The shrubs include both evergreen and deciduous forms with mainly bell-shaped blue, white, red, or occasionally yellowish summer flowers in varying sizes. They are only suitable for milder areas (or conservatories) but can be grown in large containers if moved under protection in winter. In the North, they are grown as houseplants and often summered outdoors.

SOIL Humus rich, well drained.

SITUATION Full sun or light shade, close to a south- or southwest-facing wall or other protection except in very mild, especially coastal areas. Zones 9–11.

WATERING AND FEEDING Mulch in fall and spring. Feed with a balanced rose or similar potash-rich fertilizer in mid-spring and again around midsummer. Allow dormant plants in containers to become fairly dry in winter.

PRUNING Cut back any frost-damaged shoots at least 6in./15cm. into sound wood to just above a good bud in spring. Straggly, more or less climbing forms, such as *A. megapotamicum*, may be pruned more severely, cutting back the previous season's growth by two thirds in spring. The stems will need tying in to supports.

COMMON PROBLEMS Frost damage; scale; red spider mite; and whitefly can be troublesome in warm summers.

PROPAGATION Semi-ripe cuttings in early fall.

TROUBLESHOOTING Established plants may show a tendency to become straggly. This is best combated by cutting out the oldest shoots, cutting back the remainder by about two thirds, and then routinely cutting back the previous season's growth by about half each spring.

SIZE The smallest of the common abutilons are the hybrids such as 'Kentish Belle', which reaches about 5 × 5ft./1.5 × 1.5m. in four to five years, although others such as 'Ashford Red' and 'Canary Bird' tend to be larger and similar to the *A. × hybridum* varieties (about 8–10 × 8–10ft./2.5–3 × 2.5–3m.). *A. vitifolium* is of similar speed of growth but more upright, attaining 13 × 8ft./4 × 2.5m.; the lax *A. megapotamicum* is almost a short climber, reaching about 10 × 10ft./3 × 3m. over the same timespan.

Aucuba GOLDDUST TREE

The evergreen spotted *A. japonica* 'Variegata' is one of the undervalued garden shrubs. In the best forms, it has most attractive foliage and berries and is tolerant of conditions in which very few other plants will survive.

SOIL Any, including acid, highly alkaline, and very dry.

SITUATION Light to very deep shade, intolerant of full sun. One of the few shrubs that grow beneath beech trees. Zones 6–8.

WATERING AND FEEDING Mulch in fall and spring. Feed with a balanced, general fertilizer in mid-spring.

PRUNING None necessary.

COMMON PROBLEMS A blackening of the young shoot tips, possibly caused by sunburn or a winter injury.

Aucuba japonica 'Variegata'

PROPAGATION Semi-ripe cuttings in summer or hardwood cuttings in winter.
TROUBLESHOOTING Overgrown plants may be cut back to within 1–1½ft./30–45cm. of soil level and will regenerate.
SIZE 3–5 × 3–5ft./1–1.5 × 1–1.5m. after five years (depending very much on the growing conditions); about 13 × 11ft./4 × 3.5m. after fifteen years.

Berberis thunbergii 'Rose Glow'

Berberis BARBERRY

A very large and valuable genus of deciduous and evergreen more or less spiny shrubs, with generally small leaves and small, yellow, orange, or almost reddish flowers in clusters. Many forms have attractive berries. The common species are all hardy, and some make excellent prickly hedges.
SOIL Almost any, provided it is not very heavy or water-logged.
SITUATION Sun or partial shade; full sun produces the best flowers. A few of the evergreen types are not hardy in colder areas. Zones 5–9.
WATERING AND FEEDING Mulch in fall and spring. Feed with a balanced rose or similar potash-rich fertilizer in mid-spring, and again around midsummer.
PRUNING Not normally necessary when grown as a shrub. When grown as a hedge, they should be clipped once in early fall, cutting the sides fairly hard but the leading shoots only lightly until the required height is reached.
COMMON PROBLEMS None.
PROPAGATION Semi-ripe cuttings in early fall, hardwood cuttings in winter, or by layering.
TROUBLESHOOTING Old and straggly bushes can sometimes be rejuvenated by thinning in spring, taking out some stems at or near ground level. Significant cutting back of the shoots should only be done on plants used for hedging.
SIZE There are a few dwarf forms such as *B. thunbergii* 'Atropurpurea Nana' and *B. buxifolia* 'Nana' which are unlikely to exceed about 2 × 2ft./60 × 60cm., but most of the common varieties will attain about 10 × 10ft./3 × 3m. after seven or eight years. Among commonly available types, *B. koreana*, *B. julianae*, *B × mentorensis* and some forms of *B. thunbergii* have an arching habit and will grow taller, up to about 7ft./2m. in ten years.

Buddleia BUTTERFLY BUSH

A genus of deciduous or occasionally evergreen, fairly large shrubs or almost small trees, most with large clusters of tiny, often fragrant flowers from midsummer onward according to type. The colors range from white through yellow to red, blue, and purple, and one species in particular, *B. davidii*, is especially prized for its attractiveness to butterflies.
SOIL Almost any, provided it is not very heavy or water-logged. *B. davidii* is notably lime tolerant and best in a slightly poorer soil than other types will tolerate.
SITUATION Full sun. Zones 6–9.

Buddleia – Calluna

Buddleia alternifolia

WATERING AND FEEDING Mulch in fall and spring. Feed with a balanced rose or similar potash-rich fertilizer in mid-spring, and again around midsummer.

PRUNING Varies significantly between species. *B. davidii* should have all shoots cut back to about 6in./15cm. above soil level at the end of the winter. Alternatively it may be grown on a permanent framework of stems up to 3ft./1m. above ground level, in which case, annual pruning should be to cut back to about 6in./15cm. above this main stem.

B. alternifolia grown as a normal shrub should have the flowering shoots cut back to their base after the blooms have faded and the oldest shoots cut out at the same time, but is more attractively trained as a standard (see pages18–19). When grown in this way, cut back the flowered shoots as above, and to maintain the attractive weeping habit cut out any wayward shoots in fall and again after flowering.

Other species may have old wood cut back and any necessary shaping done after flowering.

COMMON PROBLEMS Normally none, although red spider mites and Japanese beetles can damage the foliage.

PROPAGATION Semi-ripe cuttings in late summer, hardwood cuttings in winter.

TROUBLESHOOTING Old and straggly bushes are scarcely worth rejuvenating for new stock will establish easily and quickly. Most of the larger species, such as *B. globosa*, are naturally lax and straggly and for this reason not suited to small gardens.

SIZE *B. davidii*, pruned annually, should never exceed about 13 × 13ft./4 × 4m. Other species will attain about 16ft./5m. in five years; although the tree-like *B. colvilei* (Zone 9) may be taller still. On *B. alternifolia* trained as a standard, routine pruning becomes difficult if the plant is allowed to grow taller than about 8ft./2.5m.

Buxus BOX

This is one of the most useful evergreen hedging plants, and it can also make a useful specimen shrub either for shaping as topiary or, especially with the variegated forms, for foliage appeal.

SOIL Almost any, provided it is not very heavy or water-logged; valuably lime tolerant.

SITUATION Sun or partial shade; tolerant of exposure to fairly cold winds. Zones 5–9.

WATERING AND FEEDING Mulch in fall and spring. Apply a balanced, general-purpose fertilizer in early spring.

PRUNING None necessary. When grown as a hedge or for topiary, clip twice a year, first around midsummer and again in early fall; or clip once only in late summer, although this will give a tidy appearance for a shorter time.

COMMON PROBLEMS Sap-sucking box sucker and aphids can distort shoot tips and form sticky honeydew.

PROPAGATION Hardwood cuttings in late fall.

TROUBLESHOOTING Old and straggly bushes can be rejuvenated to some extent by cutting back hard in spring, but take care not to cut too far into old wood or the plant may not produce new

Buxus microphylla

Buxus sempervirens

shoots. It is best to do the job in stages, cutting back to about 2ft./60cm. above the old wood first, to see if new growth is stimulated, then cut further the following year if desired.

SIZE The small-leaved *B. microphylla* will attain about 10 × 13ft./ 3 × 4m. after many years. The common *B. sempervirens* will very slowly grow to about 16–20ft./5–6m. but the cultivars 'Myrtifolia' and 'Suffruticosa' will barely reach a third of this. Variegated forms will remain more or less dwarf.

Callistemon BOTTLEBRUSH

The evergreen *C. citrinus* is one of the relatively few Australian shrubs to be hardy in the USA, although it is reliable only in mild and coastal areas. It and *C. viminalis* are grown mostly in Florida and coastal California. It is scarcely a beautiful plant overall, but its individual red (or occasionally yellow) flowers are striking for their bottlebrush-like form.

SOIL Fertile, light, free draining.

SITUATION Full sun, preferably with the protection of a south- or south-west-facing wall. Zones 8–10.

WATERING AND FEEDING Mulch in fall and spring. Apply a balanced rose or similar potash-rich fertilizer in mid-spring, and again around midsummer.

PRUNING Cut out any frost-damaged shoots in spring.

COMMON PROBLEMS None, except frost damage.

PROPAGATION Semi-ripe cuttings in late summer.

TROUBLESHOOTING Old and straggly bushes can be rejuvenated to some extent by cutting hard back in spring, but bottlebrush shrubs usually look straggly, so you may be unable to improve the appearance as much as you might wish.

SIZE 6½ × 5ft./2 × 1.5m. after five years and perhaps double this after twenty years.

Callistemon citrinus

Calluna LING, HEATHER

Calluna is one of the two evergreen needle-leaved genera (see also *Erica*) used in gardens, with a very large number of summer-flowering cultivars all derived from the species native to Britain, *C. vulgaris*.

SOIL All varieties must have acid, free draining, humus-rich soil.

SITUATION Partial shade is tolerated but much the best results are achieved in full sun. Zones 4–6.

WATERING AND FEEDING Heathers require abundant moisture, although they are intolerant of water-logged conditions. Mulch the plants in fall and spring. Apply a balanced rose or similar potash-rich fertilizer in mid-spring, and again around midsummer. One of the best mulches is pine needles; in common with most acid-loving shrubs, heather prefer plant-derived composts to animal manures.

PRUNING Use shears to cut off dead flower heads and winter-injured stems, cutting fairly hard to just above the old wood. It is preferable to wait until spring to do this, because the dried heads can be most attractive in winter.

Calluna vulgaris 'Peter Sparkes'

931969

Calluna – Ceratostigma

REJUVENATING HEATHERS
Old plants of *Calluna* and *Erica* tend to become brown, woody, and sparse at the center. In spring, clip the plant hard with shears, then mound some good garden soil over the center (above). During that growing season the plant will send up fresh new rooted shoots (above right). Leave these plantlets to grow on where they are, or, if they are very crowded, replant them elsewhere.

COMMON PROBLEMS None, although the center of old plants may die out (see below).

PROPAGATION 2–2½in./5–6cm. long semi-ripe cuttings in late summer; or by layering.

TROUBLESHOOTING When the center of an old plant becomes brown and woody, it may be possible to rejuvenate it by shearing hard back in spring and placing a mound of soil over the center. Natural layers should form with fresh new shoots.

SIZE In general, heathers attain their maximum size – most species attain 1 × 1ft./30 × 30cm. – and optimum appearance after about five or six years, and most are best replaced after eight or nine years. There are a few dwarf forms, such as 'Pygmaea', which barely attain 6 × 6in./15 × 15cm., and a few more spreading ones, such as 'Sir John Charrington' and 'Robert Chapman', which will reach 15 × 20in./40 × 50cm. or more.

Camellia

One of the most highly prized of all evergreen shrubs, having rich, glossy foliage and beautiful flowers, of which the best may be single, double, or semi-double and pink, red, occasionally white, or mixtures of the three. These shrubs need cool but fairly mild winters, such as occur in much of the South, parts of the West Coast and even the end of Long Island, N.Y.

SOIL All varieties must have acid, free draining, humus-rich soil.

SITUATION Partial sun or shade, with some protection from wind and cold. Camellias grow best beneath the shade of other shrubs and trees in a naturally peaty soil, but they are also successful grown in an acid compost in containers. Zones 7–8.

WATERING AND FEEDING Mulch in fall and spring; apply a balanced rose or similar potash-rich fertilizer in mid-spring, and again around midsummer. One of the best mulches is white pine needles; in common with most acid-loving shrubs, they prefer plant-derived composts to animal manures. Even on naturally acid soil, they will benefit from an application of sequestered iron in spring.

PRUNING None required, although wayward shoots that affect the overall shape of the plant can be cut out after flowering.

COMMON PROBLEMS Frost damage; scale insects giving rise to sooty mold development; leaf chlorosis; bud drop. The latter is usually caused by sudden changes in temperature, or periods of heavy freezing, or some drying out of the soil.

PROPAGATION Semi-ripe cuttings in fall, or leaf-bud cuttings in early spring.

Camellia reticulata

TROUBLESHOOTING Old and misshapen bushes can sometimes be restored by hard pruning but the resulting plant is unlikely ever to achieve its original beauty.

SIZE Although several species of *Camellia* have been involved in the development of modern varieties, most have similar, fairly slow growth rates and will reach their ultimate size of about $10–13 \times 6\frac{1}{2}–10$ft./$3–4 \times 2–3$m. after fifteen or twenty years.

Ceanothus WILD-LILAC

Ceanothus impressus

Ceanothus is much prized for its unusual blue flowers, there being few other mild-climate shrubs with this color. There are late summer and fall-flowering deciduous types, and evergreen forms, some of which flower in early summer and some in late summer and fall. Although their pruning differs, both deciduous and evergreen varieties have similar requirements and in the USA are grown on the Pacific Coast.

SOIL Rich, light, free draining.

SITUATION Full sun, with some protection from cold winds; the evergreen species, which are less hardy than the deciduous types, are especially intolerant of exposure to cold winds. Zones 7–9.

WATERING AND FEEDING Mulch in fall and spring. Feed with a balanced rose or similar potash-rich fertilizer in mid-spring, and again around midsummer.

PRUNING Evergreen varieties grown as freestanding plants require little more than the cutting out of dead shoots and tidying up after flowering. When the early flowering evergreen types are grown as wall shrubs, they should be pruned harder after flowering, to within three buds of the previous season's growth. Deciduous varieties should be pruned hard in spring, again to within three buds of the previous season's growth.

COMMON PROBLEMS Frost damage, root rot, aphids and whitefly can occasionally be troublesome.

PROPAGATION Semi-ripe cuttings in summer (evergreen varieties), or hardwood cuttings in winter (deciduous varieties).

TROUBLESHOOTING After severe frost damage, especially on evergreen types, cut back at least 1ft./30cm. into unaffected wood, even if this means cutting back almost to soil level.

SIZE The most vigorous evergreen forms, such as 'Owlswood Blue', on a good site may reach up to 10×10ft./3×3m. after ten years or so, although most will barely reach half this size. The only hardy (Zones 4–6) species is the native New Jersey-tea, *C. americanus*, which grows to about 3ft./1m.

Ceratostigma SHRUBBY PLUMBAGO

There are only two or three species of *Ceratostigma*, all equally valuable for their hardiness, small size, and electric-blue flowers late in the summer. They are useful as ground covers.

SOIL Tolerates almost any, provided not very heavy or waterlogged, but performs noticeably better in rich, free draining soil.

SITUATION Tolerant of light shade but always best in full sun. Zones 5–9.

Ceratostigma – Cornus

Ceratostigma willmottianum

Chaenomeles × superba

WATERING AND FEEDING Mulch in fall and spring. Apply a balanced rose or similar potash-rich fertilizer in mid-spring, and again around midsummer.

PRUNING Routinely cut back all shoots to just above soil level in mid-spring.

COMMON PROBLEMS None.

PROPAGATION Semi-ripe cuttings in late summer.

TROUBLESHOOTING *C. plumbaginoides* is a rather creeping species and can become invasive – I have had it well established in a lawn – so its lateral extension needs limiting with a spade. Resist the temptation to treat it like a herbaceous perennial and dig it up to divide, for it re-establishes very slowly.

SIZE For *C. plumbaginoides*, see above; *C. willmottianum* spreads little and after annual pruning reaches a height of about 2–3ft./ 60cm.–1m. with each year's growth.

Chaenomeles JAPANESE QUINCE

The ornamental quinces are deciduous spring-flowering shrubs with apple-like blossom and fruits that can be cooked as substitutes for real quinces. They are most usually trained as wall shrubs, although some varieties are really too spreading for this and are better grown as freestanding shrubs.

SOIL Will grow in almost any, provided it is not very heavy or water-logged; the plants tend to suffer from leaf chlorosis on alkaline soils.

SITUATION Tolerates some shade but the flowers are always best in full sun. Although usually grown against a wall, it doesn't really need shelter in most areas. Zones 4–8.

WATERING AND FEEDING Mulch in fall and spring. Feed with a balanced rose or similar potash-rich fertilizer in mid-spring, and again around midsummer.

PRUNING On wall-trained plants, cut back the previous season's growth to two or three buds from the base after flowering, and cut out any shoots growing directly. toward or away from the wall. If space is very confined, the plant may be spur pruned after flowering by cutting back the side-shoots to 1½in./3–4cm. from their bases; the stubs that remain form the spurs. On freestanding plants, thin out overcrowded shoots (the center very easily becomes congested) and cut back the previous season's growth by about one third after flowering.

COMMON PROBLEMS Leaf chlorosis; fireblight; irregular leaf patterning caused by viruses.

PROPAGATION Semi-ripe cuttings in late summer.

TROUBLESHOOTING Old bushes become very woody and mis-shapen and are scarcely worth rejuvenating, especially when they have been trained against a wall.

SIZE Varieties derived from *C. japonica* reach about 3 × 6½ft./1 × 2m. after seven or eight years; those derived from *C. speciosa* reach about 10 × 13ft./3 × 4m. after ten years; while those from the hybrid *C. × superba* achieve about 5 × 6½ft./1.5 × 2m. in the same time, but there are more and less vigorous, and also more and less upright, forms in both of the latter species, so select carefully.

Choisya MEXICAN ORANGE

This evergreen shrub is grown both for its foliage and flowers, although the golden form, *C. ternata* 'Sundance', is much more of a foliage plant, popular on the West Coast.

SOIL Most, although best on fairly rich, well drained soil, preferably not strongly alkaline.

SITUATION Full sun with shelter, especially for the golden form. Zone 9.

WATERING AND FEEDING Mulch in fall and spring. Feed with a balanced rose or similar potash-rich fertilizer in mid-spring, and again around midsummer.

PRUNING Cut out the oldest one third of the shoots in mid-spring, after flowering.

COMMON PROBLEMS Frost damage; root and crown rot; aphids.

PROPAGATION Semi-ripe cuttings in late summer.

TROUBLESHOOTING None usually needed, although if necessary the stems can be cut hard back after flowering.

SIZE *C. ternata* will reach $6\frac{1}{2}$–10 × $6\frac{1}{2}$–10ft./2–3 × 2–3m. after about eight or ten years; 'Sundance' about two thirds of this size.

Choisya ternata

Cistus ROCKROSE

The rockroses are plants of the Mediterranean, and their bright colors and patterns are only an option for those whose garden can reproduce that region's hot dry conditions. Although strictly classed as subshrubs, they are in many ways more akin to herbaceous perennials.

SOIL Light, free draining, moderately rich to poor.

SITUATION Full sun, shelter from cold winds; good in mild, coastal gardens of southern California. Zones 9–10.

WATERING AND FEEDING Mulch in fall and spring. Feed with a balanced, general-purpose fertilizer in mid-spring, and again after midsummer. Take care not to overwater.

PRUNING Trim very lightly in spring to remove any shoots damaged in winter. Disturb the plants as little as possible; they resent being dug up or transplanted.

COMMON PROBLEMS None.

PROPAGATION Semi-ripe cuttings in summer, hardwood cuttings in winter, the species from seed.

TROUBLESHOOTING Not likely to be necessary.

SIZE Most varieties will attain a height and spread of about 3 × 3ft./1 × 1m. within three years.

Cistus × corbariensis

Cornus DOGWOOD

The deciduous shrubby dogwoods form a distinct group of varieties of two main species grown for their foliage and attractively colored stems. These species are *C. alba* and *C. stolonifera*, and they are deliberately kept small by pruning. There are other common shrubby foliage species (*C. amomum* and the creeping *C. canadensis*), and several attractive larger species that form small trees (see page 204).

Cornus – Cotoneaster

Cornus alba 'Sibirica'

SOIL Most; several of the varieties are tolerant both of heavy water-logged clay and light sandy conditions.

SITUATION Partial shade but will tolerate full sun. *C. canadensis* requires shade. Zones 2–8.

WATERING AND FEEDING Mulch in fall and spring. Feed with a balanced, general-purpose fertilizer in mid-spring, and again around midsummer.

PRUNING To obtain the brightly colored young shoots that are the principal appeal of *C. alba* and *C. stolonifera*, cut all shoots back to about 8in./20cm. above soil level in mid-spring every year. *C. canadensis* requires no pruning.

COMMON PROBLEMS None.

PROPAGATION Hardwood cuttings in winter.

TROUBLESHOOTING None needed.

SIZE *C. alba* varieties grown for their stems will be kept to about 5 × 3ft./1.5 × 1m. by annual pruning, but the yellow-stemmed *C. stolonifera* 'Flaviramea', even with pruning, will reach 6½ft./2m. in height and spreads extensively. *C. canadensis* is a ground-cover plant, reaching 8in. × 10ft./20cm. × 3m. in the same time.

Cotinus SMOKE BUSH

C. coggygria is grown equally for its feathery flowers and attractive, rounded deciduous foliage, particularly appealing in the purple-colored forms, *C.c.* 'Foliis Purpureis' and 'Royal Purple'.

SOIL Will grow in most, but best in humus-rich, slightly moist conditions.

SITUATION Tolerates partial shade but the purple of the colored foliaged forms tends to be paler there and the flowers only develop satisfactorily in full sun. Zones 5–9.

Cotinus 'Flame'

WATERING AND FEEDING Mulch in fall and spring. Feed with a balanced rose or other potash-rich fertilizer in mid-spring, and again around midsummer.

PRUNING None needed, but from time to time cut out the oldest branches in spring to induce new growth. For the best leaves on forms with good foliage (although at the expense of flowers), cut all the stems back to soil level, or to a low framework of permanent stems, in spring.

COMMON PROBLEMS None.

PROPAGATION Layering; difficult to establish from cuttings.

TROUBLESHOOTING None needed.

SIZE After about fifteen years may reach 16–20 × 16–20ft./5–6 × 5–6m., but slows down after attaining about half this size.

Cotoneaster

A large genus of very useful evergreen and deciduous shrubs with foliage, some flower and much fruiting appeal. The treatment of the various types differs in some respects and I shall, therefore, divide them into four groups:

    1 Low- to medium-growing deciduous
    2 Low- to medium-growing evergreen
    3 Tall deciduous
    4 Tall evergreen.

SOIL All groups are very tolerant of most soils; group 2 will tolerate poor soils.

SITUATION Full sun to medium shade (all groups). Some forms are very successful against walls. Zones 4–8.

WATERING AND FEEDING Mulch in fall and spring. Apply balanced rose or similar potash-rich fertilizer in mid-spring and again around midsummer.

PRUNING GROUPS 1 AND 2 None, other than occasional shaping and to keep within limits. When growing group 2 types as a hedge, clip twice, first around midsummer and again in early fall; or clip once only in late summer, although this will give a neat appearance for a shorter time.

GROUP 3 None; if used as hedging plants trim to give a very light shaping in spring.

GROUP 4 None, but some may usefully be trained. For instance, *C. floccosus* is excellent when trained against a wall, while *C. × watereri* 'Rothschildianus' can be trained on a single stem to make a fine standard plant for winter appeal (see pages 18–19).

COMMON PROBLEMS Prone to fireblight and red spider mites.

PROPAGATION Semi-ripe cuttings in late summer or hardwood cuttings in winter.

TROUBLESHOOTING None usually needed. Old and woody plants can sometimes be rejuvenated by cutting back to just above the old wood in spring, although the plants may never regain their best shape.

SIZE GROUP 1 Notably slow growing, reaching about 5 × 10ft./ 1.5 × 3m. after eighteen or twenty years.

GROUP 2 Horizontal types such as *C. horizontalis* will reach 2 × 10ft./60cm. × 3m. after about fifteen years; taller forms, such as

Cotoneaster horizontalis

Cytisus battandieri

that usually called *C.* 'Hybridus Pendulus', about 5 × 10ft./1.5 × 3m. in the same time (although this is often sold grafted as a standard).

GROUP 3 Will reach about 13 × 13ft./4 × 4m. in twenty years.

GROUP 4 Will reach 16–23 × 16–23ft./5–7 × 5–7m. after about twenty years (and about the same height if trained as a standard).

Cytisus BROOM

This is one of three important genera of deciduous or evergreen, spring-flowering shrubs referred to as brooms, *Genista* and *Spartium* being the others. They are distinctive for their yellow, white, or red pea-like flowers.

SOIL Intolerant of heavy, wet, clayey soils, and rarely successful in highly alkaline conditions.

SITUATION Full sun. The tender *C. battandieri* will benefit from some wall protection. Zones 5–9.

WATERING AND FEEDING Mulch in fall and spring. Feed with a balanced rose or other potash-rich fertilizer in mid-spring, and again around midsummer.

PRUNING None.

COMMON PROBLEMS None, although leaf chlorosis may occur in strongly alkaline conditions.

PROPAGATION Semi-ripe cuttings in early summer.

TROUBLESHOOTING Most species and varieties are short-lived or, at least, become woody and leggy after ten to fifteen years. They will not regenerate from old wood and should be replaced.

SIZE Varies considerably. The tallest species, *C. battandieri*, reaches about 20 × 20ft./6 × 6m. after eighteen or twenty years; the more or less ground-covering types, such as *C.* × *kewensis*, only about 1½ × 5–6½ft./50cm. × 1.5–2m. after five or six years. Over the same timespan the intermediate varieties of *C.* × *praecox* grow to about 5 × 6½ft./1.5 × 2m., and the slightly more vigorous *C. multiflorus*, and the varieties of *C. scoparius*, about 10 × 6½ft./3 × 2m.

Daphne

Daphnes are evergreen or deciduous, and popular principally for their intensely perfumed winter or early spring flowers. They thrive in situations that suit few other flowering shrubs, but some, such as *D. odora* (Zones 8–10), are rather tender.

SOIL Deep, rich, moist, well drained, preferably slightly acidic.

SITUATION Preferably light or medium shade; most will tolerate full sun but the perfume seems to be more apparent in a cool, more shady woodland situation. Zones 4–8.

WATERING AND FEEDING Mulch in fall and spring. Apply a balanced rose or other potash-rich fertilizer in mid-spring, and again around midsummer.

PRUNING None.

COMMON PROBLEMS None.

PROPAGATION Semi-ripe cuttings in early or mid-summer. Some species, most notably *D. mezereum*, one of the hardier species, may strike with difficulty and should be layered.

Daphne tangutica

TROUBLESHOOTING None needed. Old plants which become leggy and woody are best replaced.

SIZE All remain fairly small and after about ten years reach their maximum height, which ranges from about $1\frac{1}{2} \times 2\frac{1}{2}$ft./$50 \times 80$cm. for *D. blagayana* to about $6\frac{1}{2} \times 3$ft./2×1m. for *D. odora*.

Deutzia

A widely admired pink- or white-flowered deciduous shrub with few detracting features; nevertheless it has never really achieved the popularity that it deserves. *D. gracilis* is recommended.

SOIL Moist, fairly rich, usually good on alkaline soils, but always intolerant of dryness.

SITUATION Full sun to light shade, preferably with some shelter from cold winds. Zones 4–8.

WATERING AND FEEDING Mulch in fall and spring – this is very important as the plant is prone to suffer injury from drought. Feed with a balanced rose or similar potash-rich fertilizer in mid-spring, and again around midsummer.

PRUNING Cut back the oldest third of the shoots to soil level in spring, after flowering.

COMMON PROBLEMS None.

PROPAGATION Semi-ripe cuttings in summer or hardwood cuttings in winter.

TROUBLESHOOTING Oversized or straggly plants can usually be rejuvenated by cutting back the shoots to soil level in spring, staging the operation over a period of two years.

SIZE May reach $6\frac{1}{2} \times 3$ft./2×1m. after five years and 7×7ft./2×2m., according to species, after sixteen to eighteen years.

Deutzia × elegantissima

Elaeagnus   THORNY ELEAGNUS, RUSSIAN OLIVE

Deciduous or evergreen, medium-sized shrubs, grown principally for their attractive foliage. None of the forms is truly spectacular, but all are easy to obtain and grow. *E. pungens* 'Maculata' has very fragrant flowers in October.

SOIL Almost any, including dry, sandy conditions.

SITUATION Tolerates some shade, but always best in full sun. *E. pungens*, Zones 7–9; *E. angustifolia* (Russian Olive) Zones 2–7; *E. umbellata*, Zones 3–8.

WATERING AND FEEDING Mulch in fall and spring. Feed with a general-purpose fertilizer in mid-spring, and in midsummer.

PRUNING None, although some types can be lightly trimmed as hedging in late spring.

COMMON PROBLEMS None.

PROPAGATION Semi-ripe cuttings in summer or hardwood cuttings in winter.

TROUBLESHOOTING None needed, although old plants which become leggy and woody will usually regenerate if cut back hard in late spring. If variegated forms produce any all green shoots, these must be cut out promptly.

SIZE All will reach about $10–13 \times 10–13$ft./$3–4 \times 3–4$m. after fifteen to eighteen years.

Elaeagnus pungens 'Maculata'

Erica – Fatsia

Mixed heather border
Erica carnea

Escallonia 'Apple Blossom'

Erica HEATH

One of the two evergreen needle-leaved genera (see also *Calluna*) used in gardens, including a very large number of cultivars with white, pink, or red flowers and, sometimes, colored foliage. They are usefully divided into the winter- and spring-flowering forms derived principally from *E. carnea* and *E.* × *darleyensis*, and the summer-flowering types derived from *E. cinerea* and other species, because the soil conditions necessary differ slightly.

SOIL All winter-flowering heaths (*E. carnea* and *E.* × *darleyensis*) are tolerant of alkaline soils, provided they are moist and organic. All other varieties must have moist, acid conditions.

SITUATION Partial shade is tolerated, but much the best results are achieved in full sun. Zones 5–9.

WATERING AND FEEDING Heaths require abundant moisture, although they are intolerant of water-logged conditions. Mulch in fall and spring. Apply a balanced rose or similar potash-rich fertilizer in mid-spring, and again around midsummer. One of the best mulches is white pine needles, and generally heaths prefer plant-derived composts to animal manures.

PRUNING Use shears to cut off dead flower heads of summer varieties in early spring, cutting lightly and not very close to the old wood.

COMMON PROBLEMS None, although the center of old plants may die out. A cover of pine needles prevents winter burn.

PROPAGATION 2–2½in./5–6cm. long semi-ripe cuttings in late summer or layer.

TROUBLESHOOTING When the center of old plants becomes brown and woody, it may be possible to rejuvenate them from natural layers: see *Calluna*, page 30.

SIZE In general, heaths attain their maximum size and optimum appearance after about five or six years. They are best replaced after eight or nine years. Some, most notably the varieties of *E. carnea*, are best considered as slow-growing ground-cover plants, each reaching about 6in × 2½ft./15 × 80cm. (usually planted in groups for best effect). Others form small clumps, and the most vigorous types, such as *E. vagans* 'Mrs. D. F. Maxwell' or some forms of *E. erigena* or *E. terminalis*, will reach about 2½ × 2½ft./80 × 80cm., or even more.

Escallonia

An invaluable evergreen plant for mild West Coast areas, both as a freestanding shrub or a flowering hedge.

SOIL Tolerant of most, although generally least successful in highly alkaline conditions.

SITUATION Full sun to moderate shade, but flowers less satisfactorily in shade. Zones 8–9.

WATERING AND FEEDING Mulch in fall and spring. Feed with a balanced rose or other potash-rich general fertilizer in mid-spring, and again after midsummer.

PRUNING When grown as a freestanding shrub none is necessary, apart from the removal of frost-damaged shoots in spring; once established, the plant will benefit from the cutting back of the oldest third of the shoots in spring to stimulate new growth. When grown as a hedge, clip twice, first around midsummer and again in early fall.

COMMON PROBLEMS None, apart from some frost damage.

PROPAGATION Semi-ripe cuttings in summer or hardwood cuttings in winter.

TROUBLESHOOTING Overgrown or frost- and cold-damaged plants may be cut back to within 1–1½ft./30–45cm. of soil level, and will even regenerate after being cut back to just a few inches above soil level, although they will take up to three years to resume flowering and normal vigor.

SIZE Up to 6½ × 6½ft./2 × 2m. after five to seven years, and about 13 × 13ft./4 × 4m. after twenty years.

Euonymus SPINDLE TREE

Deciduous or evergreen, medium-sized foliage shrubs or small trees; a genus that includes some of the most useful and easy to grow variegated evergreens. There should be at least one representative of this genus in every garden.

SOIL Almost all.

SITUATION Tolerates moderate shade, but most varieties are best in full sun. *E. japonica* is a useful coastal plant, being tolerant of salt spray. Zones 4–9.

WATERING AND FEEDING Mulch in fall and spring. Apply a balanced, general fertilizer in mid-spring, and midsummer.

PRUNING Normally none, although ground-covering varieties of *E. fortunei* benefit from having upright shoots cut back in spring or early fall. *E. japonica* can be grown as a hedge; clip it twice, first around midsummer and again in early fall; or clip once only in late summer, although this will look neat for a shorter time.

COMMON PROBLEMS Mildew on *E. japonica*. Also scales and red spider mites.

PROPAGATION Semi-ripe cuttings in summer or hardwood cuttings in winter.

TROUBLESHOOTING None needed.

SIZE The ground-covering evergreen *E. fortunei* will attain about 2 × 8ft./60cm. × 2.5m. after fifteen years. The evergreen *E. japonica* may reach 10 × 10–13ft./3 × 3–4m.; the deciduous *E. europaea*, about 13 × 22ft./4 × 6.5m., and *E. alatus* about 6½ × 13ft./2 × 4m.

Euonymus fortunei 'Aurea Marginata' and 'Argentea Marginata'

Fatsia FALSE CASTOR OIL PLANT

This handsome species looks like a house plant, the only way it can be grown in the North, but, in fact, is a fairly tough and very useful evergreen shrub for difficult sites.

SOIL Tolerates most, but best on moist, rich, organic soils.

SITUATION Always best in medium or deep shade and with some shelter in cold areas; intolerant of full sun. Zone 8.

WATERING AND FEEDING Mulch in fall and spring. Feed with a balanced, general-purpose fertilizer in mid-spring, and again around midsummer.

Fatsia japonica

Fatsia – Fuchsia

Forsythia × intermedia
'Spectabilis'

PRUNING Remove suckers. Thin to show branch pattern.
COMMON PROBLEMS Snails; yellow leaves – add iron to soil.
PROPAGATION Leaf-bud cuttings in summer.
TROUBLESHOOTING None needed, but plants that have grown too large may be cut back hard and will regenerate successfully.
SIZE Will attain about 13 × 13ft./4 × 4m. in about sixteen years.

Forsythia   GOLDEN BELLS

Deciduous shrubs that light up gardens everywhere with their yellow and golden spring flowers. They are among the easiest grown and most popular of all shrubs, but the pruning still commonly causes confusion to gardeners.
SOIL Almost any, provided it is well drained and fairly deep.
SITUATION Full sun; even in partial shade, the flowering is greatly impaired. *F. suspensa* is very successful when trained against a wall; *F. × intermedia* forms a good ornamental hedge. Zones 5–8.
WATERING AND FEEDING Mulch in fall and spring. Feed with a balanced rose or similar potash-rich fertilizer in mid-spring, and again around midsummer. Take special care not to allow the plants to dry out while in flower.
PRUNING Free-standing shrubs are best pruned at least once every two or three years by cutting back the oldest third of the shoots to ground level immediately after flowering. Any overcrowded shoots should be removed at the same time. Plants trained against a wall should be clipped back hard immediately after flowering. When grown as a hedge, clip once, lightly, shortly after flowering.
COMMON PROBLEMS None; a slightly disfiguring gall that commonly appears on the shoots is harmless.
PROPAGATION Semi-ripe cuttings in late summer, or hardwood cuttings in winter.
TROUBLESHOOTING Old, congested, and woody plants can sometimes be rejuvenated by cutting the shoots back to soil level in spring. The work should be staged, cutting back one third of the shoots in each of three successive years. If the plant is very old it should be replaced.
SIZE Varies slightly between varieties. Most (including the old *F. × intermedia* 'Spectabilis', which I still consider the best) will reach about 10 × 5ft./3 × 1.5m. after five years and then 13 × 10ft./ 4 × 3m. after fifteen, but *F. suspensa* is taller and more lax (sometimes called the climbing forsythia), whereas the low, spreading 'Arnold Dwarf' barely exceeds 3 × 6½ft./1 × 2m. in five years.

Fremontodendron   FREMONTIA

Two species of evergreen or semi-evergreen shrubs with the most striking, large buttercup-yellow flowers; the color is derived, however, not from the petals but the sepals. I suspect that their reputation for being very tender is not really justified for, given some wall protection, they have survived exceedingly cold winters in my own garden in Britain.

SOIL Almost any, provided it is well drained and preferably fairly deep; they are tolerant of alkalinity.

SITUATION Full sun or very light shade. The shelter of a wall is almost essential for they are very lax and, even in a mild area, don't make successful freestanding plants. Zone 9.

WATERING AND FEEDING Mulch in fall and spring. Apply a balanced rose or similar potash-rich fertilizer in mid-spring, and again around midsummer.

PRUNING None normally necessary, apart from cutting back any stems damaged by frost; if trained against a wall in a fairly confined area, the plant may be spur pruned by cutting back the side-shoots after flowering to about 1½in./4cm. from their bases (the stubs that remain form the so-called spurs).

COMMON PROBLEMS None.

PROPAGATION Softwood cuttings in early summer.

TROUBLESHOOTING The plant has a reputation for being short-lived and there is no doubt that apparently healthy specimens will suddenly die back without warning. This may happen to individual branches as well, which should then be cut back to 5in./13cm. above their base, or above the junction with the main stem.

SIZE Attains about 10 × 10ft./3 × 3m. after five years, but plants that survive may reach 26 × 20ft./8 × 6m. after twenty years.

Fremontodendron 'California Glory'

Fuchsia

In mild or West Coast areas, the fuchsia is a hardy shrub that makes a good hedge. Elsewhere, it is a tender perennial to be taken in and out of the garden more like a pelargonium. I have included them all here, but distinguish where treatment differs.

SOIL HARDY FUCHSIAS Almost any, provided it is well drained. TENDER FUCHSIAS Treat as for hardy forms; when grown in containers they generally fare best in soil-based compost.

SITUATION Full sun or very light shade. *F. magellanica*, Zones 7–9; all other non-hardy hybrids, Zone 10.

WATERING AND FEEDING HARDY FUCHSIAS Mulch in fall and spring. Apply a balanced rose or similar potash-rich fertilizer in mid-spring, and again around midsummer.

TENDER FUCHSIAS Follow a regime for container plants giving a liquid fertilizer with high potash content once a week.

PRUNING HARDY FUCHSIAS In areas where significant damage from frost is unlikely, none is necessary. Where some frost damage is normal, either cut back in spring to at least 6in./15cm. beyond damaged shoots, or cut back to ground level in spring. When grown as a hedge, clip once in fall or early spring, cutting the sides fairly hard but the leading shoots only lightly until the required height is reached.

TENDER FUCHSIAS None normally necessary while growing outdoors. If plants are overwintered in containers under cover, cut back by at least two thirds in fall, before taking indoors.

COMMON PROBLEMS Whitefly; aphids.

PROPAGATION Softwood cuttings in summer or early spring.

TROUBLESHOOTING Very old and woody hardy plants can be rejuvenated by cutting back hard in spring.

Fuchsia 'Mrs. Popple'

Fuchsia – Hamamelis

Garrya elliptica

SIZE Varies, depending on variety. The most popular hardy varieties used for hedging are forms of *F. magellanica*, especially 'Riccartonii', which, if unpruned, in mild areas will grow quickly to reach 5 × 5ft./1.5 × 1.5m. after about ten years. Tender varieties are much smaller but it is important to choose one appropriate for your needs; the trailing, cascading, or basket varieties should be used for hanging baskets and window boxes, the upright types for other containers and for open ground planting in mild climates.

Garrya TASSEL BUSH

G. elliptica, one of several species native to West Coast regions, is a fairly hardy evergreen, although it is almost always grown as a wall shrub for the appeal of its elongated winter catkins. It can be grown as a freestanding bush but may be browned by cold winds.
SOIL Almost any, provided it is not prone to water-logging. Like all wall shrubs, the plant will benefit from a fairly high content of moisture-retaining organic matter.
SITUATION Full sun or medium shade, although the production of catkins is always best in sun. Zone 8.
WATERING AND FEEDING Mulch in fall and spring. Feed with a balanced rose or similar potash-rich fertilizer in mid-spring, and again around midsummer.
PRUNING None normally necessary, although wall-trained plants growing in a confined space will be kept tidier by having the previous season's shoots cut back to 4in./10cm. above their bases immediately after flowering.
COMMON PROBLEMS None.
PROPAGATION Semi-ripe cuttings in summer or hardwood cuttings in winter.
TROUBLESHOOTING None normally necessary. Very old or diseased wood should be cut back hard in early spring.
SIZE Attains about 10 × 6½ft./3 × 2m. after five years, and about 16 × 13ft./5 × 4m. after eighteen or twenty years.

Genista

A genus of attractive, mainly yellow-flowered spring- or summer-blooming deciduous shrubs. Some species are known as brooms, others as gorse, and yet others as greenweeds. Some forms possess greatly reduced leaves and appear almost to have leafless green stems. There is some variation in hardiness.
SOIL Almost any, but highly intolerant of water-logging.
SITUATION Full sun. Zones 4–9.
WATERING AND FEEDING Mulch in fall and spring. Feed with a balanced rose or similar potash-rich fertilizer in mid-spring, and again around midsummer.
PRUNING Inadvisable.
COMMON PROBLEMS None.
PROPAGATION Semi-ripe cuttings in summer or hardwood cuttings in winter.
TROUBLESHOOTING None normally necessary. Old and badly shaped plants should be replaced.

Genista lydia

Size The largest species, *G. aethnensis* (Zone 9), forms a small tree, reaching about 8 × 8ft./2.5 × 2.5m. after five years and up to 16 × 16ft./5 × 5m. after twenty. Other species are unlikely to exceed about 3ft./1m. in height and one, *G. sagittalis* (Zones 4–8), is lower growing still and forms good ground cover.

Hamamelis WITCH HAZEL

Witch hazels, a small group of deciduous shrubs or almost small trees, are prized for their fragrant spidery yellow or red flowers that appear on the leafless branches in winter and early spring. One species, *H. virginiana*, native to eastern North America, flowers in fall as leaves drop.

Soil Rich and preferably acid, although they are tolerant of soils around neutral provided there is a high organic matter content. Intolerant of water-logging or heavy clay.

Hamamelis mollis 'Superba'

Situation Light shade or full sun. Zones 4–8.

Watering and feeding Mulch in fall and spring. Feed with a balanced rose or similar potash-rich fertilizer in mid-spring, and again around midsummer.

Pruning None.

Common problems None.

Propagation Almost impossible from cuttings but layering is usually successful.

Troubleshooting None normally necessary. Witch hazels will not regenerate satisfactorily from old wood.

Size Slow growing in its early stages, reaching about 5 × 5ft./1.5 × 1.5m. after five years, but ultimately up to 16 × 13ft./5 × 4m. after eighteen to twenty years.

Hebe 'Midsummer Beauty'

Hebe

A large group of evergreen shrubs characterized by dense inflorescences of white or bluish flowers, the shrubby relatives of *Veronica*. Familiar types with normal leaves include 'Carl Teschner' and 'Midsummer Beauty'; the so-called whipcords have conifer-like foliage, exemplified by *H. ochracea*, *H.o.* 'James Stirling', and *H. cupressoides*. Few broadleaved species are sufficiently hardy, however, to be relied upon outdoors, except in mild or coastal areas of California.

SOIL Light, free draining, intolerant of water-logging.

SITUATION Full sun. Zones 8–9.

WATERING AND FEEDING Mulch in fall and spring. Feed with a balanced rose or similar potash-rich fertilizer in mid-spring, and again around midsummer.

PRUNING Lightly trim normal-leaved varieties in spring to encourage new shoot development. The whipcord species should not be pruned.

COMMON PROBLEMS Leaf spotting; shoot dieback.

PROPAGATION Semi-ripe cuttings in summer.

TROUBLESHOOTING Plants that are badly frost damaged or mis-shapen should be cut back almost to soil level in spring.

SIZE There are two main groups of normal-leaved hebes: the low-growing ground-cover forms such as *H. pinguifolia*, which reach their full size of about 1×3ft./30cm. $\times$ 1m. after five years; and the popular taller shrubs which attain about 3×3ft./1×1m. after a similar time and then slowly reach $5–6\frac{1}{2} \times 6\frac{1}{2}–10$ft./$1.5–2 \times 2–3$m. in fifteen to twenty years. The whipcords will reach their ultimate height and spread of $1\frac{1}{2} \times 2\frac{1}{2}$ft./$45 \times 75$cm. after five years.

Hibiscus ROSE-OF-SHARON

The hardy species is the deciduous *H. syriacus*; its flowers in white, blue, mauve, or pink have shorter trumpets than those of the popular evergreen conservatory and house plant species, *H. rosa-sinensis*, which is not hardy enough for cold areas. 'Diana' (white) and 'Blue Bird' are two outstanding summer-flowering varieties of *H. syriacus*.

SOIL Light, rich, free draining, intolerant of water-logging.

SITUATION Tolerates light shade or full sun, preferably with a little shelter. Zones 5–8.

WATERING AND FEEDING Mulch in fall and spring. Apply a balanced rose or similar potash-rich fertilizer in mid-spring, and again around midsummer.

PRUNING None necessary, although on well-established plants the previous season's shoots may be shortened by up to half in spring, to encourage a bushy habit.

COMMON PROBLEMS Japanese beetles are sometimes pests.

PROPAGATION Semi-ripe cuttings in summer.

TROUBLESHOOTING None normally necessary.

SIZE Reaches about 3×3ft./1×1m. after five years and in favored areas may attain about $10–13 \times 10–13$ft./$3–4 \times 3–4$m. after sixteen to eighteen years.

Hibiscus syriacus

Hippophaë SEA BUCKTHORN

A very familiar plant to British coastal gardeners from its natural habitat on sand dunes, but scarcely known elsewhere. It is a useful screening and winter-berrying shrub that should be better known to Americans in maritime areas.

SOIL Light, free draining; tolerant of fairly high alkalinity.

SITUATION Full sun; tolerant of exposure and salt spray. Zones 4–5.

WATERING AND FEEDING Mulch in fall and spring. Feed with a balanced rose or similar potash-rich fertilizer in mid-spring, and again around midsummer.

PRUNING None. When grown as a hedge, shear once two or three weeks after midsummer, and again in early fall.

COMMON PROBLEMS None, although a failure to form berries commonly occurs because the sexes are on different plants; both male and female are required for fruiting.

PROPAGATION From seed; difficult from cuttings.

TROUBLESHOOTING None normally necessary, but very old and woody plants may regenerate if cut hard back into the old wood in spring.

SIZE Reaches about $6\frac{1}{2} \times 6\frac{1}{2}$ft./$2 \times 2$m. after five years and ultimately 20×20ft./6×6m. after about fifteen years.

Hippophaë rhamnoides

Hydrangea

One of the most useful groups of deciduous flowering shrubs, with one related common climber (see page 91). Hydrangeas may grow inadequately or produce flowers of the wrong color if the soil and site do not meet their requirements.

SOIL Rich, moist but not prone to water-logging. Hydrangeas are tolerant of acidity and alkalinity but the flower color of many popular mop-heads and some lacecap varieties will vary with soil conditions. To obtain the desirable blue, acidic soil must be used; any lime present will turn them red. A proprietary "blueing powder" will help to correct this, but is never as successful as growing the plants on a naturally acidic soil.

SITUATION Sun to light shade; most varieties are tolerant of exposure and salt spray. Zones 4–9.

WATERING AND FEEDING Mulch in fall and spring. Apply a balanced rose or similar potash-rich fertilizer in mid-spring, and again around midsummer.

PRUNING Most species and varieties require little, with the following exceptions. On established plants of the mop-head and lacecap varieties of *H. macrophylla*, cut out up to one-third of the oldest or weakest nonflowered shoots each year, in late spring or early summer, to a few inches above soil level. At the same time, cut off dead flower heads, cutting back to a strong pair of new leaves. Since buds form in the previous season, prune *after* flowering. Prune *H. paniculata* in mid-spring, cutting back the previous season's growth to within three buds of the base.

COMMON PROBLEMS Leaf tattering caused by capsid bugs; powdery mildew in hot summers.

Hydrangea (lacecap)

Hydrangea – Kerria

Hypericum olympicum

PROPAGATION Semi-ripe cuttings in late summer.

TROUBLESHOOTING Old, woody, or winter-damaged plants of most species will regenerate if cut back hard in mid-spring but flowering may be set back by one or two years.

SIZE Varies according to species, although most types, including the mop-head and lacecap varieties of *H. macrophylla*, will fairly quickly reach about 3×3ft./1×1m. and then eventually, after about fifteen years, reach $6\frac{1}{2} \times 6\frac{1}{2}$–$8$ft./$2 \times 2$–$2.5$m. Among other popular forms, *H. involucrata* is perhaps the smallest, eventually reaching about 3×3ft./1×1m., while *H. paniculata* is the largest, reaching about 13×13ft./4×4m. in fifteen to eighteen years.

Hypericum ST JOHN'S WORT

A genus of evergreen and deciduous flowering shrubs, grown for their yellow-orange flowers and, in the case of the very popular *H. calycinum*, as a very tough ground cover.

SOIL Almost any, *H. calycinum* especially being tolerant of extremes of acidity, alkalinity, and dryness.

SITUATION Most forms prefer light shade, although *H. calycinum* is tolerant of deep shade. Zones 4–8.

WATERING AND FEEDING Mulch in fall and spring. Feed with a balanced rose or similar potash-rich fertilizer in mid-spring, and again around midsummer.

PRUNING Varies with species. *H. calycinum* and the varieties grown for their colored foliage should be cut back to soil level in spring in every other year, to encourage vigorous new shoot growth. The varieties grown for flowers and fruit can be similarly treated but will, consequently, remain fairly small; they are better pruned annually, in spring, cutting back the oldest one third of the shoots to soil level.

COMMON PROBLEMS Rust.

PROPAGATION Semi-ripe cuttings in summer or hardwood cuttings in winter. *H. calycinum* produces abundant suckers, which are readily removed and replanted.

TROUBLESHOOTING Old, woody, or neglected plants will regenerate if cut back hard in early spring.

SIZE Most forms grow fairly slowly to reach about 3×3ft./1×1m. after ten years, but *H. calycinum* is vigorous and will reach about 1×3ft./30cm. $\times 1$m. after three or four years.

Jasminum

There are two common and popular outdoor jasmines: the yellow, early spring-blooming *J. nudiflorum* and the white-flowered, fragrant, summer jasmine, *J. officinale*. The latter is rather more tender, and is often classed as a climber, but, although its shoots are certainly lax, I always think it is better considered as a wall shrub. Both are excellent plants, although not all gardens suit them equally.

SOIL Almost any, especially for *J. nudiflorum*, which will tolerate rather poor conditions. *J. officinale* is less tolerant of extremes of dryness or water-logging.

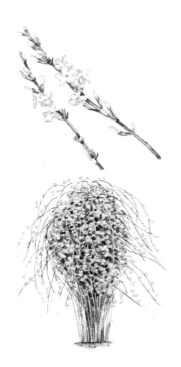

Jasminum nudiflorum

SITUATION Full sun to light shade; *J. nudiflorum* is the more shade-tolerant of the two. *J. officinale* (Zones 7–10) must have some shelter (Zones 5–10).

WATERING AND FEEDING Mulch in fall and spring. Feed with a balanced rose or similar potash-rich fertilizer in mid-spring, and again around midsummer.

PRUNING *J. nudiflorum*: when it is grown freestanding, I prefer to cut back the oldest third of the stems to ground level every spring, but leave the previous season's flowered shoots. When trained against a wall, I treat it like a hedge and clip it hard immediately after the flowers fade. *J. officinale*: cut back the long, whippy shoots by up to two thirds in mid-spring.

COMMON PROBLEMS None. Winter cold may damage shoots; cut out in mid-spring.

PROPAGATION Semi-ripe cuttings in summer.

TROUBLESHOOTING Old, woody, or neglected plants will usually regenerate if cut back hard in early spring.

SIZE *J. nudiflorum* will reach about 5 × 5ft./1.5 × 1.5m. after five years and about twice this after twenty. *J. officinale* is roughly twice as fast growing and vigorous, ultimately reaching as much as 33 × 33ft./10 × 10m., although it is much better pruned back.

Kalmia latifolia

Kalmia CALICO BUSH, MOUNTAIN-LAUREL

The exquisitely beautiful, spring-flowering evergreen *K. latifolia* is a relative of rhododendrons and azaleas. It makes a good companion to them and requires very similar conditions. Unfortunately, if the natural garden soil is unsuitable, it doesn't, in my experience, grow well in a container.

SOIL Deep, rich, acid and moist.

SITUATION Light shade. Zones 4–9.

WATERING AND FEEDING Mulch in fall and spring. Feed with a balanced rose or similar potash-rich fertilizer in mid-spring, and again around midsummer; or use the fertilizer Hollytone.

PRUNING Remove fading flowers to aid next year's bloom.

COMMON PROBLEMS Leaf spot in full sun.

PROPAGATION Seeds in sphagnum moss.

TROUBLESHOOTING None normally necessary.

SIZE Fairly slow growing: reaches about 5 × 5ft./1.5 × 1.5m. after five years, twice this after about fifteen years.

Kerria JAPANESE-ROSE

Perhaps the easiest and least demanding flowering garden shrub, the deciduous, yellow, spring-flowering *K. japonica* has the merit of an upright then arching green cane-like habit. 'Pleniflora' has double flowers and 'Aureo-variegata', yellow and green leaves.

SOIL Almost any; tolerant of dryness and water-logging, acidity and alkalinity.

SITUATION Full sun to moderate shade. Zones 5–8.

WATERING AND FEEDING Mulch in fall and spring. Apply a balanced rose or similar potash-rich fertilizer in mid-spring, and again around midsummer.

Kerria japonica 'Pleniflora'

Laurus nobilis

PRUNING Cut back the oldest third of the shoots to soil level immediately after flowering.

COMMON PROBLEMS None.

PROPAGATION Semi-ripe cuttings in late summer, hardwood cuttings in winter, or from rooted suckers.

TROUBLESHOOTING None normally necessary.

SIZE Fast growing, reaching its ultimate height of about 8–10ft./2.5–3m. in under five years. It will then spread slowly to form a clump about 10ft./3m. in diameter after twenty years.

Laurus SWEET BAY, BAY LAUREL

One of two evergreen shrubs popularly known as laurels, *L. nobilis* has been grown in gardens for centuries. It is almost the only large shrub routinely used as a herb but it is a valuable ornamental, too; carefully clipped specimens in pots command very high prices. It is much tougher than it is often given credit for and, even when damaged, has great powers of regeneration.

SOIL Almost any, provided it is not very wet.

SITUATION Tolerates full sun to deep shade, but foliage is browned by exposure to cold winds. Zones 7–9.

WATERING AND FEEDING Mulch in fall and spring. Feed with a balanced, general fertilizer in mid-spring.

PRUNING None is necessary but plants can be clipped or pruned to shape in spring. When grown as a hedge, clip once in early fall, cutting the sides fairly hard but the leading shoots only lightly until the required height is reached.

COMMON PROBLEMS Scale insect, leading to sooty mold.

PROPAGATION Semi-ripe cuttings in summer.

TROUBLESHOOTING Cold-damaged or overgrown plants may be cut back hard into the old wood, and will regenerate.

SIZE Reaches 5×3ft./1.5×1m. after five years but left unpruned will become a tree of 40×30ft./12×9m. after about 30 years.

Clipping Lavender

AFTER FLOWERING Keep plants compact by shearing them over quite hard.

Lavandula LAVENDER

There are several species and cultivars of lavender and they are grown as herbaceous perennials in the North. In mild climates, dwarf compact cultivars of *L. angustifolia*, such as 'Hidcote', 'Compacta', and 'Munstead', are suitable for hedging.

SOIL Prefers a light, free draining soil, but will tolerate almost any provided it is not very wet.

SITUATION Full sun. Zones 5–9.

WATERING AND FEEDING Mulch in fall and spring. Feed with a balanced rose or similar potash-rich fertilizer in mid-spring, and again after midsummer.

PRUNING None is necessary but a light trim in mid-spring will encourage a bushy habit and hard clipping after the flowers have faded – just cutting into the woody growth at the base of the flower spikes – will create the neatest appearance. When grown as a hedge, clip once immediately after flowering. If flowers are required for potpourri, they must be cut just as they open fully.

COMMON PROBLEMS Winter dieback in cold climates.

PROPAGATION Semi-ripe cuttings in summer.

TROUBLESHOOTING Old and woody plants usually regenerate satisfactorily if cut back hard in spring, cutting about 2in./5cm. into the woody tissue.

SIZE In mild climates hedging varieties may reach 2×2ft./60×60cm. in four years; taller types about 3×3ft./1×1m. in ten years.

Lavatera TREE MALLOW

A varied genus of plants that includes some popular bedding annuals and biennials, as well as the species considered here. Of those seen most commonly, *L. olbia* (of which 'Rosea' is the best known) is shrubby and *L. thuringiaca* (of which 'Barnsley' is the most familiar) is herbaceous, but it is impossible to draw a hard and fast line between the two species. Their soil and site requirements are similar and rather critical if the best results are to be achieved. Plants in the closely related genus *Malva*, also known as mallows, may be treated similarly.

Lavatera olbia 'Rosea'

SOIL Tolerant of a range of conditions from rich to moderately poor, but must be free draining. Particularly successful in alkaline conditions. The commonest reason for failure is when the plants are growing in heavy clay or strongly acidic soil.

SITUATION Full sun to light shade with shelter from cold winds. Shrubby forms suit mild West Coast gardens. Zones 9–10.

WATERING AND FEEDING Mulch in fall and spring. Feed with a balanced, general-purpose fertilizer in mid-spring, and again after midsummer.

PRUNING Prune in spring, preferably by cutting one third of the shoots back to just above soil level, then cutting the remainder into healthy wood about 1ft./30cm. beyond the limits of any frost or cold damage; or cut the entire plant back to about 1ft./30cm. above soil level.

COMMON PROBLEMS None.

PROPAGATION Semi-ripe cuttings in early summer or hardwood cuttings in winter.

TROUBLESHOOTING Overgrown, damaged, or straggly plants can usually be rejuvenated by cutting them back to about 1ft./30cm. above soil level in spring, and feeding well.

SIZE Up to $6\frac{1}{2}–10 \times 6\frac{1}{2}–10$ft./$2–3 \times 2–3$m. after five years without hard pruning; will attain about $5–6\frac{1}{2} \times 5$ft./$1.5–2 \times 1.5$m. in a single season if pruned hard.

Leycesteria HIMALAYAN HONEYSUCKLE

A greatly underrated but valuable, hardy deciduous shrub that is tolerant of difficult sites and very useful for flower and foliage interest at the back of a border or in a slightly shady corner. *L. formosa* is the most common species.

SOIL Almost any, provided it is not highly alkaline.

SITUATION Full sun or medium shade. Zone 7.

WATERING AND FEEDING Mulch in fall and spring. Apply a balanced rose or similar potash-rich fertilizer in mid-spring, and again after midsummer.

Leycesteria formosa

Ligustrum ovalifolium

Ligustrum ovalifolium 'Aureum'

Lonicera nitida 'Baggesen's Gold'

PRUNING Cut back all shoots to a few inches above soil level in early spring.

COMMON PROBLEMS None.

PROPAGATION Does not strike easily from cuttings, and is usually grown from seed.

TROUBLESHOOTING Old and neglected plants will usually regenerate satisfactorily if cut back to soil level in spring.

SIZE With annual pruning, will attain about $6\frac{1}{2} \times 3$ft./2×1m. each season, after the first two years.

Ligustrum PRIVET

The evergreen Japanese privet (*L. ovalifolium*) is the hedging plant of the past. It still has its devotees, but there are now many better plants for the purpose. The golden variety justifiably remains popular as a specimen shrub.

SOIL Almost any, provided it is not highly alkaline.

SITUATION Full sun to fairly deep shade. Zones 7–9.

WATERING AND FEEDING Mulch in fall and spring. Apply a balanced, general fertilizer in mid-spring.

PRUNING No pruning is actually necessary, but privets will almost always require some shaping which can be done in spring. When grown as a hedge, clip several times starting just after the time when the last frost is likely to occur, and stop at the first frost in the fall.

COMMON PROBLEMS Aphids, leading to sooty mold.

PROPAGATION Semi-ripe cuttings in midsummer or hardwood cuttings in winter.

TROUBLESHOOTING Old, woody, and neglected plants usually regenerate if cut back hard into the old wood in spring.

SIZE In the unlikely event of never being pruned, privets will reach about 10×10ft./3×3m. after five years and double this after sixteen to eighteen years.

Lonicera HONEYSUCKLE

Although *Lonicera* is best known as a genus of climbing honeysuckles, there are several evergreen and deciduous shrubby species, some very hardy and familiar, others more tender and less common but still highly desirable.

SOIL Most, provided it is not very dry or water-logged.

SITUATION Full sun to light shade. Zones 3–8.

WATERING AND FEEDING Mulch in fall and spring. Feed with a balanced, general fertilizer in mid-spring.

PRUNING No pruning is normally necessary with the deciduous types, although up to one third of the oldest shoots may be removed each spring to encourage new growth. The evergreen *L. nitida* (Zone 7) may be treated similarly but is also often used as a hedge. In this case, clip several times starting just after the last frost and stopping at the first frost in the fall.

COMMON PROBLEMS None.

PROPAGATION Semi-ripe cuttings in midsummer or hardwood cuttings in winter.

TROUBLESHOOTING Old, woody, and neglected plants can sometimes be rejuvenated if cut back hard in spring, but very old and misshapen plants should be replaced.

SIZE Most of the common deciduous and evergreen forms will reach about $3 \times 6\frac{1}{2}$ft./1×2m. after five years and about $6\frac{1}{2}$–10×13ft./2–3×4m. after fifteen years. The major exception is the semi-evergreen *L. pileata*, which is a ground-cover plant eventually reaching about 3×13ft./1×4m.

Mahonia OREGON GRAPE

The most familiar mahonia is *M. aquifolium*, one of the toughest of all evergreen shrubs and one that will grow, and even flower, nearly anywhere. It has several larger-leaved relatives, more beautiful in bloom but also rather more tender.

SOIL Most will tolerate a wide range of soils but are least successful in very dry sites.

SITUATION *M. aquifolium* (Zones 5–8) tolerates part sun to deep shade; the other species and varieties prefer light to deep shade, with some shelter from cold winds. Zones 6–8.

WATERING AND FEEDING Mulch in fall and spring. Feed with a balanced rose or similar potash-rich fertilizer in mid-spring, and again after midsummer.

PRUNING No pruning is necessary on *M. aquifolium*, unless it is grown as a hedge. But on *M. aquifolium*, *M. × media* 'Charity', *M. lomariifolia*, *M. bealei*, and related plants, a more compact habit will be encouraged by cutting back nonflowering shoots by about one half in mid-spring, at least in the early years. If a tall plant is required to fill a sheltered corner, this is not necessary.

COMMON PROBLEMS Rust on *M. aquifolium*.

PROPAGATION Very difficult to strike from cuttings, although semi-ripe wood in early summer may be successful; otherwise propagate by layering.

TROUBLESHOOTING Old, woody, and neglected plants can sometimes be rejuvenated if cut back hard in spring but very old and misshapen plants should be replaced.

SIZE *M. aquifolium* reaches its maximum height of about 3–4ft./ 1–1.2m. within three or four years but then creeps slowly outward, reaching about 10ft./3m. ultimately. The other common species will reach about $5 \times 6\frac{1}{2}$ft./1.5×2m. after five years and 10–13×10ft./3–4×3m. after twenty, although hybrids such as 'Charity' may reach half as much again.

Myrica WAX MYRTLE, BAYBERRY

A variable but particularly useful genus of deciduous and evergreen shrubs or, in a few cases, small trees, that will grow in conditions too wet for most others. Their flowers are interesting if unspectacular, but the deciduous *M. gale*, the sweet gale or bog myrtle, has delightfully perfumed leaves; the other American species (the evergreen *M. californica*, *M. cerifera* known as the wax myrtle, and *M. pensylvanica*) bear characteristic, wax-coated fruits.

SOIL Wet, boggy, acidic; intolerant of alkalinity.

Mahonia × media 'Charity'

Myrica pensylvanica

Myrica – Paeonia

Nandina domestica

SITUATION Full sun or very light shade. *M. californica*, Zone 8; *M. cerifera*, Zone 7; *M. gale*, Zone 4; *M. pensylvanica*, Zones 2–6.

WATERING AND FEEDING Mulch in fall and spring unless growing in very boggy conditions with constant surface water. Feed with a balanced rose or similar potash-rich fertilizer in mid-spring, and again around midsummer.

PRUNING Varies considerably between species. None is required for *M. gale* and may result in branch die-back. The other two related American species, *M. cerifera* and *M. pensylvanica*, may be used as hedging or trained on single stems to form round-headed standards: in both cases clip in late spring and early fall.

COMMON PROBLEMS None.

PROPAGATION Semi-ripe cuttings in early spring, or from seed.

TROUBLESHOOTING Old or damaged plants of all species except *M. gale* will regenerate if cut back to soil level, preferably spreading the work over two or three years. *M. gale* cannot be rejuvenated satisfactorily.

SIZE *M. gale* will reach its full size of about 3–5 × 3ft./1–1.5 × 1m. after about eight years. Over about sixteen years, *M. pensylvanica* will attain roughly 10 × 6½ft./3 × 2m., *M. californica* 26–33 × 26ft./8–10 × 8m., and *M. cerifera* up to 33 × 33ft./10 × 10m. in mild West Coast areas.

Nandina HEAVENLY BAMBOO

A genus of one, more or less evergreen, bamboo-like species, *N. domestica*, is grown for its foliage in cooler areas but with the added bonus of flowers and bright red fruits in mild climates.

SOIL Tolerates most, although best on well drained but moist, acidic soils.

SITUATION Full sun but shelter from cold winds. Zones 6–9.

WATERING AND FEEDING Mulch in fall and spring. Feed with a balanced rose or similar potash-rich fertilizer in mid-spring, and again around midsummer.

PRUNING It is sensible to cut away dead flowered or fruiting stems, and to cut back very old shoots to soil level in spring.

COMMON PROBLEMS None.

PROPAGATION By division in spring, or from seed.

TROUBLESHOOTING Damaged or overgrown plants may be cut back to soil level and should regenerate satisfactorily.

SIZE 3–4 × 3–4ft./1–1.2 × 1–1.2m. after fifteen years.

Olearia DAISY BUSH

Olearia macrodonta

Pretty evergreen flowering shrub for the California coast's mild-climate gardens, but too tender to be of much use anywhere else unless it can be given good protection.

SOIL Tolerates a wide range of soils but is always best in free draining, rich, and slightly acidic conditions.

SITUATION Full sun but shelter from cold winds. Zones 9–10.

WATERING AND FEEDING Mulch in fall and spring. Apply a balanced rose or similar potash-rich fertilizer in mid-spring, and again after midsummer.

PRUNING Once plants are established, cut back the oldest third of the shoots to soil level in late spring.

COMMON PROBLEMS None.

PROPAGATION Semi-ripe cuttings in summer or hardwood cuttings in winter.

TROUBLESHOOTING Old, woody, and neglected plants can sometimes be rejuvenated if cut back hard in spring but very old and misshapen plants should be replaced.

SIZE In coastal gardens, attains about 3 × 3ft./1 × 1m. after five years and 13 × 13ft./4 × 4m. after eighteen to twenty years.

Pachysandra

A very low-growing, ground-cover shrub, useful for dry and difficult areas, although tolerant of a wide range of conditions.

SOIL Tolerates many, but best on moist, rich, organic soils.

SITUATION Light to deep shade; a useful plant for moist areas under trees. Zones 3–8.

WATERING AND FEEDING Mulch in fall and spring. Feed with a balanced general fertilizer in mid-spring.

PRUNING None necessary.

COMMON PROBLEMS Foliage yellows in sun and very dry soil.

PROPAGATION Division (treat like a herbaceous perennial).

TROUBLESHOOTING Old and straggly plants may be rejuvenated by cutting them back to soil level in spring and applying both a mulch and a general fertilizer.

SIZE Slower growing than is often claimed, especially the variegated form, which can be very slow indeed. The normal species will attain about 8in. × 2½ft./20 × 80cm. after five years, and about 1 × 6½ft./30cm. × 2m. after fifteen or seventeen years, although as ground cover a large number of individual plants would be used.

Pachysandra terminalis 'Variegata'
Pachysandra terminalis

Paeonia TREE PEONY

The so-called tree peonies are genuine shrubs, superb in flower in the right conditions. Sadly, some of the best forms tend to be rather scarce.

SOIL Tolerates a wide range, provided it is not very heavy or water-logged, but less successful in highly alkaline conditions.

SITUATION Full sun to light shade, although with some shelter from cold winds. Zones 5–8.

WATERING AND FEEDING Mulch in fall and spring. Feed with a balanced rose or similar potash-rich fertilizer in mid-spring, and again after midsummer.

PRUNING None necessary or even advisable, as the plants may be seriously checked by it.

COMMON PROBLEMS Shallow planting; set roots 6in./15cm. deep.

PROPAGATION Not possible. The true species are propagated from seed; most of the Chinese and Japanese varieties by grafting.

TROUBLESHOOTING None should be necessary, but dead or damaged branches should be cut back to their base. Many tree peonies have such heavy double blooms that they may require staking during flowering time.

Paeonia lutea

Philadelphus coronarius

Phlomis fruticosa

SIZE The modern Oriental varieties (which are grafted onto herbaceous peony rootstocks), and the true species, including the exceptionally lovely *P. suffruticosa*, as well as the more common *P. lutea*, will attain about 5 × 5ft./1.5 × 1.5m. after ten to twelve years, and its variety *Ludlowii* may eventually grow to twice this.

Philadelphus MOCK ORANGE

Also mistakenly known as syringa, philadelphus is among the most rewarding of deciduous, hardy summer-flowering shrubs.
SOIL Most, but succeeds best on more or less neutral, well drained rich loams.
SITUATION Full sun to medium shade; variegated and golden-leaved forms scorch in full sun and cold winds. Zones 5–8.
WATERING AND FEEDING Mulch in fall and spring. Feed with a balanced rose or similar potash-rich fertilizer in mid-spring, and again after midsummer.
PRUNING After flowering in late spring to early summer, cut back old wood that has borne blooms to a new shoot or bud.
COMMON PROBLEMS Aphids.
PROPAGATION Semi-ripe cuttings in summer or hardwood cuttings in winter.
TROUBLESHOOTING Old, congested, and very woody plants can be rejuvenated by initiating annual pruning as above.
SIZE The small shrubby forms, such as 'Manteau d'Hermine', are slow growing and will reach 2 × 2ft./70 × 70cm. after about five years and slightly over 3ft./1m. ultimately. Half as fast and large again is a slightly taller group, with 'Belle Etoile' the best-known variety; the largest group, including 'Beauclerk', 'Virginal', and *P. coronarius* 'Aureus', will reach 5 × 3ft./1.5 × 1m. after five years and 10–13 × 10–13ft./3–4 × 3–4m. after sixteen to eighteen years.

Phlomis JERUSALEM SAGE

Great, gaunt, and ungainly it may be, yet many gardeners love the Jerusalem sage for its whorls of flowers in pastel shades. It is mostly grown in California where it thrives in sun and sand.
SOIL Light, free draining.
SITUATION Full sun. Zones 8–10.
WATERING AND FEEDING Mulch in fall and spring. Feed with a balanced, general-purpose fertilizer in mid-spring, and again after midsummer.
PRUNING Cut out damaged or overcrowded shoots in spring. Remove faded flowers to encourage repeat summer bloom.
COMMON PROBLEMS None.
PROPAGATION Division in spring, semi-ripe cuttings in summer, hardwood cuttings in winter, or from seed.
TROUBLESHOOTING None normally necessary but woody and unkempt plants may regenerate if up to one third of the shoots are cut back to just above soil level in fall or early spring.
SIZE The common, true Jerusalem sage, *P. fruticosa*, will reach 4 × 3ft./1.2 × 1m. after three years, although there are related and slightly smaller species.

Photinia

One of the few evergreen (or in a few instances, deciduous) shrubs in which the primary appeal derives from the color of the young shoots in spring, although the summer flowers and fall red berries are showy. *P. × fraseri* has red foliage and stem color in spring.
SOIL Most, but succeeds best on acidic soils, and generally unsuccessful with any alkalinity.
SITUATION Full sun to light shade. Zones 6–9.
WATERING AND FEEDING Mulch in fall and spring. Feed with a balanced, general fertilizer in mid-spring.
PRUNING None necessary.
COMMON PROBLEMS Fireblight.
PROPAGATION Semi-ripe cuttings in summer.
TROUBLESHOOTING Rarely necessary, but old plants will usually respond well to being cut back hard in spring.
SIZE Up to 5 × 6½ft./1.5 × 2m. after five years, 16 × 13ft./5 × 4m. after twenty years.

Pieris ANDROMEDA

Like *Photinia*, some cultivars of the evergreen genus *Pieris* are appreciated for the color of their young shoots, but others are worth having for their delicate tresses of cream spring flowers. Although the plant is hardy, the young shoots can be damaged by late freezes and the soil and site requirements are fairly exacting.
SOIL Moist, rich, acidic; will not flourish in very dry conditions and is intolerant of any alkalinity.
SITUATION Light shade; shelter from cold winds. Zones 5–8.

Photinia davidiana

WATERING AND FEEDING Maintain a permanent mulch of decaying oak leaves, leafmold or white pine needles. Feed with cottonseed meal or azalea-camellia fertilizer in early spring.
PRUNING None necessary.
COMMON PROBLEMS Lacebugs infest foliage when site is too sunny and dry.
PROPAGATION Semi-ripe cuttings in summer or by layering.
TROUBLESHOOTING None necessary.
SIZE Varies slightly but most cultivars will attain 2–3ft. × 3ft./60cm.–1m. × 1m. after about five years, and perhaps double this after eighteen or twenty years.

Pittosporum

A delightful and delicately foliaged evergreen, much beloved of flower arrangers but with rather exacting requirements.
SOIL Fairly rich, free draining, suitable for most soil types but rather intolerant of high alkalinity.
SITUATION Full sun or light shade with some shelter from cold winds; very successful in maritime areas. Zones 9–10.
WATERING AND FEEDING Mulch in fall and spring. Feed with a balanced, general fertilizer in mid-spring.
PRUNING None necessary, but can be trimmed as a hedge: clip twice, first around midsummer and again in early fall.

Pieris japonica 'Pink Delight'

Pittosporum – Pyracantha

Pittosporum tenuifolium

COMMON PROBLEMS Very susceptible to aphids and scales.
PROPAGATION Semi-ripe cuttings in late summer.
TROUBLESHOOTING None normally necessary, but overgrown or very woody plants regenerate if cut back to about 1ft./30cm. above soil level in spring. Very large plants are best treated in two stages: cut back to about 5ft./1.5m. in the first year and then back to 1ft./30cm. in the following year, if they have satisfactorily produced new shoots.
SIZE Most, including the popular *P. tobira* 'Variegata', will reach about 5–6½ × 3ft./1.5–2 × 1m. in favorable, mild areas after five years, and about 20 × 8–10ft./6 × 2.5–3m. after twenty.

Potentilla   CINQUEFOIL

Among the most useful and adaptable of free-flowering, small deciduous shrubs. They are suitable for most gardens, provided care is taken in siting them. Generally do well in the Midwest.
SOIL Preferably light and free draining; intolerant of water-logging or high alkalinity.
SITUATION Full sun; potentillas flower much less satisfactorily in even light shade. Zones 2–7.
WATERING AND FEEDING Mulch in fall and spring. Feed with a balanced rose or similar potash-rich fertilizer in mid-spring, and again after midsummer.
PRUNING None necessary, but most varieties usually produce more flowers and maintain a more effective, neater shape if the oldest one third of the shoots are regularly cut back to just above soil level each spring.
COMMON PROBLEMS None.
PROPAGATION Semi-ripe cuttings in late summer or hardwood cuttings in winter.
TROUBLESHOOTING Old, overgrown, or very woody plants will usually regenerate satisfactorily if cut back to just above soil level in spring, although the task is better staged over two or three years. Very large and neglected plants should be replaced. Even young potentillas look dead or moribund in winter and there is a temptation to cut them back hard in the belief that they have suffered frost damage. Always wait until the buds have burst (which in some cultivars may be quite late), as this will reveal those parts that have truly been killed back.
SIZE Varies considerably. Some dwarf or almost ground-covering varieties, such as *P. fruticosa* 'Manchu', will slowly reach about 8in × 2½ft./20 × 75cm., but most of the common bush varieties will reach about 4 × 4ft./1.2 × 1.2m. after eight or nine years.

Potentilla fruticosa 'Elizabeth'

Prunus

Most of the *Prunus* species and cultivars grown in gardens are tree-sized (see pages 214 and Tree Fruit) but there are a few important types that are classed as shrubs: the cherry laurel, *P. laurocerasus*, a one-time favorite hedging plant; the Portugal laurel, *P. lusitanica*, used as a specimen shrub and for topiary; and some dwarf, flowering species, such as flowering almond, *P. glandulosa*.

Prunus mume 'Beni-chidori'

SOIL Almost any, although *P. glandulosa*, *P. laurocerasus*, and *P. tenella* are less successful in strongly alkaline conditions.

SITUATION Full sun or light shade. Cherry and Portugal laurels tolerate deep shade, one of their chief merits. Zones 6–8.

WATERING AND FEEDING Mulch in fall and spring. Feed with a balanced, general fertilizer in mid-spring.

PRUNING The laurels do not require any pruning but can be cut to shape as necessary and, if required, clipped as hedges or specimens. When that is the case, clip once in early fall, with pruning shears to avoid disfiguring the large leaves. Among the dwarf, flowering species, only *P. × cistena*, *P. glandulosa*, and *P. triloba* require or indeed tolerate pruning. Between one third and one half of the shoots should be cut back by about half, immediately after flowering.

COMMON PROBLEMS Peach leaf curl and mildew will affect some species but laurels are generally trouble free.

PROPAGATION Laurels and some other species may be propagated from semi-ripe cuttings, in early summer, but a few of the flowering species are notoriously tricky.

TROUBLESHOOTING Old, overgrown, or very woody laurels will usually regenerate satisfactorily if cut back to just above soil level in spring. This may also be successful on species tolerant of pruning; others, such as the treelike *P. mume*, are best replaced.

SIZE Unpruned, cherry laurel will reach 10 × 10ft./3 × 3m. after five years and 26–33 × 26ft./8–10 × 8m. after eighteen or twenty. Portugal laurel and *P. mume* will attain a little over half these sizes, while the remaining species will reach about 3 × 3ft./1 × 1m. after five years, and double this ultimately.

Pyracantha FIRETHORN

Popular and hardy, ornamental evergreen shrubs, grown in part for their flowers but more importantly for their red, orange, or yellow berries, which are retained well into the winter when birds allow. They are often grown as wall shrubs.

SOIL Almost any, although intolerant of high alkalinity.

Pyracantha rogersiana

SITUATION Full sun to deep shade, although with increasingly fewer flowers and fruits, the greater the shade. Zones 6–9.

WATERING AND FEEDING Mulch in fall and spring. Feed with a balanced rose or similar potash-rich fertilizer in mid-spring, and again after midsummer.

PRUNING None required when grown as a freestanding specimen. When grown as an informal hedge, shear twice, first around midsummer and again in early fall. When grown as a wall shrub, shape the plants by cutting shoots as hard back as necessary in very early spring.

COMMON PROBLEMS Fireblight; scab sometimes disfigures the fruits and causes them to drop; scales.

PROPAGATION Semi-ripe cuttings in summer.

TROUBLESHOOTING Misshapen or overgrown plants will generally respond to being cut back hard in early spring, although flowering and fruiting will be reduced for one or two seasons.

SIZE About 6½ × 5ft./2 × 1.5m. after five years, 13 × 10–13ft./4 × 3–4m. after about twenty years.

Rhamnus BUCKTHORN

Not the most familiar of ornamental shrubs, but the buckthorns have much to commend them. In milder gardens (Zones 7–9), the variegated evergreen forms can be most appealing.

SOIL Almost any, although the evergreen forms are intolerant of water-logging.

SITUATION Light to moderate shade, with effective shelter from cold winds. Hardy species such as *R. frangula*, Zones 2–7.

WATERING AND FEEDING Mulch in fall and spring. Feed with a balanced, general fertilizer in mid-spring.

PRUNING None required, although evergreen species may be lightly trimmed to shape in spring. Deciduous species when used in informal hedges: shear twice, the first time two or three weeks after midsummer, the second in early fall; or shear once only in late summer, although this will give a neat appearance for a shorter time.

COMMON PROBLEMS None.

PROPAGATION Semi-ripe cuttings in late summer or hardwood cuttings in late winter.

TROUBLESHOOTING None normally necessary.

SIZE Will attain $6\frac{1}{2} \times 5$ft./2×1.5m. after five years, up to 16×13ft./5×4m. after sixteen to eighteen years.

Rhamnus cathartica

Rhododendron

The largest and most valuable group of evergreen flowering shrubs in appropriate soil conditions, although some species and cultivars are much hardier than others. I also include here those shrubs known as azaleas, some of which are evergreen and some deciduous, as they are technically part of the genus.

SOIL Acidic, organic, moist but not prone to water-logging.

SITUATION Light to moderate shade; azaleas are generally more tolerant than rhododendrons of full sun. Many rhododendrons will thrive successfully only in mild areas and, in general, it is the larger, treelike species and cultivars with very large leaves that are among the most tender. Zones 5–7, depending on the species or cultivar.

WATERING AND FEEDING Maintain a permanent mulch of oak leaves, pine needles or ground bark. Peat moss is not a good mulch but should be mixed in soil at planting time. Feed lightly with cottonseed-meal or a special evergreen fertilizer like Holly-tone in early spring or after flowering.

PRUNING None required, although careful removal of dead flower heads improves the appearance of plants and encourages new flower buds to develop. You will find, of course, that this is all but impossible on very large plants or on an extensive collection, or on azaleas.

COMMON PROBLEMS None, if plants have been properly set out and cared for but pests and diseases can occur. Consult a County Extension Specialist for local advice.

PROPAGATION Seeds sown in sphagnum moss; layering; also evergreen azalea cuttings in peat moss and sand enclosed in plastic propagating box.

TROUBLESHOOTING None normally necessary, although old plants will often regenerate after being cut back hard into the old wood in spring, with the operation staged over three years.

SIZE Varies widely from dwarf, rock garden shrubs, such as *R. impeditum*, to species that eventually can become multi-stemmed trees 16ft./5m. tall. Carefully check the label when buying plants, especially if you live in a mild climate, and be prepared to increase the predicted ultimate size of your plant by about half as much again, as there is a tendency for some nurseries to underestimate the growth of rhododendrons.

Azalea 'Merlin'

Rhus – Rosa

Rhus glabra 'Laciniata'

Ribes sanguineum

Rhus STAGHORN SUMAC

The deciduous staghorn sumac is sometimes classed as a small tree, although in most gardens it normally attains only large shrub size. It is grown essentially for its vivid fall foliage colors but unfortunately has a stark winter appearance and a habit of suckering, especially if its roots are damaged or disturbed.

SOIL Any.

SITUATION Full sun or light shade. Zones 3–9.

WATERING AND FEEDING Mulch in fall and spring. Apply a general fertilizer in mid-spring but feeding is rarely needed.

PRUNING None required, although plants can be cut back to ground level each spring to stimulate the production of new shoots with larger-than-normal leaves.

COMMON PROBLEMS None.

PROPAGATION Semi-ripe cuttings in summer, hardwood cuttings in winter, or from suckers.

TROUBLESHOOTING None normally necessary, although old plants will regenerate after being cut back to about $1\frac{1}{2}$ft./45cm. above soil level in spring.

SIZE Without pruning, the stagshorn sumach (*R. typhina*) will attain about $6\frac{1}{2} \times 6\frac{1}{2}$ft./$2 \times 2$m. after five years and around $20–23 \times 16$ft./$6–7 \times 5$m. after eighteen to twenty years.

Ribes FLOWERING CURRANT

The deciduous and hardy, spring-blooming flowering currants will grow in most situations, but their ultimate size is not always fully appreciated. They also have a valuable and slightly more tender evergreen relative in *R. speciosum*, the fuchsia-flowered gooseberry, a native of California's southern coast.

SOIL Will tolerate most, but less successful in dry conditions.

SITUATION Full sun or light shade; *R. speciosum* (Zones 9–10) requires some shelter and *R. sanguineum* (Zones 6–8) performs best as a wall shrub.

WATERING AND FEEDING Mulch in fall and spring. Feed with a balanced rose or similar potash-rich fertilizer in mid-spring.

PRUNING Cut out the oldest one third of the shoots in spring, after flowering, to prevent the plants from becoming leggy and unkempt. *R. speciosum* will generally require lighter pruning, and in most areas this may only mean cutting out those parts killed by winter cold. When flowering currants are grown as an informal hedge, clip once lightly, shortly after flowering.

COMMON PROBLEMS Aphids, red spider mites and white pine blister rust on some species.

PROPAGATION Semi-ripe cuttings in summer or hardwood cuttings in winter.

TROUBLESHOOTING Old and overgrown plants can usually be rejuvenated by cutting back hard to just above soil level in spring, spreading the work over two spring seasons.

SIZE Most flowering currants, including *R. sanguineum* 'Pulborough Scarlet', will attain about 5×5ft./1.5×1.5m. after five years and about 8×8ft./2.5×2.5m. after twelve or fifteen years.

Romneya TREE POPPY

The Californian tree poppy (*R. coulteri*) is one of those misnamed plants, a shrub called a tree but having much in common with a flowering herbaceous perennial. It is undeniably lovely with huge white flowers, but will not be successful if the soil is wrong – although it can become too vigorous once established in good conditions. It is also known as Matilija poppy.

Soil Moist, rich, acid, or alkaline; *Romneya* will not tolerate a clay soil or one prone to water-logging.

Situation Full sun. Zones 8–10, also 6–7 with winter mulch.

Pruning Cut back to soil level in early spring.

Common problems None.

Propagation Root cuttings in winter; one of the classic plants for this method of propagation and often given to horticulture students to practice on.

Troubleshooting None should be necessary; old and overgrown plants may be divided in spring.

Size Attains 4ft./1.2m. in height but spreads invasively and can become 6½–10ft./2–3m. across after ten or fifteen years.

Romneya coulteri

Rosa ROSE

As a group, roses are justifiably the most popular of all garden plants. But they do comprise a large number of sub-groups, and while their soil and site requirements are fairly similar, their ultimate sizes, pruning and winter care in cold climates differ. In fact, culture can differ from region to region; consult the County Extension Specialist for local advice, including hardiness, winter protection.

Soil Although tolerant of a wide range of soil types, they will always be most successful in a rich, moisture-retentive soil, but this could range from an organic loam to a heavy clay. Light soils will produce good roses provided large quantities of organic matter are incorporated. Roses are least successful on very acidic or very alkaline soils.

Situation Full sun or light shade; some varieties in almost all groups are successful in deeper shade. Others, most notably the tea roses and some of the less common species, are more tender and require shelter from cold winds. Overall, the rugosas and rugosa hybrids are the most tolerant of exposure. For Zones, see above.

Watering and feeding Mulch in fall and spring. Feed with a balanced rose fertilizer in mid-spring and in midsummer.

Pruning Varies considerably among groups although, on all types, any very long and whippy shoots that are not to be used to form part of the permanent framework should be cut back by about half in fall, to minimize damage caused to the plant's overall stability by winter gales. Most garden roses are grafted onto rootstocks of different varieties, chosen for their rooting rather than flowering attributes. Suckers may arise from these below soil level and must be pulled away promptly.

Rosa

HYBRID TEAS In spring, cut back any damaged shoots to soil level, cut out any very feeble or spindly shoots, and then cut back all remaining shoots by about half to a healthy bud, cutting slightly less for vigorous, strongly growing varieties and slightly more for weaker growing ones.

FLORIBUNDAS In spring, cut out one third of the shoots to soil level, cutting out principally the oldest but also removing any diseased or damaged ones. Then cut back the remaining shoots by

Roses: pruning hybrid teas

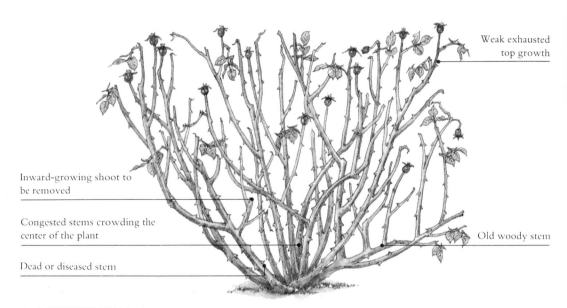

Weak exhausted
top growth

Inward-growing shoot to
be removed

Congested stems crowding the
center of the plant

Old woody stem

Dead or diseased stem

▲ **ASSESSMENT** Hybrid tea roses are vigorous plants, and at pruning time in spring will look a mass of tangled stems. They can be pruned hard, to stimulate plenty of new growth on which the summer's flowers will be borne.

▶ **AFTER PRUNING** Cut back to soil level no more than one third of the shoots, removing any showing signs of damage from rubbing or disease, and those that look feeble or spindly. This will leave about two thirds of the stems: cut these back to tiny pink buds low down on the stem and facing away from the center of the plant. For vigorous varieties cut to a bud about half way up the stem; for weaker varieties prune harder, to a bud about a third of the way up.

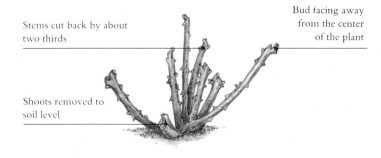

Stems cut back by about
two thirds

Bud facing away
from the center
of the plant

Shoots removed to
soil level

approximately one third, cutting slightly less for vigorous, strongly growing varieties and slightly more for weaker growing ones. Always cut back to strong, outward-facing buds.

SHRUB ROSES Although this is a highly diverse group, including, among the more familiar types, rugosas, albas, damasks, noisettes, bourbons, musks, centifolias, a number of hybrids or seedlings derived from them, and a few so-called ground-cover or procumbent varieties, they may all be treated similarly. Little

Roses: pruning floribundas

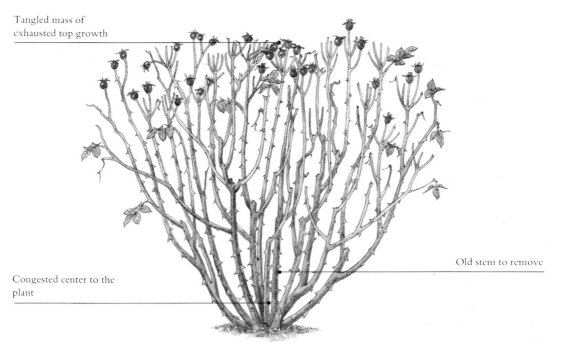

Tangled mass of exhausted top growth

Old stem to remove

Congested center to the plant

▲ **ASSESSMENT** Floribundas produce their flowers in clusters, so at pruning time in spring there will be a tangled mass of top growth. The aim of pruning is to remove all this tired growth, and stimulate new growth from the base.

▶ **AFTER PRUNING** Cut back to soil level one third of the stems, removing the oldest and any showing signs of damage. Cut the remaining shoots back to buds that face away from the plant's center, and are about two thirds of the way up the stem. Cut strong varieties back by slightly less, and weaker ones by slightly more.

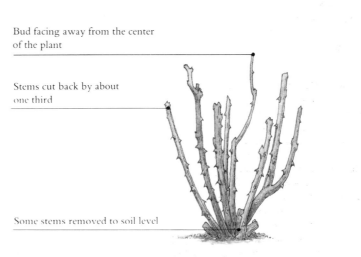

Bud facing away from the center of the plant

Stems cut back by about one third

Some stems removed to soil level

Rosa

pruning is needed although, every two or three years, the oldest shoots or any that are damaged or diseased should be pruned to soil level to stimulate the production of new growth. Any abnormally long shoots that were cut back in the fall (see page 61), should also be pruned to soil level in the spring. It is important not to leave shoots only partially cut back on shrub roses, as this will result in an unsightly proliferation of twiggy growth. Shrub roses should not be dead-headed after the flowers have faded as, in many instances, they produce very attractive hips in the fall. The old fruits will drop, shrivel or be eaten by birds during the winter, and as there are usually so many of them, it is only worth cutting off the more unsightly dead heads in spring.

Roses: pruning shrubs

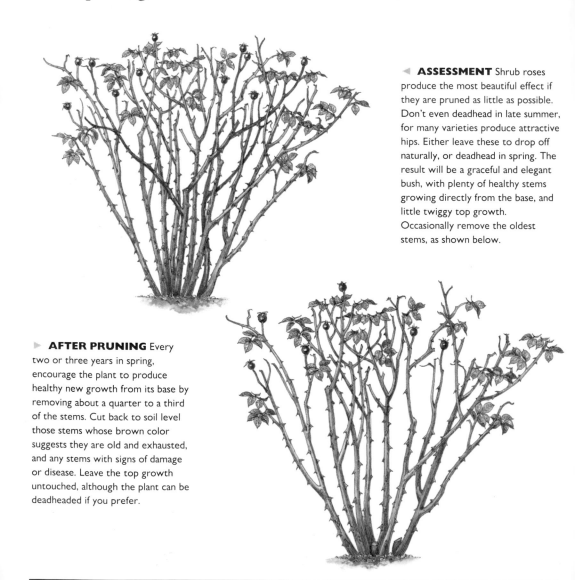

◄ **ASSESSMENT** Shrub roses produce the most beautiful effect if they are pruned as little as possible. Don't even deadhead in late summer, for many varieties produce attractive hips. Either leave these to drop off naturally, or deadhead in spring. The result will be a graceful and elegant bush, with plenty of healthy stems growing directly from the base, and little twiggy top growth. Occasionally remove the oldest stems, as shown below.

► **AFTER PRUNING** Every two or three years in spring, encourage the plant to produce healthy new growth from its base by removing about a quarter to a third of the stems. Cut back to soil level those stems whose brown color suggests they are old and exhausted, and any stems with signs of damage or disease. Leave the top growth untouched, although the plant can be deadheaded if you prefer.

Roses: troubleshooting

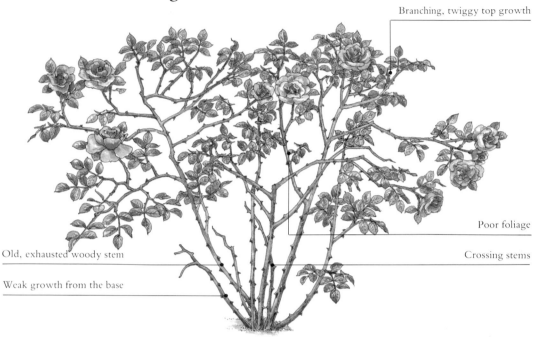

Branching, twiggy top growth

Poor foliage

Old, exhausted woody stem

Crossing stems

Weak growth from the base

▲ **ASSESSMENT** This shrub rose shows the results of poor pruning in the past: the stems have been repeatedly cut back to remove the top growth, so the plant has produced branching, twiggy growth at the tops of the stems, but little new shoot growth from the base. Its exhausted stems have bowed under the weight to unbalance its shape. Flowering is good, but the foliage is poor due to inadequate feeding and mulching. Remedial pruning needs to be combined with careful feeding, watering and mulching.

◄ **AFTER PRUNING, 1ST SPRING** The oldest stems have all been removed, and the weak shoots from the base cut out. The remaining stems are left untouched. Depending on the vigor of the plant, between one and two thirds of the stems can be removed in the first pruning.

► **AFTER PRUNING, 2ND SEASON** The initial pruning and feeding will throw up new shoots from the base. At the second pruning time, another old stem can be cut out completely, and the plant progressively renewed.

Rosa – Salix

Rosa 'Alec's Red'

MINIATURES These scaled-down versions of floribundas or hybrid teas require less true pruning and more of a tidying up in spring. They are all slightly more prone than their larger counterparts to frost damage and, inevitably, there will be some dead shoots to be cut out in spring. Their growth also tends to be more congested and so, at the same time, the twigs may be thinned out. Some hybrids tend to produce long flowering shoots, and these should be cut back to a bud just above soil level, after the flowers have faded in the fall.

STANDARD AND HALF-STANDARD ROSES These are artificial productions comprising a selected variety grafted at the desired height on the stem of a rootstock. They should be pruned as described for the variety, except that pruning back "to soil level" should be read as pruning back to the point of grafting.

COMMON PROBLEMS Mildew; aphids; black spot; rust; rose chafer; Asiatic and Japanese beetles; earwig; sawfly.

PROPAGATION Hardwood cuttings in early winter, although these are difficult to strike successfully from hybrid teas and floribundas.

TROUBLESHOOTING Old and overgrown plants can often be rejuvenated by cutting back the shoots to just above soil level in spring; spread the work over three seasons so that no more than one third of the shoots is cut out at any one time. Although there are some notable and fine very old rose specimens, they are generally plants that have been tended throughout their lives and my feeling is that a neglected rose more than eight or ten years old is best replaced. A regular spray program for rose pests is required.

SIZE Enormously variable, so check label descriptions. As a general guide, most will attain their final height in three to five years (allowing for pruning of those for which it is needed). Miniatures reach about 1×1 ft./30×30 cm., hybrid teas and floribundas about $3 \times 2\frac{1}{2}$ ft./1 m. $\times 80$ cm., and shrubs about $5-6\frac{1}{2} \times 5$ ft./$1.5-2 \times 1.5$ m., but there are larger and smaller varieties in all of these groups.

Rosmarinus ROSEMARY

Although usually grown as a herb, rosemary also makes a most useful evergreen foliage shrub, tolerant of a wide range of conditions, and is particularly attractive as a low hedge or pot plant.

SOIL Will tolerate most, although never very successful in waterlogged or very highly alkaline conditions.

SITUATION Full sun or very light shade. Zones 7–9.

WATERING AND FEEDING Mulch in fall and spring. Feed with a balanced, general fertilizer in mid-spring.

PRUNING Cut out the oldest one third of the shoots in spring. When grown as hedges, clip twice, first around midsummer and again in early fall.

COMMON PROBLEMS None.

PROPAGATION Semi-ripe cuttings in early summer.

TROUBLESHOOTING Overgrown plants can usually be rejuvenated by cutting back hard to just above soil level, spreading the work over two consecutive spring seasons.

Rosmarinus officinalis

Size Most varieties will attain their ultimate height of about 5 × 5ft./1.5 × 1.5m. after five or seven years in mild climates but there are a few lower-growing forms, the best known being the ground-covering 'Prostratus'.

Rubus FLOWERING BRAMBLE

Although most of the hardy deciduous *Rubus* species and cultivars in gardens are grown for their soft fruit, there are a few worthy of including where space permits for their flowering and ground-covering attributes, although they are rare in US nurseries.
Soil Will tolerate most soils, although most species suffer from nutrient deficiencies in strongly alkaline conditions and are fairly intolerant of dryness.
Situation Light to moderate shade, although will tolerate full sun and deeper shade. Zones 5–7 and 9, depending on species.
Watering and feeding Mulch in fall and spring. Feed with a balanced rose or other potash-rich fertilizer in mid-spring.
Pruning Varies with species. Those such as *R. cockburnianus*, grown for their white stems, should be cut back to soil level in early spring. The ground-covering *R. tricolor* needs no pruning. Those types grown principally for their flowers, such as the popular *R. × tridel* 'Benenden', should have the oldest third of the shoots cut back to soil level each spring. Popular on the West Coast is the evergreen, creeping *R. calycinoides*, which requires little pruning.
Common problems None.
Propagation Semi-ripe cuttings in summer or hardwood cuttings in winter.
Troubleshooting Old and overgrown plants of all types can be rejuvenated by cutting back to just above soil level in spring.
Size With the pruning regime suggested, *R. cockburnianus* will reach about 10 × 10ft./3 × 3m. after five years. Unpruned, *R. tricolor* will soon reach its ultimate height of about 2½ft./75cm. and will spread to about 10–13ft./3–4m. after twelve years. *R. × tridel* 'Benenden' will reach about 3 × 3ft./1 × 1m. after five years and 10 × 10ft./3 × 3m. after fifteen years.

Rubus cockburnianus

Salix WILLOW

There are numerous deciduous willows suitable for growing as garden shrubs; a few larger species make good trees (see page 216), while others are most inappropriate for any garden use. Tolerant of a wide range of conditions, they are particularly useful for heavy and wet sites, and some are very hardy.
Soil Will tolerate most, although particularly successful in wet or even water-logged soils.
Situation Full sun to moderate shade. Zones 1, 5–6, 8–9.
Watering and feeding Mulch in fall and spring. Feed with a balanced rose or other potash-rich fertilizer in mid-spring.
Pruning Varies with species. Many willows require no pruning. This applies to all of the dwarf species, such as *S.* 'Boydii', the low-growing types like *S. lanata* and *S. helvetica* (even when

Salix helvetica

grown grafted atop an upright stem as a standard), and to larger species grown for their overall form, foliage effect and catkins, such as *S. fargesii*, *S. gracilistyla* and its form 'Melanostachys'. The latter species, however, does respond well to hard pruning to keep the plants manageable, and other common and popular species that benefit from pruning are *S. exigua*, *S. irrorata* and *S. udensis* (previously *S. sachalinensis*). All of these should be pruned to about 1ft./30cm. above soil level every three years, in early spring. This will produce the attractively colored shoots that will then gradually fade between prunings.

COMMON PROBLEMS Many species suffer from leaf-attacking insects and fungal leaf spots, which may cause some disfigurement as the summer progresses. Also borers.

PROPAGATION Hardwood cuttings in winter, layers or suckers; willows root more readily from cuttings than any other shrub.

TROUBLESHOOTING Old and overgrown plants of all types will regenerate extremely well if cut back hard to just above soil level in spring.

SIZE Varies greatly, so check label descriptions. The genus includes prostrate forms like *S. repens* ($6\frac{1}{2}$ft./2m. spread after five years); small, slow-growing shrubs such as *S. helvetica* ($2\frac{1}{2} \times 2\frac{1}{2}$ft./ 80×80cm. after five years), and robust, vigorous species, such as *S. gracilistyla* 'Melanostachys', ($7 \times 6\frac{1}{2}$ft./2.2×2m. after five years).

Sambucus ELDER

The hardy, deciduous elderberries, *S. nigra* from Europe and *S. canadensis*, the American native, are scarcely worthy garden plants except for large, country places, but selected foliage forms and a related species, *S. racemosa*, make most attractive garden shrubs with careful pruning.

SOIL Almost any, including wet and dry sites.

SITUATION Light shade; tolerant of moderate shade, but golden-foliaged varieties tend to be scorched in full sun. Zones 3–9.

WATERING AND FEEDING Mulch in fall and spring. Apply a balanced, general fertilizer in mid-spring.

PRUNING There are two options. If the oldest one third of the shoots is pruned to soil level each year, in spring, the plants will reach a greater height but the leaves will be generally less attractively colored and smaller. By cutting all the shoots back to soil level each spring, the best foliage will be obtained but the plants will remain much smaller.

COMMON PROBLEMS Aphids.

PROPAGATION Semi-ripe cuttings in late summer or hardwood cuttings in winter.

TROUBLESHOOTING Old and overgrown plants of all types regenerate successfully if they are cut back hard to just above soil level in spring.

SIZE With complete annual pruning, all forms will reach about $6\frac{1}{2} \times 3$ft./2×1m. each year. With partial pruning, they will attain a maximum of about $10–13 \times 6\frac{1}{2}$ft./$3–4 \times 2$m. Unpruned, *S. racemosa* will reach about 20×13ft./6×4m. after twenty years, and *S. nigra* and *S. canadensis* about half as tall again.

Sambucus racemosa 'Plumosa Aurea'

Santolina COTTON LAVENDER

Often seen in the herb garden, this makes a useful silver-foliaged small shrub for other places, too, provided the dry and sunny conditions so beloved of Mediterranean plants can be supplied. It is sometimes grown as an ornamental border plant, and makes an interesting change from the more familiar dwarf box.

Soil Light, free draining, and neutral.

Situation Full sun or very light shade. Zones 6–9.

Watering and feeding Mulch in fall and spring. Feed with a balanced, general fertilizer in mid-spring.

Pruning Trim lightly with shears in late spring, cutting just a few inches above the base of last year's growth.

Common problems None.

Propagation Semi-ripe cuttings in summer.

Troubleshooting Old plants should be replaced; as with most shrubby herbs, the effective life is only four or five years, or less where summers are hot and humid.

Size Within five years, will attain about $1\frac{1}{2} \times 2\frac{1}{2}$ft./50 × 75cm.

Santolina neapolitana 'Edward Bowles'

Sarcococca EVERGREEN SWEET

Also known as sweet boxes, these are among the lesser known of the easily grown and widely available garden shrubs. They are worthy of much wider note for their fragrant late winter flowers.

Soil Organic and fertile soil is required but they are tolerant of acidity and alkalinity.

Situation Moderate to full shade. Zones 6–8.

Watering and feeding Mulch in fall and spring. Feed with a balanced rose or other potash-rich fertilizer in mid-spring.

Pruning None necessary.

Common problems None.

Propagation Semi-ripe cuttings in late summer, hardwood cuttings in winter, or by suckers.

Troubleshooting If old plants become congested and flowering diminishes, cut back the oldest third of the shoots to about 4in./10cm. above soil level after flowering in spring.

Size *S. confusa* is a slow-growing dwarf species that will attain about 5×5ft./1.5×1.5m. after fifteen years. *S. hookeriana* variety *humilis* is also slow-growing and remains at 2ft./60cm.

Senecio

This is a large genus of annuals, perennials, shrubs, and vines best known to American gardeners for the gray-leaved dusty miller, a summer bedding plant and the florist's cineraria, a pot plant with showy daisy flowers. One of the shrub species, popular in English gardens and in mild regions of the West Coast, is the yellow-flowered, grayish-green-leaved *S. greyi* (also known as *S. compactus*). Do not allow it to become unkempt and straggly.

Soil Tolerates most, if not too rich, cold, or water-logged.

Situation Full sun to very light shade; the plant is tolerant of salt spray and is therefore a useful seaside plant. Zones 8–10.

Sarcococca confusa

Senecio – Spartium

Senecio greyi

WATERING AND FEEDING Mulch in fall and spring. Feed sparingly with a potash–rich fertilizer in mid–spring.

PRUNING Cut back old growth in spring to maintain an attractive and compact shape.

COMMON PROBLEMS None.

PROPAGATION Semi-ripe cuttings in summer.

TROUBLESHOOTING Straggly and misshapen plants, provided they are not very old and woody, can generally be rejuvenated if cut back to about 1½ft./45cm. above soil level in spring.

SIZE Will grow fairly swiftly to reach about 3–5 × 3–5ft./1–1.5 × 1–1.5m. after four or five years.

Skimmia

Skimmias are extremely popular and widely grown small, evergreen, berrying shrubs with specific soil and site requirements. The male flowers of *S. japonica* are very fragrant.

SOIL Always best in moist, organic acid soil; intolerant of dryness and of impoverished or alkaline conditions, which result in small, yellowed foliage.

SITUATION Light to moderate shade; in full sun, the foliage yellows most unattractively. Zones 7–9.

WATERING AND FEEDING Mulch in fall and spring. Feed with a balanced rose or other potash–rich fertilizer in mid–spring.

PRUNING None necessary.

COMMON PROBLEMS Leaf chlorosis, as described above. A failure to form berries arises with *S. japonica* unless both male and female plants are grown in close proximity to each other. *S. reevesiana* has perfect flowers, so berries always form on each plant, so to guarantee flowers choose this kind.

Skimmia japonica 'Rubella'

PROPAGATION Semi-ripe cuttings in late summer or hardwood cuttings in winter.

TROUBLESHOOTING If old plants become congested and flowering diminishes, cut back the oldest third of the shoots to about 4in./10cm. above soil level immediately after flowering.

SIZE Both species are slow-growing, *S. japonica* in both male and female plants attaining an ultimate height of 3–5 × 3–5ft./ 1–1.5 × 1–1.5m. in about twelve years. *R. reevesiana* is a smaller species remaining at about 2ft./60cm.

Sorbus reducta

Sorbus

Most of the common *Sorbus* species grown in gardens will eventually reach tree size (see page 217) but one exception, *S. reducta*, is a worthy and attractive, deciduous, suckering species with foliage, blossom, and fruiting appeal. Two others are *S. tianshanica* and *S. vilmorinii* with similar characteristics.

SOIL Almost all.

SITUATION Full sun or light shade. Zone 6.

WATERING AND FEEDING Mulch in fall and spring. Apply a balanced rose or other potash-rich fertilizer in mid-spring.

PRUNING None necessary.

COMMON PROBLEMS None.

PROPAGATION From suckers.

TROUBLESHOOTING None normally necessary, but old or overgrown plants can be rejuvenated by cutting hard back to just above soil level in spring.

SIZE Slow growing and spreading, reaching about 10in. × 1½ft./ 25 × 50cm. after five years and about 2½ × 6½ft./75cm. × 2m. after sixteen to eighteen years.

Spartium

A one-species genus as far as gardens are concerned, *S. junceum* is a summer-flowering yellow broom, relatively easy to grow in climates similar to its native Mediterranean region, but sharing the same soil and site requirements as the other related broom genera *Cytisus* and *Genista*.

SOIL Light, free draining, tolerant of high alkalinity but not of water-logging.

SITUATION Full sun or light shade. Tolerates salt spray so an excellent plant for coastal gardens. Zone 8.

WATERING AND FEEDING Mulch in fall and spring. Feed with a balanced rose or other potash-rich fertilizer in mid-spring.

PRUNING Some pruning needed when growth becomes straggly.

COMMON PROBLEMS None.

PROPAGATION Difficult from cuttings; semi-ripe cuttings in summer are the only ones worth trying.

TROUBLESHOOTING None normally necessary; old and overgrown plants should be replaced.

SIZE Reaches about 6½ × 3ft./2 × 1m. after six or eight years and twice this eventually, although plants this large are likely to be leggy and unattractive and should be replaced.

Spartium junceum

Spiraea – Symphoricarpos

Spiraea × arguta

Spiraea

A large genus of hardy deciduous shrubs, suitable for a wide range of sites and grown principally for their feathery spring and summer flowers. They are commonly described as "small" but many will eventually grow fairly tall and be wide spreading.

Soil Almost all; least successful in highly alkaline conditions.

Situation Full sun or light shade. Zones 3–8.

Watering and feeding Mulch in fall and spring. Feed with a balanced rose or other potash-rich fertilizer in mid-spring, and again after midsummer.

Pruning Spiraeas that flower in spring on old wood should be pruned immediately after flowering, by cutting back the oldest third of the shoots to soil level. Forms that flower after midsummer should have all shoots pruned to about 8in./20cm. above soil level in early spring.

Common problems None.

Propagation Semi-ripe cuttings in summer or hardwood cuttings in winter.

Troubleshooting None normally necessary but overgrown plants can be rejuvenated by cutting all shoots back to just above soil level in spring; this is most successful on late-flowering varieties. With spring-flowering types, the operation is best spread over two or three years.

Size There are a few relatively dwarf forms, such as S. × bumalda, which will attain about 3×3ft./1×1m. after ten years, but most, including the two bridal wreaths, S. × arguta and S. vanhouttei, will reach this in half the time, and $6\frac{1}{2}$–$8 \times 6\frac{1}{2}$–8ft./1×1m. after fifteen or twenty years.

Stephanandra   CUTLEAF STEPHANANDRA

A genus with two familiar, hardy and easy to grow yet rather different, deciduous species worthy of a place in most gardens for their foliage: S. incisa (most usually seen in its variety 'Crispa'), and S. tanakae, which has the added attraction of winter stems the color of mahogany. The former is one of the best and most underappreciated of deciduous, moderately vigorous, ground-cover shrubs.

Soil Almost all, provided not very dry.

Situation Full sun or light shade. Zones 3–8; S. tanakae, 6.

Watering and feeding Mulch in fall and spring. Feed with a balanced, general fertilizer in mid-spring.

Pruning None necessary for S. incisa 'Crispa'. On S. tanakae, cut the oldest third of the shoots to soil level each spring, to encourage the production of the young brown shoots in winter.

Common problems None.

Propagation Hardwood cuttings in winter; or rooted tips of 'Crispa'.

Troubleshooting None normally necessary but overgrown or, in the case of S. incisa 'Crispa', very congested plants can be rejuvenated by cutting some or all shoots back to just above soil level in spring.

Stephanandra tanakae

Spiraea – Symphoricarpos

SIZE *S. incisa* 'Crispa' forms a dense ground-covering mound, about $1\frac{1}{2} \times 2\frac{1}{2}$ft./$50 \times 75$cm. after five years and $3–5 \times 3–5$ft./$1–1.5 \times 1–1.5$m. after twenty years. *S. tanakae* will attain about 5×3ft./1.5×1m. after five or seven years and perhaps $10 \times 6\frac{1}{2}$ft./3×2m. after fifteen years, in good conditions.

Stranvaesia CHINESE STRANVAESIA

One species and four or five varieties of a very attractive, hardy evergreen shrub, grown for the value of both its foliage and flowers, followed by Christmas-red berries. *S. davidiana* variety *undulata* is slower-growing than the species.

SOIL Almost all, although least successful in dry conditions.

SITUATION Full sun or moderate shade. Zones 6–8.

WATERING AND FEEDING Mulch in fall and spring. Feed with a balanced rose or other potash-rich fertilizer in mid-spring.

PRUNING None required.

COMMON PROBLEMS Fireblight, the very damaging disease that also affects fruit trees in the rose family; it is sensible not to plant stranvaesias in areas near commercial apple or pear orchards.

PROPAGATION Semi-ripe cuttings in summer or by layering.

TROUBLESHOOTING Old and neglected plants may be rejuvenated by cutting back the oldest shoots to soil level in spring.

SIZE Reaches $6\frac{1}{2} \times 5$ft./2×1.5m. after five years, and about $23 \times 13–16$ft./2×1.5m. after twenty years. *S. davidiana* var. *undulata* reaches about 3ft./1m.

Stranvaesia davidiana

Symphoricarpos SNOWBERRY

The hardy, deciduous snowberry is aptly named, for its large globular fruits are usually snow white and have the merit of hanging on the plant through much of the winter as birds seem largely to ignore them. It makes a good freestanding shrub, or a useful informal hedging plant.

SOIL Any, including very dry.

SITUATION Full sun to deep shade. Zones 3–8.

WATERING AND FEEDING Mulch in fall and spring. Feed with a balanced rose or other potash-rich fertilizer in mid-spring.

PRUNING None necessary for freestanding shrubs, although up to a third of the oldest stems can be cut back to soil level in spring to stimulate new growth. For hedges, clip twice, first around midsummer and again in early fall.

COMMON PROBLEMS None.

PROPAGATION Semi-ripe cuttings in summer or hardwood cuttings in winter.

TROUBLESHOOTING Old and neglected plants may be rejuvenated by cutting them back to soil level in spring.

SIZE The commonest species, *S. rivularis* (now *S. albus laevigatus*), is a suckering and somewhat invasive plant that can reach $8 \times 10–13$ft./$2.5 \times 3–4$m. after fifteen years. But there are other species and varieties, including the popular *S. × doorenbosii* varieties with pink fruits, and the Indian-currant, or coralberry, *S. orbiculatus*, with purple-red berries, that only attain half this size.

Symphoricarpos × doorenbosii

Syringa 'Louis van Houtte'

Syringa LILAC

Lilacs are among the most familiar, hardy and fragrant of all deciduous flowering shrubs. In many sites they can attain the size of small trees, and for this reason, and because they are much less attractive when out of flower, they are unwise choices for small gardens. Almost all of the common cultivars are derived from the species *S. vulgaris*, to which my remarks below refer, although there are many other attractive species and cultivars, much less known and less widely available.

SOIL Always best in rich, organic soils that are slightly acid, neutral or slightly alkaline. Add limestone to very acid soils.

SITUATION Full sun or moderate shade. Zones 3–8.

WATERING AND FEEDING Mulch in fall and spring. Feed with a balanced rose or other potash-rich fertilizer in mid-spring.

PRUNING Except for standards, lilacs are no longer grafted on privet or wild lilac rootstock, but suckers will arise and should be carefully cut away in spring and fall. Lilacs can be left for many years without pruning but are always better if up to one third of the oldest or weakest shoots are cut back to their bases each year, in spring. The flower heads are most unattractive when they fade, and, if practicable, should be cut off after flowering – which is a good reason for routine annual pruning, as the job of dead heading is so much easier on a smaller plant.

COMMON PROBLEMS None.

PROPAGATION Semi-ripe cuttings in late summer. Also by suckers dug from nongrafted plants.

TROUBLESHOOTING Old and overgrown plants may be rejuvenated by cutting back the oldest shoots to soil level and reducing the remainder by half in spring, although it will be two or three years before the plant returns to its full flowering potential.

SIZE Unpruned, reaches 5 × 3ft./1.5 × 1m. after five years, and 16 × 16ft./5 × 5m. after twenty years.

Tamarix TAMARISK

Deciduous shrubs with a very distinctive feathery appearance of both foliage and flower heads. Invaluable in areas that approximate to their natural coastal habitats. *T. ramosissima* is the most hardy species for most of North America.

SOIL Light, free draining, even sandy, especially intolerant of heavy, water-logged conditions.

SITUATION Full sun or light shade; always best in maritime gardens where its tolerance of sea breezes and salt spray make it particularly invaluable. Zones 2–7 for *T. ramosissima*.

WATERING AND FEEDING Mulch in fall and spring. Apply a balanced rose or other potash-rich fertilizer in mid-spring.

PRUNING None necessary to encourage flowering but the plants then tend to become leggy and straggly. The species that bloom after midsummer should have all the old flowered shoots cut back in spring, to reduce their length by at least half. Spring-blooming types should be pruned after they have flowered by cutting the oldest third of the shoots back by at least half. When grown as a

Tamarix pentandra

hedge, either leave quite informal as a simple screen, with almost no clipping at all, or, for a more compact hedge, clip twice, first around midsummer and again in early fall.

COMMON PROBLEMS None.

PROPAGATION Hardwood cuttings in early winter.

TROUBLESHOOTING Neglected plants may be rejuvenated by cutting back up to one third of the oldest shoots to soil level and reducing the remainder by half, in spring.

SIZE Pruned, tamarisk remains at a height and spread of about 5 × 5ft./1.5 × 1.5m. after five years, and about 13 × 13ft./4 × 4m. after sixteen or eighteen years.

Thymus THYME

Thymes are most usually seen in the herb garden but they make attractive, small evergreen shrubs for other areas too, particularly where their fragrance can be appreciated – such as the rock garden, between paving stones, and in wall crevices.

SOIL Light, free draining and preferably alkaline; intolerant of heavy, water-logged or strongly acid conditions.

SITUATION Full sun or very light shade. Zones 3–9.

WATERING AND FEEDING If grown as flowering ornamentals, mulch in fall and spring. Feed with a balanced rose or other potash-rich fertilizer in mid-spring, and again after midsummer. If grown principally for culinary use, substitute a balanced general fertilizer, and apply it in spring only.

PRUNING Trim back dead flower heads with shears.

COMMON PROBLEMS None.

PROPAGATION Semi-ripe cuttings in summer.

TROUBLESHOOTING None necessary. After five or six years, old plants should be replaced.

SIZE Varies according to species and cultivars. Within their five- or six-year lifespan, the more vigorous bush forms of *T. vulgaris* will reach 10 × 8in./25 × 20cm.; the creeping forms, such as *T. × citriodorus* 'Doone Valley', about 2 × 10in./5 × 25cm.

Thymus 'Doone Valley'

Ulex GORSE

To my mind, the deciduous, spiny gorse could be grown much more extensively in larger gardens. It is somewhat coarse in appearance but undeniably beautiful in flower, and it provides a most effective screen or barrier when mass planted; also, it is tolerant of a wide range of conditions.

SOIL Most types, but least successful in strongly acid conditions.

SITUATION Full sun or very light shade; shelter from very cold winds but highly tolerant of coastal wind. Zones 6–8.

WATERING AND FEEDING Mulch in fall and spring. Feed sparingly with a balanced rose or other potash-rich fertilizer in mid-spring.

PRUNING None necessary.

COMMON PROBLEMS None.

PROPAGATION Semi-ripe cuttings in summer or hardwood cuttings in winter.

Ulex europaeus 'Plenus'

Ulex – Vinca

Vaccinium myrtillus

TROUBLESHOOTING Neglected plants may be rejuvenated by cutting them back to soil level after flowering. This is particularly worth doing, as the plant is not very widely stocked by garden centers, especially in USA, where it is not well known.

SIZE Reaches $2\frac{1}{2} \times 3$ft./75cm. $\times$ 1m. after five years, and about $6\frac{1}{2} \times 10$ft./2 $\times$ 3m. after fifteen years.

Vaccinium

If you have the correct conditions, the bilberry and its allies, including the blueberry, will thrive in your garden. The deciduous types will provide superb fall colors and, in many instances, repay you with a fruit crop. Unfortunately they are fussy plants, and if you do not have precisely the right conditions, there is little point in trying to grow them.

SOIL Highly acid, moist, organic; a shortcoming in any of these respects will not be tolerated.

SITUATION Full sun or very light shade; the plants require shelter from very cold winds. Zones 3–7.

WATERING AND FEEDING Mulch in fall and spring. Feed with a balanced rose or other potash-rich fertilizer in mid-spring.

PRUNING Little needed if plants are grown as ornamentals.

COMMON PROBLEMS None.

PROPAGATION Semi-ripe cuttings in early summer or hardwood cuttings in fall.

TROUBLESHOOTING If plants become very woody and congested, they can usually be rejuvenated by cutting the old wood back to soil level in late winter.

SIZE Varies considerably and label information should be read carefully. The American highbush blueberry (*V. corymbosum*) will reach 5×5ft./1.5 $\times$ 1.5m. after about ten years but annual pruning can restrict this height. The bilberry, *V. myrtillus*, will never exceed a quarter of this.

Viburnum

A large genus of hardy evergreen and deciduous shrubs that includes some of the best medium and large species for gardens. They are suitable for most types of garden soil and site, and offer both flower and foliage appeal in return for relatively little effort or attention. The flowers of many species are very fragrant.

SOIL Almost any.

SITUATION Generally best in light shade but most are tolerant of full sun and slightly deeper shade. Hardiness varies according to species but many thrive in Zones 4–8.

WATERING AND FEEDING Mulch in fall and spring. Apply a balanced rose or other potash-rich fertilizer in mid-spring.

PRUNING None necessary.

COMMON PROBLEMS None.

PROPAGATION Semi-ripe cuttings in early summer or hardwood cuttings in winter.

TROUBLESHOOTING Overgrown and congested plants are readily rejuvenated by cutting the oldest shoots back to soil level in late winter, but it is best if the operation is spread over three years to give the plant time to recover.

SIZE Varies considerably, although most viburnums eventually make fairly large plants. Check label descriptions in each instance, but most will reach about 5×3ft./1.5×1m. after five years and around $10–16 \times 10–13$ft./$3–5 \times 3–4$m. after fifteen years. Notably lower and slower-growing types among common species are the evergreen *V. davidii* and the deciduous *V. carlesii* (which occurs in several named varieties); both forms will attain about $5–6\frac{1}{2} \times 5–6\frac{1}{2}$ft./$1.5–2 \times 1.5–2$m. over the same timespan.

Vinca PERIWINKLE

Two popular species most useful as ground covers, often under trees. They are more like evergreen perennials than subshrubs. *V. major*, the less hardy, is widely used on the West Coast. Both share attractive (often variegated) foliage and blue flowers in spring.

SOIL Humus-rich soil that does not readily dry out.

SITUATION Generally best in light shade but tolerant of full sun and deep shade if soil contains ample organic matter. Zones 7–9 for *V. major*, and Zones 5–9 for *V. minor*.

WATERING AND FEEDING Mulch newly set (about 12in./30cm. apart) plants. If the plants are under deciduous trees, the fall leaf fall will supply a permanent decaying mulch. Feeding is usually not needed in humus-rich soils until the clumps have formed a ground-covering carpet. Then apply a potash-rich food in early spring.

Viburnum plicatum 'Mariesii'

Vinca major

PRUNING Use shears or a strimmer to cut *V. major* back to soil level every two or three years, in early spring. *V. minor* rarely needs trimming.

COMMON PROBLEMS Rust disease can be serious on *V. major* but I have never known it so on *V. minor*.

PROPAGATION Semi-ripe cuttings in early summer, hardwood cuttings in winter, or from natural layers.

Vinca – Dwarf conifers

Weigela florida

Pleioblastus auricomus (Arundinaria viridistriata)

TROUBLESHOOTING Overgrown plants are readily rejuvenated by trimming them back to soil level in spring, then providing mulch and a general fertilizer.

SIZE Both common species are fairly fast growing. Individual plants reach their ultimate size of about $1\frac{1}{2} \times 3$ft./50cm. × 1m. for *V. major* and about 6in. × $2\frac{1}{2}$ft./15 × 80cm. for *V. minor* in under five years, but usually mass planted for ground cover.

Weigela

Deciduous, spring- and summer-flowering shrubs tolerant of a wide range of conditions.

SOIL Almost any, except very dry ones.

SITUATION Best in full sun; tolerates light shade. Zones 5–8.

WATERING AND FEEDING Mulch in fall and spring. Feed with a balanced rose or other potash-rich fertilizer in mid-spring, and again after midsummer.

PRUNING None is really necessary but once plants are established, they will benefit from having the oldest third of the shoots cut back to their base each year after flowering.

COMMON PROBLEMS None.

PROPAGATION Semi-ripe cuttings in late summer, hardwood cuttings in winter.

TROUBLESHOOTING Old plants can be rejuvenated by pruning as outlined above, although the modern varieties are better than many of those planted fifteen or twenty years ago, so really old stock is best replaced.

SIZE The most popular weigela is 'Bristol Ruby', which will reach $3–5 \times 3–5$ft./$1–1.5 \times 1–1.5$m. after five years, and $6\frac{1}{2}–8 \times 6\frac{1}{2}–8$ft./$2–2.5 \times 2–2.5$m. after about fifteen years. Few others are likely to be larger than this and some, such as 'Eva Supreme', may be about three quarters of this height.

Bamboos

Bamboos are woody grasses. They comprise a huge group of plants in a huge range of sizes, among which the biggest and most attractive are often not hardy. Some of the hardy genera are invasive and, overall, bamboos should be chosen and positioned with care.

SOIL Best in rich, moist loam, but tolerate most, provided it is not too dry or subject to water-logging.

SITUATION Light to moderate shade; shelter from cold winds. Hardiness varies from Zone 10 to Zones 7–8, according to genera.

WATERING AND FEEDING Mulch in fall and spring. Feed with a balanced, general-purpose fertilizer in mid-spring and again after midsummer. Take care not to allow the soil to dry out, particularly until the plants are well established.

PRUNING Thin out dead canes in spring by removing the oldest and most damaged; do not cut back the whole plant to soil level annually. Some bamboos flower regularly, some irregularly and some hardly ever, but in all cases, after flowering, cut back the old flowered stems. In some species, flowering seems to occur on all shoots at the same time and no leafy shoots are then produced. In such instances, the entire plant will have to be cut back to soil level and may, in fact, appear dead, but it will usually grow again the following year. While a few bamboos do die after flowering, this does not seem to occur with any of the common hardy types.

COMMON PROBLEMS None.

PROPAGATION Division in fall or spring; use a spade to sever the roots, which on large plants can be very tough.

TROUBLESHOOTING Not likely to be necessary.

SIZE Varies widely among species; as a guide, although almost all bamboos extend laterally, the less vigorous hardy forms such as the dwarf varieties of *Pleioblastus auricomus* (previously *Arundinaria viridistriata*) will only reach about $2\frac{1}{2} \times 1\frac{1}{2}$ft./75 × 40cm. in three years, whereas the more vigorous species, such as *Drepanostachyum falconeri* (previously *Arundinaria falconeri*), can reach 33ft./10m. in height and $6\frac{1}{2}$ft./2m. in spread after the same time.

Dwarf conifers

This is a large and heterogeneous group of plants comprising dwarf, or very slow-growing, variants of coniferous trees. They are grown in much the same way as more conventional shrubs and, as a group, are probably the most widely represented shrubs in gardens after roses. Their colors and overall growth habits can be useful in mixed plantings. They are adaptable to a wide range of conditions, although most share one or two drawbacks.

SOIL Most, although best on fairly rich, well drained soil, preferably slightly acidic; least successful on highly alkaline or heavy water-logged soils.

SITUATION Full sun or light shade; although some are tolerant of considerable exposure to low temperatures, almost all tend to be browned by cold or salt-laden winds. Zones 3–8 for many.

WATERING AND FEEDING Mulch in fall and spring. Apply a balanced, general fertilizer in mid-spring. Feed sparingly.

PRUNING Not necessary, although all may be trimmed lightly in late spring or late summer to maintain a neat appearance. Some prostrate forms occasionally produce upright shoots, and these must be cut out.

COMMON PROBLEMS Red spider mite; cold wind damage; foliage browning from fungal root decay in wet soils.

PROPAGATION Almost impossible to strike from cuttings without a facility for misting.

TROUBLESHOOTING I am persuaded that broken, misshapen, browned or otherwise damaged plants should be replaced as they rarely regenerate and recover their shape satisfactorily.

SIZE Varies greatly with genus and overall habit. There are upright conical, globular, pyramidal, or umbrella-shaped cultivars, as well as horizontal and truly prostrate types. Read label information carefully and then allow for growth of at least half as much again. Also check if the plant is a genuine dwarf selection or, like the popular Korean fir, *Abies koreana*, just a slow-growing one that will eventually become a tree.

Juniperus scopulorum 'Skyrocket'

Thuja plicata 'Collyer's Gold'

Juniperus horizontalis

Dwarf conifers

CLIMBERS

Actinidia
Ampelopsis
Clematis
Hedera
Hydrangea
Lonicera
Parthenocissus

Passiflora
Rosa
Solanum
Tropaeolum
Vitis
Wisteria

Principles of Care

There are few, if any, gardens that are not enhanced by some climbing plants. Not only do they increase the overall growing area, they also cover unsightly walls and other structures that are best concealed. In reality they are simply shrubs with weak stems which have adopted the habit of growing on some form of natural or artificial support, but this lifestyle does impose certain constraints.

Soil and site requirements

I can perhaps best describe in general terms the soil and site requirements for climbers by saying that the recommendations I make for shrubs apply even more strongly to climbers. Their habit of growing against a vertical support almost invariably means that they will be growing in soil that is drier than that in the open garden. Extra attention must therefore be given to watering and mulching, not only for the general well-being of the plants but also to ensure that there is no premature drop of flowers or fruit.

Where a climber is supported by another plant it will inevitably be competing with its host not only for water but also for nutrients. Compensation must therefore be made by watering regularly in summer and by applying fertilizer assiduously at the suggested times. While I recommend general-purpose or rose fertilizers, a liquid feed is also beneficial in cases where the soil is especially dry and a solid formulation would merely lie on the surface.

Aspect is also of particular importance to climbers, especially those grown against walls, for the wall itself will on the one hand afford shelter from cold winds, but on the other cast shade. While a north-facing wall is often considered one of the harshest situations in the garden, in practice far more problems are likely to arise with climbers grown against east-facing walls, where the rapid thawing of frozen tissues early on spring mornings can cause considerable damage. Tender climbing plants will therefore almost always do better on a north-facing than an east-facing aspect.

Climbing plants can be grown in containers in just the same way as other shrubs, but the same constraints apply: they must be grown in a good soil-based mixture and kept well watered, mulched, and fed. The types of shrub that generally fare least satisfactorily in containers (mainly deep-rooting varieties) will similarly fare badly as their climbing counterparts; roses are the best and most important examples of this. Climbers are sometimes grown in containers because the ground in the chosen site is paved or otherwise covered. There are few instances, however, where a couple of slabs or a small area of concrete or tarmac can't be removed to allow the plant to be grown directly in the soil.

Pruning and support

All the general comments that I have made concerning pruning of shrubs (see pages 15–17) are also relevant to climbers, but it is important to bear in mind that if a plant needs heavy pruning to restrict its size it is probably growing in the wrong place. I make a significant distinction between vigorous, straggly climbers that are best grown over a large support such as an old tree or a very large pergola, which need little if any pruning, and the less-rampant varieties that, with a modest amount of pruning, can be trained over a small archway or wall-mounted trellis. Trying to grow a vigorous climber such as *Clematis montana* in a confined space, against a house wall for instance, is a recipe for problems, and you can do no better than learn from nature's example and grow them as they grow in the wild – allowing them free rein to scramble over a tree stump, a rock face, or even a rough slope.

If a climber can't be pruned because it is too big, too inaccessible, or so entangled with another plant that to prune would harm the other, leave well alone. Flowering may in due course be impaired and some dead growth may become apparent, but by removing as much dead material as possible and paying extra attention to feeding and watering you will probably achieve a more satisfactory result in the long term.

There is a widespread tendency among gardeners to use inadequate supports for climbers; trellises are usually far too feebly constructed and poorly fixed, wall nails too small and insufficiently anchored, and even training wires often too thin. Choose trellis that is held together with something rather stronger than tacks, and attach it to wooden battens to separate it from the wall surface and therefore allow the free circulation of air around the plant.

Supporting and training climbers

◀ **USING WIRES** Wires tied tautly between ring-headed screws offer permanent and unobtrusive means of support for climbing plants. The screws should be screwed into purpose-made wall plugs. Tie the plant stems on to the wires as they become robust enough. Either use string tied in a figure-of-eight so that the knot cannot rub the plant stem; or use proprietary metal ties.

► **USING TRELLIS** More decorative than wires, trellis is an effective means of support for less robust climbers. Always fix the trellis on to battens, so that it stands away from the wall: this ensures a good flow of air and reduces the chance of disease. Each year at pruning time cut out any shoots that have forced themselves behind the trellis.

▼ **TRAINING PLANTS** If left to themselves, most climbers would bear flowers only at the tips of their shoots. To encourage flowering along the full length of every stem, bend them down horizontally and tie them to the support. Buds will break into growth all along the stem.

Free-standing structures

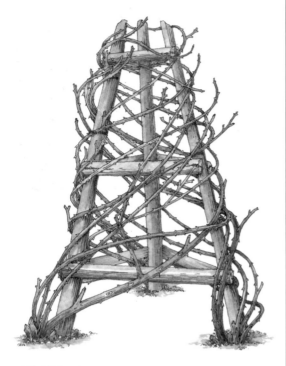

TRAINING THE PLANTS Climbing plants grown up pergolas or other freestanding structures need to have their stems trained down nearly horizontally to encourage flowering all along their length. While each shoot is still young and pliable, wind it around the upright and tie it in.

When supporting climbers on wires, choose the plastic-coated wire sold specifically for training (rather than for tying) and attach it to screw-pattern vine eyes plugged into the wall or, if necessary, to straining bolts. Check all the ties by which individual shoots are attached to the supports at least once each year. The girth of the stems of a vigorous climber can increase considerably during the course of a season and the tie that was loose one fall can become a garotte by the next.

There is one important group of climbing plants, among which ivies are the best known, that require no artificial support for they have self-clinging aerial roots. While it is often said that ivy will damage brickwork, this is true only where bricks are crumbly or mortar is loose, as is often the case on old buildings, but it is worth pointing out that ivy can cause superficial if not structural damage to paint-work such as window frames.

Complaints are sometimes made because newly-planted, self-clinging climbers refuse to climb, but there is nothing abnormal in this and the plants must simply be left to their own devices.

I have mentioned the growing of *Clematis montana* over trees, and this is a perfectly acceptable practice with almost any climber, vigorous or not. But never try to grow a climber over a young, small, or feeble tree as the host plant will suffer. As a general rule, a tree or large shrub about 16ft./5m. tall will usually be robust enough to support any except the most aggressive of climbers.

COMMON PROBLEMS

While climbing plants in general are no more susceptible to pest and disease attack than other plants, again, their habit tends to magnify the problems. The environment close to a wall or other support is not only drier than that in the open, it also tends to be warmer, and while it offers shelter to plants it encourages problems, too. Aphids, red spider mite, and other pests are often more prevalent, or at least appear rather earlier in the season, in such situations than in the open garden.

Among diseases, powdery mildew is the most common since it is one of the relatively few that require dry, hot conditions for maximum proliferation. As with pests, it tends to be seen on climbers before it appears on plants in more exposed positions, and it may well be that climbers provide a sheltered habitat for mildew and other garden pests and diseases which allows them to survive the winter. The dense foliage of some evergreen climbers, for example, can harbor colonies of snails. On the other hand, because the soil in which climbing plants grow is usually much drier than elsewhere, those root-decaying fungi that thrive in stagnant, water-logged conditions tend to be less prevalent.

With any climbing or wall-trained plant, it is vital to pay careful and regular attention to ties, not only because of the straightforward injury they may inflict on the plant if they are allowed to get too tight, but also because abrasion of the bark may admit decay or canker-causing fungi that will then spread into healthy tissues.

Actinidia

A genus with two popular and fairly hardy deciduous species, grown for rather different purposes. *A. kolomikta* is an ornamental with appealingly variegated foliage; *A. chinensis* (now sometimes called *A. deliciosa*) is the Chinese gooseberry or kiwi fruit. You will need both male and female plants to effect pollination and fruit production. Although there is now a hermaphrodite form, it has not been available long enough to be assessed properly.

SOIL Moist, fairly rich, intolerant of very dry conditions.

SITUATION South- or south-west-facing wall. The variegation of *A. kolomikta* is not usually apparent on plants under four to five years old. Zones 4–8 for *A. kolomitka*; 7–9 for *A. chinensis*.

WATERING AND FEEDING Mulch in fall and spring. Feed with a balanced rose or similar potash-rich fertilizer in mid-spring, and again around midsummer.

PRUNING AND SUPPORT For *A. kolomikta*, no pruning is necessary; train and prune *A. chinensis* as a grapevine. Support by tying to horizontal wires pegged to a wall.

COMMON PROBLEMS None.

PROPAGATION Semi-ripe cuttings in summer.

TROUBLESHOOTING Overgrown and neglected plants will usually regenerate satisfactorily if cut back very hard in spring.

SIZE The species *A. kolomikta* reaches about 5 × 5ft./1.5 × 1.5m. after five years, and then rather slowly will ultimately reach about 20 × 20ft./6 × 6m. *A. chinensis* is very vigorous and can reach 50 × 40ft./15 × 12m. eventually, although it should never be allowed to attain anything like this if pruned annually.

Actinidia kolomikta

Ampelopsis   PORCELAIN AMPELOPSIS

Ampelopsis brevipedunculata

Some species of *Parthenocissus* are sometimes called *Ampelopsis* but I am restricting this account to *A. brevipedunculata*, a hardy deciduous twining tendril climber, usually with good fall leaf color and suitable for sites where its vigor can be allowed free rein.

SOIL Most, provided neither very wet nor very dry.

SITUATION Best in very light shade; the variegated 'Elegans', requires some shelter. Zones 4—9.

WATERING AND FEEDING Mulch in fall and spring. Feed with a balanced general fertilizer in mid-spring.

PRUNING AND SUPPORT No pruning is necessary with the green-leaved species, although it can be cut back as necessary in spring to maintain it within bounds. The variegated 'Elegans' performs best when a proportion of the previous season's lateral shoots is cut back each spring, to within two buds of the base. This will produce plenty of young shoots with good leaf variegation. The best support is provided by horizontal wires pegged to a wall, pergola or fence.

COMMON PROBLEMS None.

PROPAGATION Semi-ripe cuttings in summer.

TROUBLESHOOTING Over vigorous plants will usually regenerate satisfactorily if cut back hard in spring.

SIZE About 5 × 5ft./1.5 × 1.5m. after five years, the variegated form eventually attaining about 13 × 13ft./4 × 4m. after eighteen or twenty years, and the green-leaved species perhaps twice as much.

Clematis

A genus of twining, deciduous or evergreen plants which comprises the largest and most popular group of flowering climbers, with a very wide range in flower type and considerable variation in vigor. While the soil requirements are fairly constant, some species must have shelter. Pruning methods vary but are in essence perfectly logical.

SOIL Tolerates most, but always best in moderately alkaline, rich, deep loam; much less satisfactory in acid or poor soils.

SITUATION Varies; none except the very vigorous forms, such as the cultivars derived from *C. montana* or *C. tangutica*, are very wind tolerant; they are easily torn from their supports in windy conditions. The evergreen forms are mostly tender, with species such as the vigorous *C. armandii* being suitable for the Pacific Northwest and Southeast (Zones 7–8) and *C. dioscoreifolia* requiring even warmer regions (Zones 9–10). Most other clematis are suited to the colder Zones 3–8. Some large hybrids give their best flower color when the head of the plant is in the shade. For this reason, they thrive well on a north-facing wall; as also do the bell-flowered hybrids of *C. alpina*. Double- and semi-double-flowered hybrids should have a south- or south-west-facing position. All clematis benefit from having the roots and lower part of the stem shaded.

The vigorous hybrids and species are best grown through or over some other vegetation, such as a large old tree or hedge. Only the less vigorous types, including most of the large-flowered hybrids, are really satisfactory trained against a wall. On a wall, trellis raised on battens gives the most effective support for growing clematis.

WATERING AND FEEDING Mulch in fall and spring. Feed with a balanced rose or other potash-rich fertilizer in spring, and midsummer.

Planting clematis

PLANT DEEPLY To help clematis establish well, dig a hole much deeper than usual and bury the bottom 6in./15cm. of stem below the soil surface. This helps minimize the likelihood of clematis wilt.

Clematis 'Etoile Violette'

PRUNING Clematis are divided into three main groups for pruning purposes, each method of pruning depending entirely on the time of flowering and vigor of the hybrid or species.

GROUP 1 These are the evergreen forms and the varieties derived from *C. alpina*, *C. macropetala*, and *C. montana*. They all flower early in the year, on the previous year's wood, and pruning comprises the cutting back immediately after flowering of all weak and dead stems to just above a bud. Large, well-established plants growing where they may be allowed free rein (which certainly should mean most specimens of the very vigorous *C. montana* type) need not be pruned.

Pruning clematis, group 1

PRUNE AFTER FLOWERING

The flowers of clematis in this group will all have been borne on growth made in the previous season, so the plant may need a tidy up after flowering to help it to produce plenty of healthy new wood to flower the following year. Therefore where practical, cut back some of the flowered stems to just above a bud. These varieties can be left completely unpruned if space allows.

Old flowered shoots can be left or cut back to a bud

The plant will quickly produce a tangled mass of stems that can be difficult to prune

Clematis

Pruning clematis, group 2

▶ **EARLY SPRING** Clematis in this group produce their flowers on wood made the previous season, but they need to be pruned early in the year, before they flower, to keep them tidy and to encourage new growth. Cut out completely any dead or weak stems. Cut back remaining stems by about 10in.–1ft./ 25–30cm., to a strong pair of buds. Although a few buds will be removed by pruning in this way, there will be plenty left to produce flowers.

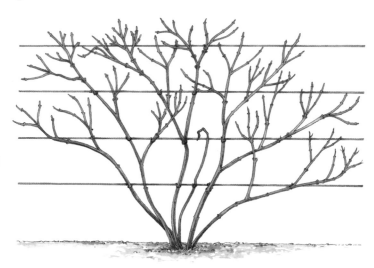

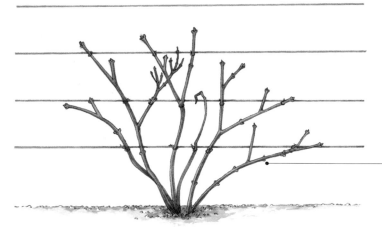

◀ **AFTER PRUNING** The plant will not be significantly reduced in size, but buds all along the stems will now break and flower. New growth should now be produced from the base of the plant.

The buds along the stems
should now break

GROUP 2 These also produce their flowers on the previous season's wood, and comprise the early and mid-season single-flowered hybrids, and the double- and semi-double-flowered hybrids. These should be pruned in early spring by cutting out any dead or weak stems and cutting back the remainder by about 10in.–1ft./25–30cm., to just above a strong pair of buds. Any remaining dead leaf stems should be cut away and the stems retied to their supports, allowing plenty of space between each.

GROUP 3 These plants are the hybrids of the C. × *jackmanii* type, the late large-flowered hybrids, the hybrids derived from *C. viticella* and *C. texensis*, the late-flowering species such as *C. tangutica*, and the so-called herbaceous types. They all flower late in the season on the current year's wood, and their top growth dies back during the winter. Pruning comprises cutting back all of the previous season's growth, in early spring, to just above a pair of strong buds about 2½ft./75cm. above soil level.

Pruning clematis, group 3

▲ **EARLY SPRING** The clematis in this group are the most vigorous forms, and require the most drastic pruning. By late winter or early spring, all the top growth will have died off but green buds will be appearing along the stems. Cut the plant back to the lowest strong pair of buds, ideally about 2½ft./75cm. above soil level. If left unpruned, group 3 clematis become very untidy indeed, with new growth always at the top of the plant and tangled up with dead stems.

► **AFTER PRUNING** The plant will look very insubstantial, but will quickly put on a great deal of top growth again, and will throw up new stems from the base of the plant. If slugs and snails are a problem in your garden, ensure adequate protection while the shoots are developing low down on the stems.

COMMON PROBLEMS Mildew; clematis wilt – plants suddenly die back without warning. If this occurs, immediately cut back to sound wood close to soil level and drench the area with a systemic fungicide. Plants generally recover, but if the effects are repeated, uproot and destroy the plant and before replanting with fresh stock, dig a hole of 1ft./30cm. all round and replace the soil with fresh from elsewhere in the garden. Always plant clematis with the bottom 6in./15cm. of the stem buried below soil level, to aid new root development (see page 86).

PROPAGATION Softwood cuttings in early summer, cut internodally, is the best method although it is less successful with large-flowered hybrids; layering is also generally satisfactory.

TROUBLESHOOTING Old and overgrown plants can almost always be rejuvenated by cutting them back as hard as desired in early spring. One season's flowers may be lost but there will be ample opportunity to re-establish the correct pruning regime.

Clematis – Lonicera

Hedera colchica 'Sulphur Heart'

SIZE Varies greatly, depending on variety and how assiduously it is pruned. Pruned as I have suggested, and provided that the very vigorous types are not planted against a wall, it should be possible to restrict most varieties to a wall space of between $6\frac{1}{2} \times 3$ft./2×1m. and about 13×13ft./4×4m. If unpruned, the most vigorous forms such as *C. tangutica*, or the hybrids of *C. montana*, will cover an old tree of 16×16ft./5×5m. in about seven years.

Hedera IVY

The ivies, as a group, include some of the best, most reliable and attractive of evergreen climbers; certainly of the evergreen self-clinging climbers. They are grown almost entirely for their foliage appeal and three species and their many cultivars are suitable for many different garden purposes.

SOIL Any, although some ivies are difficult in dry soil.

SITUATION Full sun to light or deep shade, depending on cultivar; the larger-leaved and variegated forms are generally better in full sun but are liable to be browned if exposed to cold winds. In the wild, ivies grow on trees but this is not a practice to be encouraged in gardens. Young trees are likely to suffer adversely from the competition, while older ones may become unstable. *H. canariensis* Zones 9–10; *H. colchica*, Zone 7; *H. helix*, Zones 5–9.

WATERING AND FEEDING Until the plant is well established mulch in autumn and spring, and feed with a balanced general fertilizer in mid-spring.

PRUNING AND SUPPORT No pruning is necessary but ivies may be sheared in spring to remove winter-damaged leaves. The small-leaved varieties may be trimmed with shears but pruners should be used on large-leaved forms. Ivies are firmly self-clinging once established, so are best not grown over wooden or other structures of limited durability. They will damage old and crumbly bricks and mortar but are perfectly safe on sound brickwork. When first planted, some ivies fail to climb and no amount of tying up will induce them to do so. After a year or two, however, during which time they form a mound of growth, they begin to climb of their own accord.

COMMON PROBLEMS None.

PROPAGATION Semi-ripe cuttings in summer or from naturally formed layers.

TROUBLESHOOTING Overgrown and neglected plants will usually regenerate satisfactorily if cut back very hard in spring.

SIZE Varies greatly, depending on type and climate, so check label information carefully. Without pruning, certainly most forms of *H. helix*, will reach about $6\frac{1}{2} \times 6\frac{1}{2}$ft./$2 \times 2$m. after five years, $10–13 \times 10–13$ft./$3–4 \times 3–4$m. after ten years, and perhaps 26×26ft./8×8m. after twenty, although the popular 'Goldheart' is rather more vigorous and more upright in habit. The most vigorous ivy that I have grown is the large-leaved *H. canariensis* 'Gloire de Marengo', which reached 20×20ft./6×6m. after ten years and showed no signs of abating. At the other extreme some of the small-leaved cultivars, such as 'Crippsii', will barely reach $6\frac{1}{2} \times 6\frac{1}{2}$ft./$2 \times 2$m. after fifteen years.

Hydrangea   CLIMBING HYDRANGEA

Although most of the familiar hydrangeas are shrubs, there is one self-clinging climber, *H. anomala petiolaris*, and a few similar plants in the closely related genus *Schizophragma*; less hardy so best in the South.

SOIL Rich and moist, at least until plants are well established, but not prone to water-logging; tolerant of acidity and alkalinity.

SITUATION Full sun to moderate shade; this plant grows very well against a north-facing wall. Zones 5–7.

WATERING AND FEEDING Mulch in fall and spring. Feed with a balanced rose or similar potash-rich fertilizer in mid-spring.

PRUNING None necessary but prune as hard as desired in spring.

COMMON PROBLEMS None.

PROPAGATION By layering.

TROUBLESHOOTING Old, woody or winter-damaged plants will regenerate if cut back hard in spring.

SIZE About 6½ × 6½ft./2 × 2m. after five years, 23 × 23ft./7 × 7m. after ten, and 40–46 × 40–46ft./12–14 × 12–14m. ultimately.

Hydrangea petiolaris

Lonicera   HONEYSUCKLE

Although there are some fine shrubby and evergreen species, it is as deciduous or semi-evergreen climbers that the honeysuckles are best known. They have some great merits, most importantly the fine perfume that most possess. Against this must be set the fact that they are rather unkempt plants and never at their best when forced to grow up a trellis on a wall, in limited space.

SOIL Always best in a moist, organic loam and rarely successful in very dry or very wet conditions.

SITUATION Full sun to moderate shade; most climbing honey-suckles are naturally woodland plants. Zones 4–8 for most hardy.

WATERING AND FEEDING Mulch in fall and spring. Feed with a balanced rose or similar potash-rich fertilizer in mid-spring, and again around midsummer for less vigorous vines.

PRUNING AND SUPPORT The best support is provided by an old tree, a large hedge or a large and substantial fence. They thrive and flower without pruning, but vigor and appearance of established plants are improved if the oldest one third of the shoots is cut back to soil level every spring.

COMMON PROBLEMS Mildew; aphids.

PROPAGATION Semi-ripe cuttings in summer, but some varieties are notoriously difficult to strike. Layering may be successful.

TROUBLESHOOTING Fairly old and overgrown plants can usually be rejuvenated by cutting them back to soil level in spring, spreading the work over two consecutive springs. Very old plants with a really stout, woody trunk are best replaced.

SIZE Varies considerably, depending on variety. As a guide, forms of the common *L. periclymenum* will reach about 6½ × 6½ft./2 × 2m. after five years, 13 × 13ft./4 × 4m. after ten years and perhaps 20 × 20ft./6 × 6m. eventually. A strong spreader that can take over in a small property is *L. japonica*. It is considered a weed in much of the Northeast but its floral scent is lovely.

Lonicera periclymenum

Parthenocissus – Rosa

Parthenocissus tricuspidata

Parthenocissus   WOODBINE

This group of invaluable deciduous climbers has suffered a fair number of name changes over the years, but most are known collectively by the common name of woodbines.

SOIL Most, but least successful where very dry.

SITUATION Full sun to light shade. Zones 7–9 for *P. henryana*; Zone 3 for *P. inserta*; Zones 3–9 for *P. quinquefolia*, Virginia creeper; Zones 4–8 for *P. tricuspidata*, Boston-ivy.

WATERING AND FEEDING Mulch in fall and spring. Apply a balanced general fertilizer in mid-spring.

PRUNING AND SUPPORT The most popular species, *P. tricuspidata*, is self-clinging but, like ivies, should not be planted against unsound brickwork. *P. henryana* and *P. quinquefolia* require support on wires at least when young, while *P. inserta* will require wire support permanently. No pruning is necessary but all species may be clipped in spring or summer to keep them within bounds.

COMMON PROBLEMS None.

PROPAGATION Semi-ripe cuttings in summer or by layering.

TROUBLESHOOTING Plants that have outgrown their allotted space may be cut back hard and will rejuvenate satisfactorily. If necessary, plants may also be cut back to soil level in spring and will regrow, although the work is best spread over two years.

SIZE Early establishment may be slow but all forms should reach $6\frac{1}{2} \times 6\frac{1}{2}$ft./$2 \times 2$m. after five years, 16×16ft./5×5m. after ten years and 33×33ft./10×10m. after twenty years.

Passiflora   PASSION FLOWER

There can be few plants as compelling in bloom as the exotic and bizarre passion flowers. *P. caerulea* can be grown as a house or greenhouse plant in the North, outdoors in the South.

SOIL Most, but least successful where very dry or very alkaline.

SITUATION Full sun to light shade; in mild but frost-prone areas, it must be grown against a warm south-west-facing wall. Passion flowers usually flower best when their roots are confined to an area of about $1\frac{1}{2} \times 1\frac{1}{2}$ft./$45 \times 45$cm. by paving slabs sunk vertically in the soil to create a bottomless pit. Zone 10.

WATERING AND FEEDING Mulch in fall and spring. Feed with a potash-rich fertilizer in mid-spring, and around midsummer.

PRUNING AND SUPPORT Best trained loosely against horizontal wires. No pruning is necessary to encourage flowering but there will almost inevitably be some shoot death from frost damage; such dead or damaged growth should be cut back to within 2ft./60cm. of soil level in spring.

COMMON PROBLEMS Apart from frost, virus often causes leaf crumpling; various insects may tatter the leaves.

PROPAGATION Semi-ripe cuttings in summer.

TROUBLESHOOTING Plants that have outgrown their allotted space may be cut back to soil level and will usually rejuvenate.

SIZE Up to $6\frac{1}{2}–10 \times 6\frac{1}{2}–10$ft./$2–3 \times 2–3$m. after five years and $20–23 \times 20–23$ft./$6–7 \times 6–7$m. in mild areas after fifteen or eighteen years.

Passiflora caerulea

Rosa ROSE

There are climbing forms of most of the roses also grown as bushes, and they have much of their cultivation in common. Additionally, there are a few roses derived from species that exist only in a climbing or scrambling form.

SOIL Although tolerant of a wide range of soil types, climbing roses – like bush roses – will always be most successful in a rich, moisture-retentive soil, but this could range from an organic loam to a heavy clay. Light soils will produce good roses provided large quantities of organic matter are incorporated; this is especially important for climbing roses, which tend to be grown in places that are inherently very dry, such as close to walls or other supports. Roses are least successful on very acidic soils, while in very alkaline soils they may suffer from severe leaf chlorosis.

SITUATION Full sun or light shade. Some cultivars are successful in deeper shade, but produce fewer flowers, while some, most notably the tea roses and some of the less common species, are more tender and require winter protection. Zones 5–9 for many.

WATERING AND FEEDING Mulch in fall and spring; mulching and watering is especially important for climbing roses. Feed with a balanced rose or similar potash-rich fertilizer in mid-spring, and in midsummer.

PRUNING CLIMBERS These require much less pruning than their bush counterparts and, in general, pruning in the fall should comprise the shortening of any very long and whippy shoots followed, in spring, by the cutting out of dead or diseased stems and light cutting back of the tips of old flowered shoots. Pruning of the very vigorous near-species, such as *R. filipes* 'Kiftsgate', will quickly become impractical.

Some varieties of climbing rose, especially certain climbing hybrid teas, develop a permanent framework of stems that produces each year a regular pattern of side-shoots on which the flowers are borne. These side-shoots, once flowered, should be cut back in the spring of the following year to within 2in./5cm. of their junction with the main stems.

RAMBLERS True rambling roses are pruned differently for, instead of bearing their flowers on side-shoots from a permanent framework, most produce long new shoots each year on which the flowers are borne, and once those flowers have faded, these shoots will not flower again and are of no further use. The precise method of pruning varies among varieties, but as so few different types of rambler are now grown (they are very prone to mildew and flower once only in early summer), I will restrict this description to the commonest of those still found. On large old plants of 'Dorothy Perkins' or 'American Pillar', cut all flowered stems back to soil level after flowering. On younger plants, cut back flowered side-shoots to within about 4in./10cm. of their junction with main stems. On 'Albertine', 'Albéric Barbier', 'Pink Perpétué', and 'New Dawn', cut back up to one third of the old flowered stems to soil level after flowering, and cut back the flowered side-shoots on the remainder to within about 4in./10cm. of their junction with the main stems.

Rosa – Solanum

Pruning climbing roses

▶ **SPRING** Identify the permanent framework of stems which each year produce side-shoots on which flowers are borne. The permanent stems should be tied down horizontally, with all the flowering side-shoots growing vertically. Each spring, any weak or diseased main stems should be cut out but on a healthy, established rose, no main stems at all need be cut. Then cut back all the side-shoots hard, to a bud within 2in./5cm. of the junction with the main stems.

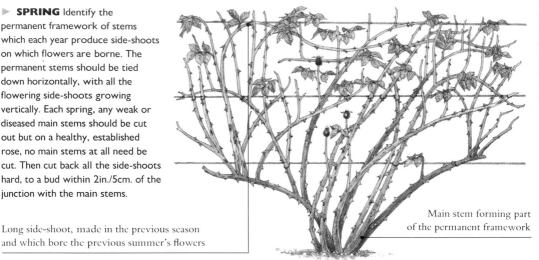

Long side-shoot, made in the previous season and which bore the previous summer's flowers

Main stem forming part of the permanent framework

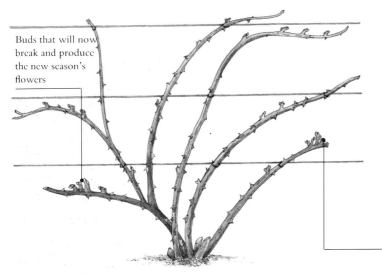

Buds that will now break and produce the new season's flowers

◀ **AFTER PRUNING** Re-tie all the main stems that remain, pulling them down to the horizontal and ensuring that the ties are quite loose and will not chafe the stems. New side-shoots will now develop from this permanent framework, to flower later in the year. In the fall, tip back any excessively long side-shoots to avoid wind damage during the winter.

Stubs of previous year's side-shoots

COMMON PROBLEMS Aphids; mildew (especially serious on climbers and ramblers); black spot; rust; and many beetles.

PROPAGATION Hardwood cuttings in early winter, although these are often very difficult to strike from climbing hybrid teas and floribundas.

TROUBLESHOOTING Old and overgrown plants can often be rejuvenated by cutting back the shoots to just above soil level in spring, spreading the work over three years so that no more than one third of the shoots is cut out at any one time. Although there are some notable and fine very old rose specimens, generally they have been tended throughout their lives, and my feeling is that a neglected rose more than eight or ten years old is best replaced.

The commonest problem with climbing roses is that all of the flowers are borne at the top of the plant. This is remedied very easily by pulling down the vertical shoots and tying them horizontally to cover the wall or other support. Buds will then break along the whole length of the stem. As with bush forms, most climbing roses are grafted onto rootstocks of different varieties, chosen for their rooting rather than their flowering attributes. Suckers may arise from these and must be pulled off.

SIZE Enormously variable so it is important to check label descriptions. The shortest-growing climbers, commonly called pillar roses, will not attain a height of much more than 6½ft./2m. The majority of modern climbers will reach about 16ft/5m. but some of the older varieties and some of the species are very much more vigorous and can attain as much as 50ft./15m.

Solanum

The climbing solanums are deciduous or semi-evergreen relatives of the potato, and immediately recognizable as such from the form of their flowers. They are vigorous, but reliably hardy only in milder areas. *S. crispum*, the so-called climbing potato, tends to grow more in the form of a lax shrub but I find it is better treated as a climber.

Solanum crispum 'Glasnevin'

SOIL Most, but least successful where very dry.
SITUATION Full sun to light shade, and always best against a warm south- or south-west-facing wall. Zone 10.
WATERING AND FEEDING Mulch in fall and spring. Feed with a balanced rose or similar potash-rich fertilizer in mid spring, and again around midsummer.

Solanum – Vitis

Tropaeolum speciosum

PRUNING AND SUPPORT Best trained loosely against horizontal wires. Solanum is very free-flowering but rather ungainly in its growth habit, so annual pruning is necessary each spring to keep it compact and tidy. Cut out completely one or two of the oldest stems, to a vigorous young shoot. Cut back very straggly or overlong stems, and stems growing forwards away from the wall, to a junction with strong young growth. Tie in all new shoots.
COMMON PROBLEMS None.
PROPAGATION Semi-ripe cuttings in early summer.
TROUBLESHOOTING Plants that have outgrown their allotted space may be cut back hard, and will usually rejuvenate.
SIZE Varies slightly between species, the more shrubby *S. crispum* generally being rather less vigorous than *S. jasminoides*, which will reach $6\frac{1}{2} \times 6\frac{1}{2}$ft./$2 \times 2$m. after five years, and perhaps 16×16ft./5×5m. after twenty years.

Tropaeolum NASTURTIUM

Perhaps best known in the form of the species grown as annuals – the nasturtium and the canary creeper. But there are related and valuable perennial climbing species, too, most notably the orange-yellow *T. tuberosum* and the more hardy, scarlet-flowered *T. speciosum*, the Scots or Chilean flame flower. The latter's common names betray its fondness for a mild, moist climate.
SOIL Tolerates a wide range but must be free draining, yet moist and preferably organic; intolerant of alkalinity.
SITUATION Full sun to light shade with shelter from cold winds; preferably sited so that its roots are in shade. Zones 7–9.
WATERING AND FEEDING Mulch in fall and spring. Feed with a balanced rose or similar potash-rich fertilizer in mid-spring, and again around midsummer.
PRUNING AND SUPPORT No pruning is needed as the growth above ground dies down in the winter. They are best allowed free rein over some natural support such as a large evergreen hedge or coniferous tree.
COMMON PROBLEMS None.
PROPAGATION Basal cuttings in spring: take a nonflowering shoot from the base of the plant, or even just below ground level.
TROUBLESHOOTING Unlikely to be necessary.
SIZE Will attain an annual height of about 10ft./3m. after four or five years, and a similar spread depending on the support.

Vitis GRAPE VINE

The best known and most important species of *Vitis* is the grape-vine, although there are one or two ornamental species, most notably the large-leaved *V. coignetiae*, crimson glory vine.
SOIL Most, but least successful where very dry or water-logged.
SITUATION Full sun to light shade, but in northern areas it always grows best, and grape production is always better, against a warm south- or south-west-facing wall. Zones 5–8.
WATERING AND FEEDING Mulch in fall and spring. Feed with a balanced rose or similar potash-rich fertilizer in mid-spring, and

Regular annual pruning of outdoor vines

▶ **WINTER** Once the basic fan framework of the vine is established (see page 98), prune in winter to remove all of the previous season's growth: cut back all the extension growth on the main stems or rods to a strong pair of buds; and cut back the strongest side-shoots to two buds from their junction with the main rod.

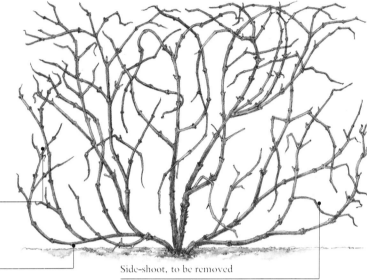

Last season's extension growth, to be cut back completely

Main stem or rod

Side-shoot, to be removed

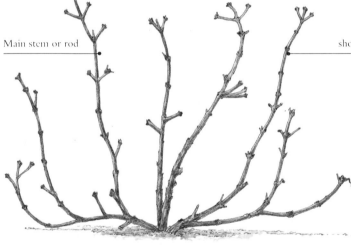

Main stem or rod

Buds will break to become side-shoots: these should be thinned out in spring

▶ **AFTER PRUNING** The basic framework of stems or rods will now be clear. Further pruning is required in spring: thin out the side-shoots as they elongate to leave one for every 1½ft./45cm. of rod length. Tie the side-shoots to the wires.

again around midsummer. Fruiting vines benefit from considerable additional watering when in fruit.

PRUNING AND SUPPORT Although fruit of sorts will be produced with little or no pruning, the fruiting varieties soon become an unkempt mess and both for the best appearance and best crop, it is worth taking a little care to train and prune vines correctly. In North America, home garden grape culture differs from region to region. Consult the County Extension Specialist for local recommendations for cultivar selection, pruning, pests. This is one pruning regime among many based on the principle of encouraging fruit-bearing wood to grow on stems one year old; sometimes those stems may be reduced to a spur.

Vitis – Wisteria

Vitis coignetiae

In the first season after planting, loosely tie in all shoots to a system of horizontal support wires. In the following winter, select the strongest two or three of these shoots, cut them back by about half, spread them so they are spaced more or less equidistantly, and tie them to the support wires in a fan pattern. These will form the main stems or rods of the vine and each season's extension growth on them should be cut back by about half each winter until they are as long as space allows. Thereafter all the extension growth should be cut back each time.

Also each winter, cut back side-shoots to two buds from their bases. In the spring, after the side-shoots have begun to elongate, prune to leave one side-shoot for every 1½ft./45cm. of rod length, tie them to the support wires and pinch out the tips when they have reached their allotted length. Thereafter, every winter, cut back these side-shoots to two buds from the base, and every spring thin out the side-shoots as before.

The foliage ornamental *V. coignetiae* may also be pruned in this way for the neatest effect, but it may equally be allowed to ramble, unpruned, over an archway, pergola or similar support, if space permits. The southern muscadine grape *V. rotundifolia* (Zones 6–8) is also often allowed to ramble over pergolas or trellises, but can become too rampant without some pruning.

COMMON PROBLEMS Mildew; gray mold on fruit.

PROPAGATION Semi-ripe cuttings in early summer; the best results are usually obtained from "eyes", 1–1½in./2.5–4cm.-long cuttings taken to include a node with buds.

TROUBLESHOOTING Provided they are not very old and woody, plants that have outgrown their allotted space may be cut back hard to soil level and will usually rejuvenate satisfactorily.

SIZE Vines really should be pruned to keep them within an allotted space, and a wall area of about 10–13 × 6½–10ft./3–4 × 2–3m. should be manageable. Unpruned, a grapevine will reach about 10 × 10ft./3 × 3m. in five years, 20 × 20ft./6 × 6m. after ten years, and perhaps 33 × 33ft./10 × 10m. ultimately. The ornamental *V. coignetiae* will grow faster and larger than a fruiting vine, probably by about half as much again. Its fruits are inedible.

Wisteria

The queen of climbers, the deciduous twining wisteria is a fine and very hardy fragrant flowering plant, but it is also a vigorous one and must be allowed space. It is usually grown against a wall, but can be trained as a standard around a central support.

SOIL Most, provided there is adequate rooting depth; dryness is tolerated once the roots are well established.

SITUATION Full sun to moderate shade; although flowering is undoubtedly best on a south- or south-west-facing wall, I have a very successful and free-flowering old plant facing north-east. Zones 4–9, depending on species.

WATERING AND FEEDING Water and feed until established and preferably permanently. Mulch in fall and spring. Feed with a balanced rose or similar potash-rich fertilizer in mid-spring. Contrary to opinion, wisteria will not flower better if starved.

Regular annual pruning of established wisteria

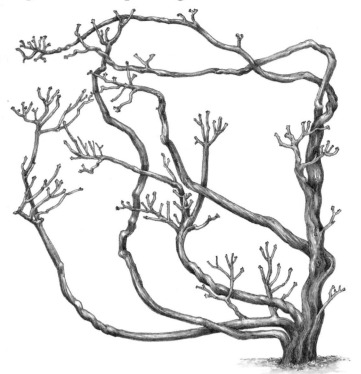

AFTER PRUNING, WINTER
Wisterias are vigorous and should be pruned hard in winter. Identify the stems which make up the permanent framework, and the side-shoots that flowered the previous season. Cut back all these side-shoots to three buds from their junction with the main stems (see inset, above). The plant will be much reduced in bulk, but will produce plenty of shoot growth for pruning in the summer (see text).

PRUNING AND SUPPORT A very stout system of support wires will be required initially. Thereafter, mature wisteria stems are best supported by being tied carefully and individually to stout supports pegged to the wall. In the first season after planting, loosely tie in all shoots to the support wires. In the following winter, select three to five shoots to form the main framework of the plant (depending on space available), cut them back by about half, spread them so they are spaced more or less equidistantly, and tie them to the support wires. Thereafter, each summer cut back all long, whippy side-shoots to about 10in./25cm. long, except for any that you require to fill in gaps in the main framework. In the following winter, cut these shortened shoots back further to three buds from the base. But no matter how careful your pruning, a wisteria is unlikely to flower in under five to seven years.

COMMON PROBLEMS None.

PROPAGATION By layering or by semi-ripe cuttings taken in late summer.

TROUBLESHOOTING Not necessary as established wisterias are all but indestructible, but damaged or overgrown plants may be cut back very hard into old wood, in spring, and will regenerate. Train a wisteria to standard or tree form to save space.

SIZE Without pruning, will reach about 16 × 16ft./5 × 5m. after five years, 33–40 × 33–40ft./10–12 × 10–12m. after ten years, and up to 65 × 65ft./20 × 20m. ultimately.

PERENNIALS

Acanthus	Kniphofia
Achillea	Lamium
Aconitum	Ligularia
Alcea	Limonium
Alchemilla	Lobelia
Anemone	Lupinus
Anthemis	Lychnis
Aquilegia	Meconopsis
Artemisia	Mentha
Aster	Nepeta
Astilbe	Oenothera
Astrantia	Omphalodes
Bellis	Paeonia
Bergenia	Papaver
Campanula	Penstemon
Centranthus	Perovskia
Chrysanthemum	Phlox
Coreopsis	Phormium
Delphinium	Platycodon
Dicentra	Polygonatum
Digitalis	Polygonum
Doronicum	Pulmonaria
Echinacea	Ranunculus
Echinops	Romneya
Epimedium	Rudbeckia
Eryngium	Ruta
Erysimum	Salvia
Euphorbia	Sanguinaria
Geranium	Stachys
Geum	Thalictrum
Gypsophila	Verbascum
Helenium	Veronica
Helleborus	Yucca
Hemerocallis	Ferns
Heuchera	Grasses
Hosta	Sedges and rushes

Principles of care

Herbaceous perennials are ornamental plants that have no above-ground woody framework and, with a few exceptions, die down at the end of the growing season to survive as an underground rootstock; they are generally differentiated from so-called bulbous plants (see pages 142–65) by the absence of any swollen, food storage structure. They were once grown only in borders (a use now in revival in the USA) but are now used with shrubs in mixed plantings, the shrubs providing a permanent framework after the perennials have died down; or occasionally the more 'architectural' species might be grown as isolated specimens. Most herbaceous perennials (and certainly the taller types) are unsuitable subjects for growing in containers.

SOIL AND SITE REQUIREMENTS

There are species, cultivars and varieties suitable for all types of soil but common causes of failure are inappropriate soil or site conditions. Few herbaceous perennials will tolerate more than light shade, and among those few it is important to distinguish between the species that are tolerant of dry shade and those that must have moisture.

FEEDING AND WATERING

Herbaceous perennials need to be fed, certainly once and preferably twice each year, with a balanced, general-purpose fertilizer if they are to give of their best. Very vigorous or fast-growing types will also benefit from a foliar application of liquid fertilizer during the summer months, although I don't consider this essential and have not included it in my advice on individual species. Few types are well adapted

Providing wrap-around support

▲ **SPRING** As growth appears, push three to five canes into the ground around the plant and tie string loosely around, keeping the top string below the top of the leaves. Ideally, start with short canes, and exchange them for progressively longer ones as the plant grows up.

▶ **SUMMER** Add more string to keep the plant well supported; its leaves will soon conceal the string and canes.

to very dry soils and almost all will therefore benefit from the application of a moisture-retaining mulch in spring. If organic mulching material is in short supply, it may be confined to the area around the root crown of each plant but, ideally, the soil surface over the entire bed should be mulched to improve root growth and limit water loss by evaporation.

In very dry seasons it may be necessary to use hoses or sprinklers (if permitted), but if the plants need regular watering even in the course of a normal summer it generally means that they have not been chosen correctly for the soil conditions, or perhaps have been inadequately mulched in advance.

GENERAL MANAGEMENT

Most perennials require cutting down to soil level at the end of the growing season, but for all but the very hardiest kinds this operation is better left until the spring in areas subject to cold winters. The dead shoot growth will provide some protection against penetrating frost, and any seed-heads will offer food for birds. Additional protection can be provided by a fall organic mulch mounded around the root crowns. In the case of the relatively small number of evergreen perennials, dead leaves should be cut away but under no circumstances should the plant be cut back to ground level.

A number of perennials require staking, although the trend in recent years has been toward lower-growing cultivars with stiffer, more self-supporting stems. Staking can be by means of individual (and preferably unobtrusive) canes, or by a wrap-around support of wire rings in which the entire clump is more loosely confined: canes and string are the cheapest but most fiddly method, interlocking metal stakes the most elegant.

PROPAGATION

Almost all types of perennials benefit from being lifted and divided every few years, the frequency of this operation varying with the vigor of the plant and, to a lesser extent, the growing conditions. Division is also the most reliable method of propagation, although a considerable number of perennials (especially the true species) can be propagated from seed; for others softwood cuttings are the best method. The many cultivars with fully double flowers produce no seed and can only, therefore, be multiplied by division.

Acanthus BEAR'S BREECHES

A small genus of large, rather glossy, and prickly-leaved, semi-evergreen plants with tall spikes of white, pinkish, or mauve flowers. *A. mollis* is the commonest species, but *A. spinosus* is more stately. Bear's breeches are usually grown at the back of borders large enough to accommodate their rather gaunt appearance, and although they are hardly graceful plants, they are usefully large, easy to grow, and invariably cause comment.

SOIL Deep, rich, preferably well drained.

SITUATION Always performs best in full sun, but will tolerate light shade, and needs it in hot summers. Zones 9–10.

WATERING AND FEEDING Mulch in fall and spring. Feed with a balanced, general-purpose fertilizer in mid-spring and again around midsummer.

MANAGEMENT Cut back dead flower spikes after flowering. In winter in colder areas, the crowns may need mulch protection. Little staking is necessary.

COMMON PROBLEMS None.

PROPAGATION Division in fall or spring but root cuttings in fall are better; can be grown from seed.

TROUBLESHOOTING None necessary.

SIZE Reaches 1–1.5m. × 50cm./3–5 × 1½ft. in three years.

Acanthus mollis

Achillea – Alchemilla

Achillea filipendulina

Achillea YARROW

A rather large genus of semi-evergreen, rather stiff-stemmed hardy perennials. Perhaps the most familiar but often invasive is *A. millefolium*, milfoil or yarrow, but there are several useful and versatile, if unexciting, medium-sized border perennials, such as *A. filipendulina*, with white, yellow, or pinkish hybrids.

SOIL Light, preferably fertile soil, but tolerant of fairly thin, poor, and alkaline conditions.

SITUATION Always performs best in full sun, although will also tolerate light shade. Zones 3–7.

WATERING AND FEEDING Mulch in fall and spring. Feed with a balanced, general-purpose fertilizer in mid-spring, and again around midsummer.

MANAGEMENT Cut back dead flower spikes after flowering; only taller forms require staking.

COMMON PROBLEMS None.

PROPAGATION Basal cuttings in spring or early summer, or division in fall or spring every two to three years.

TROUBLESHOOTING None necessary.

SIZE Varies with cultivar; taller forms such as *A. filipendulina* 'Gold Plate' reaches $5 \times 1\frac{1}{2}$ft./1.5m. $\times$ 50cm. in three years, but many others, such as the newer German Galaxy hybrids, will not exceed 2×1ft./60 $\times$ 30cm.

Aconitum MONKSHOOD

Deciduous perennials with characteristically hooded flowers in shades of blue or white. The roots are poisonous and the plants rather sinister in appearance, but because they are easy to grow and relatively trouble free – qualities that are ever more valuable in the modern garden – I am convinced that this is one of the herbaceous genera most likely to stage a comeback.

SOIL Moist, well drained, rich, organic, intolerant of light or poor soils or of water-logging.

SITUATION Full sun or light shade. Zones 3–8.

WATERING AND FEEDING Mulch in fall and spring. Feed with a balanced, general-purpose fertilizer in mid-spring and again around midsummer. It is very important not to allow the soil to dry out in summer.

MANAGEMENT Thin out the flower spikes in spring to leave five or six per mature plant, then cut back dead flower spikes after flowering; only taller forms require staking. *A. uncinatum*, native to the Southeast of the USA, is a scrambling plant, best grown in wilder parts of the garden over and through shrubs.

COMMON PROBLEMS None.

PROPAGATION Division in spring, some forms from seed.

TROUBLESHOOTING None necessary.

SIZE Varies considerably among species and cultivars (nomenclature among monkshood is often confused, especially in garden catalogues). Among the commoner forms available from nurseries are *A. × bicolor* 'Bressingham Spire', 3×3ft./90 $\times$ 90cm. or so; *A. carmichaellii* (syn. *A. fischeri*), about $5 \times 1\frac{1}{2}$ft./1.5m. $\times$ 50cm.

Aconitum napellus

Alcea HOLLYHOCK

Familiar garden plants for many years, hollyhocks have come to be identified with the cottage style of garden. Most are actually biennial, although some are short-lived perennials. All grow so large, however, that they are more conveniently considered with other herbaceous perennials. Rust disease can be a very serious problem on hollyhocks in many gardens.

SOIL Well drained, fairly rich; hollyhocks are tolerant of some dryness and are successful when grown close to walls, but they are intolerant of wet, heavy soils.

SITUATION Full sun or very light shade. Zones 3–9.

WATERING AND FEEDING Mulch in fall and spring. Feed with a balanced, general-purpose fertilizer in mid-spring, and again around midsummer, or apply a liquid fertilizer high in potash at three-week intervals during rapid growth in summer.

MANAGEMENT Cut off dead flower spikes after flowering; pull away lower leaves if they show signs of rust early in the season, as it is from these that the disease spreads up the plant. Collect and destroy old foliage in fall to lessen the amount of disease surviving the winter.

COMMON PROBLEMS Rust; whitefly.

PROPAGATION Only possible from seed.

TROUBLESHOOTING If individual plants become severely affected by rust, destroy them before the disease spreads to others.

SIZE The best and most common forms, including the popular biennial *A. rosea* 'Chater's Double', will reach about 6½–8 × 2ft./2–2.5m. × 60cm. by flowering time in the second year.

Alcea rosea

Alchemilla LADY'S MANTLE

Deciduous but, nonetheless, one of the most useful and pretty of all ground-cover plants, extremely easy to grow, and tolerant of a wide range of conditions. Lady's mantles self-seed freely, and seedlings may need to be removed where not wanted.

SOIL Most, but least successful in very dry or very wet conditions, and best in deep, rich loams.

SITUATION Full sun to moderate shade. Zones 4–8.

WATERING AND FEEDING Mulch in spring before the foliage emerges (mulching in fall is not really practical because of the ground-covering leaves). Feed with a balanced, general-purpose fertilizer in mid-spring. Where space is not restricted and growth need not be curtailed, a second feed after midsummer can usefully be applied.

MANAGEMENT In late fall or early winter, cut back foliage with shears once it has died down and browned.

COMMON PROBLEMS None.

PROPAGATION Division in spring or fall, or by the many self-sown seedlings.

TROUBLESHOOTING Not likely to be necessary.

SIZE The common *A. vulgaris* (syn. *mollis*) attains 1½ × 1½ft./50 × 50cm. after two years; the less vigorous *A. alpina* will spread to a similar size, but only attain half the height.

Alchemilla vulgaris (syn. mollis)

Anemone – Aquilegia

Anemone × hybrida

Anemone   JAPANESE ANEMONE

There are several quite distinct sub-groups in the genus *Anemone* (see also page 147), and the most useful border plant is that generally known as the Japanese anemone, *A. × hybrida*. Its white or pink flowers are among the delights of the garden in late summer, but the plant is almost too easy to grow and its invasive nature requires watching.

SOIL Almost any, tolerant of fairly wet and fairly dry conditions and also of moderate acidity and alkalinity.

SITUATION Full sun to light shade. Zones 5–8.

WATERING AND FEEDING Mulch in fall and spring. Feed with a balanced, general-purpose fertilizer in mid-spring, and again around midsummer.

MANAGEMENT Cut back dead flower stems after flowering and cut foliage back to soil level as soon as it browns with frost. In mild winters, the foliage will persist for several months. The plants do not require staking. Where Japanese anemones threaten to become invasive they are best divided every three years; but on the whole they dislike disturbance, and in a semi-wild situation they can be allowed free rein.

COMMON PROBLEMS None.

PROPAGATION Division in fall or spring.

TROUBLESHOOTING None necessary.

SIZE Will reach 3–5 × 1½–2ft./1–1.5m. × 50–60cm. in three years, depending on the growing conditions.

Anthemis

This is a genus of feathery-foliaged, evergreen, ground-covering plants, of which the most common and important is the herb camomile (now known as *Chamaemelum*): in its flowering forms, it is sometimes grown for culinary use or at the front of the border, but in its nonflowering form, *C. nobile* 'Treneague', is used for small, ornamental lawns in England.

SOIL Free draining, fairly rich, light; will fail miserably on cold or wet soils.

SITUATION Full sun to very light shade; camomile lawns succeed only in full sun and with shelter from cold winds. Zones 5–8.

WATERING AND FEEDING Mulching is seldom practicable (and certainly not on ornamental lawns) because of the close mat of foliage, so assiduous watering is essential, especially during dry spells in spring. Feed with a balanced, general-purpose fertilizer in mid-spring and apply liquid feed during the summer.

MANAGEMENT Little attention is needed on flowering forms other than lightly trimming the plants back in spring. Camomile lawns should be trimmed very lightly in summer with shears or with a rotary lawn mower with the blades set high. Weed control (including the control of grasses) is important, but must be done by hand.

COMMON PROBLEMS None.

PROPAGATION Basal cuttings in early summer, or some forms from seed.

Chamaemelum nobile 'Flore Pleno'

TROUBLESHOOTING Not likely to be necessary; camomile will suffer if the growing conditions are unsuitable, and in such circumstances there is no point in persevering. Camomile lawns will not take heavy wear.

SIZE Individual plants will attain 4 × 18in./10 × 45cm. in two years; for lawns, they should be spaced 20cm./8in. apart.

Aquilegia   COLUMBINE

Hardy, deciduous, spring-flowering border plants, among my personal favorites for their easy maintenance. The older forms are indispensable cottage garden plants, and although they tend to be short-lived, they easily self-seed and spread.

SOIL Most, equally successful on light and heavy soil provided it is not seriously water-logged.

SITUATION Full sun to moderate shade; I grow the old 'granny's bonnet' varieties (*A. vulgaris*) well under trees. Zones 5–9.

WATERING AND FEEDING Mulch in fall and spring. Feed with a balanced, general-purpose fertilizer in mid-spring and again after midsummer.

MANAGEMENT Cut back dead flower heads after flowering and before the seed is shed; divide every three years or, if mixed color varieties are being grown, simply discard old plants and make use of self-sown seedlings. If rain or wind make the taller forms flop, light staking will keep them neat.

COMMON PROBLEMS Aphids; columbine leafminer.

PROPAGATION See above. Can be grown from seed.

TROUBLESHOOTING Not likely to be necessary.

SIZE Most of the commoner border varieties, including *A. vulgaris*, will attain 3 × 1½ft./1m. × 50cm. after two years.

Aquilegia vulgaris

Artemisia 'Powis Castle'

Artemisia

More or less hardy clump-forming plants, most with grayish or silvery evergreen foliage, and usually grown to provide contrast with other, grander plants. Like so many silver-leaved species, they are only really successful when conditions are similar to those in Mediterranean gardens. Although this is a fairly large genus, with some dwarf alpine species, most of the common border types can be divided into the more herbaceous, clump-forming varieties, and the larger, more woody, semi-shrub forms.

SOIL Light, free draining; successful in alkaline conditions.

SITUATION Full sun to very light shade. Most kinds Zones 3–9; *A. absinthium* 'Lambrook Silver', Zones 4–9; *A.* 'Powis Castle', Zones 6–8.

WATERING AND FEEDING Mulch in fall and spring. Feed with a balanced fertilizer in mid-spring, and after midsummer.

MANAGEMENT Trim lightly in spring; divide every three or four years in spring.

COMMON PROBLEMS None.

PROPAGATION Basal cuttings in early summer; or division of young plants in spring. Old plants are difficult to divide.

TROUBLESHOOTING Not likely to be necessary; old and woody plants can be cut hard back to soil level in spring and will often rejuvenate, but they are best discarded and replaced.

SIZE Most of the commoner border cultivars, including *A. absinthium* 'Lambrook Silver', will reach about $2\frac{1}{2} \times 1\frac{1}{2}$ft./80 × 50cm. in three years; the more shrubby forms, including *A.* 'Powis Castle', will reach about 3×3ft./1 × 1m. in the same time.

Aster MICHAELMAS DAISY

Not to be confused with the annual China asters in the genus *Callistephus*, this is the genus of Michaelmas daisies, among the most dependable of border perennials for the fall. Select varieties that have some resistance to mildew.

SOIL Almost any, provided it is not very heavy or water-logged.

SITUATION Full sun to light or partial shade. Mostly Zones 3–8.

WATERING AND FEEDING Mulch in fall and spring. Feed with a balanced, general-purpose fertilizer in mid-spring, and again after midsummer.

MANAGEMENT Cut back to soil level after flowering. Taller varieties will need some wrap-around support. Divide every four or five years.

COMMON PROBLEMS Mildew; best avoided by not growing the *A. novi-belgii* varieties.

PROPAGATION Division in spring or from basal cuttings in spring.

TROUBLESHOOTING Not likely to be necessary; old and very woody plants should be discarded.

SIZE The taller-growing forms of *A. novae-angliae* will reach about $2\frac{1}{2}$–3×2ft./75–90 × 60cm. in two or three years. The dwarf *A. × thomsonii* 'Nanus' will only reach about $1\frac{1}{2} \times 1\frac{1}{2}$ft./50 × 50cm. in the same time. There are many cultivars of varying heights.

Aster novae-angliae

Astilbe FALSE SPIREA

The feathery-flowered hardy astilbes are among the more instantly recognizable herbaceous perennials. They are colorful, sometimes too colorful, and very easy to grow – provided you appreciate that they are demanding in their site requirements.

SOIL Moist and rich; these are really plants for boggy conditions or near the water garden, but they will succeed in a normal border with fairly rich soil that does not dry out.

SITUATION Will tolerate full sun and also moderate shade but I find them best in light shade. Zones 3–8.

WATERING AND FEEDING Mulch in fall and spring. Feed with a balanced, general-purpose fertilizer in mid-spring, and again about midsummer. If grown as a border plant, water in dry spells.

MANAGEMENT Leave dead flower spikes to provide interest during the winter and then cut back in spring. Disturb and divide as infrequently as possible – only when plants are old and stunted.

COMMON PROBLEMS None, except for mice in some regions.

PROPAGATION Division in fall or spring; the species may be grown from seed.

TROUBLESHOOTING Not likely to be necessary.

SIZE Apart from a few, less common, dwarf forms, most will reach about 3 × 3ft./1 × 1m. in three years.

Astilbe × arendsii

Astrantia MASTERWORT

Never distinguished but always interesting, always easy and, I think, among the prettiest of hardy deciduous perennials.

SOIL Tolerates most, provided not subject to water-logging; successful in relatively poor soils, although they will require some additional feeding.

SITUATION Tolerates full sun but performs best in light to moderate shade. Zones 5–8.

WATERING AND FEEDING Mulch in fall and spring. Feed with a balanced, general-purpose fertilizer in mid-spring, and again in midsummer.

MANAGEMENT Leave dead flower spikes until well into the fall to provide interest and then cut back to soil level. Divide in spring every four or five years.

COMMON PROBLEMS None.

PROPAGATION Division in fall or spring, or from seed.

TROUBLESHOOTING Not likely to be necessary.

SIZE Reaches 2½ × 1½ft./75 × 45cm. in three years.

Bellis ENGLISH DAISY

For many gardeners, the genus *Bellis* is the daisy that they eradicate from their lawns, but it has attractive relatives that make cheerful clump-forming, extremely hardy perennials – some commonly grown as biennials.

SOIL Any, but least successful in highly acid soils.

SITUATION Full sun to moderate shade; fully hardy and tolerant of cold winds. Zones 3–10.

Astrantia major

Bellis – Centranthus

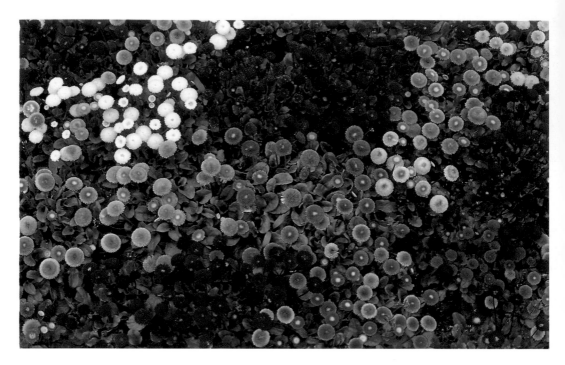

Bellis perennis

WATERING AND FEEDING Mulch in fall and spring. Feed with a balanced, general-purpose fertilizer in mid-spring, and again in midsummer.

MANAGEMENT Deadhead regularly during the summer; divide every four or five years.

COMMON PROBLEMS None.

PROPAGATION Division in fall or spring, or from seed.

TROUBLESHOOTING Not likely to be necessary.

SIZE Reaches 8 × 8in./20 × 20cm. in two years, and if grown as perennials will slowly spread by about 10cm./4in. per year.

Bergenia

If your requirement is for a hardy, evergreen, ground-cover perennial with large leaves and good, if not spectacular, flowers, then bergenias are for you. And especially so if you require plants that are happy in shade.

SOIL Any, including heavy clay; the attractive leaf colors seem to develop best in poorer soils.

SITUATION Full sun to moderate shade; although leaf color is probably best in full sun, I have obtained good results in shade from such purple-foliaged forms as *B.* 'Bressingham Ruby'. The large leaves can be damaged and tattered in strong or cold winds so bergenias are best in a spot with some shelter. Zones 4–9.

WATERING AND FEEDING Mulch in fall and spring. Feed with a balanced, general-purpose fertilizer in mid-spring, and again in midsummer.

MANAGEMENT Deadhead after flowering; divide every four or five years.

COMMON PROBLEMS None.

Bergenia 'Ballawley'

PROPAGATION Division in fall or spring.
TROUBLESHOOTING Not likely to be necessary.
SIZE Most varieties will attain about $1-1\frac{1}{2} \times 1-1\frac{1}{2}$ft./30–45 $\times$ 30–45cm. in three years.

Campanula BELLFLOWER

The genus *Campanula* is a large one and includes a number of popular, hardy varieties for the border, all fairly adaptable; other members are discussed with rock garden plants (see page 170).
SOIL Tolerates most, but unsatisfactory in very wet or very acid conditions; usefully tolerant of high alkalinity.
SITUATION Full sun to moderate shade, preferably with some shelter from strong winds. Zones 3–8.
WATERING AND FEEDING Mulch in fall and spring. Feed with a balanced, general-purpose fertilizer in mid-spring, and again in midsummer.
MANAGEMENT Cut back old flowered stems to soil level after flowering. Divide every four or five years. In my experience, campanulas are extremely difficult to stake, as their flowering stems are pliable and bend as soon as they begin to grow. Wrap-around support is not effective and the only real solution, if you want to stake the plant, is to use several tiers of the criss-cross, trivet-style supports, placed one above the other as the stems elongate. Some campanulas can be grown without any staking, and for *C. persicifolia*, in particular, it is rarely necessary.
COMMON PROBLEMS Mildew; slugs.
PROPAGATION Division in fall or spring; some varieties from seed.
TROUBLESHOOTING Not likely to be necessary.
SIZE The common border perennials are varieties of *C. latifolia*, *C. lactiflora* and *C. persicifolia*, which will attain a height of 4ft./1.2m. and a spread of 2ft./60cm. within two or three years.

Campanula latifolia

Centranthus VALERIAN

Among the most delightful sights on old or ruined buildings are the clumps of red and white valerian growing from gaps in the stonework and mortar. Where similar conditions can be met in the garden they will thrive – and also self-seed rather aggressively.
SOIL Light, free draining, alkaline; preferably rather poor.
SITUATION Full sun to very light shade. Zones 4–9.
WATERING AND FEEDING Mulch in fall and spring. Feed with a balanced, general-purpose fertilizer in mid-spring, and again in midsummer.
MANAGEMENT Cut down to soil level in fall. The flower stems tend to flop outward toward the end of the flowering period and are best supported with wrap-around support. Divide every three years.
COMMON PROBLEMS None.
PROPAGATION Division in fall or spring, or from seed.
TROUBLESHOOTING None normally necessary.
SIZE Will reach $3 \times 2\frac{1}{2}$ft./1m. $\times$ 70cm. after two years.

Centranthus ruber

Chrysanthemum

Florists' chrysanthemum

Chrysanthemum

Although botanists have now split up the old genus *Chrysanthe-mum* into smaller groups, I am retaining it here to cover the plants that might be used in a mixed border – *C. rubellum*; the hardy shasta daisy varieties derived from *C.* × *superbum* (*C. maximum*); the less than hardy marguerites (*C. frutescens*); and the early-flow-ering florists' or 'border' chrysanthemums, in a wide range of flower size and form. I am excluding the late-flowering florists' chrysanthemums, which are raised in pots for blooming in a cool greenhouse, as these tend to be a specialist's plant.

Soil Widely tolerant of soil types, provided it is well drained, fairly rich, and neither highly acidic nor alkaline.

Situation Full sun to light shade, preferably with some shelter from cold winds. Most hardy species, Zones 5–9.

Watering and feeding *C. rubellum and shasta daisies* Mulch in fall and spring. Feed with a balanced, general-purpose fertilizer in mid-spring, and again after midsummer.

Marguerites When in open ground, mulch in fall and spring. Feed with a balanced, general fertilizer in spring and again after midsummer. When grown in pots, use a synthetic soil mix such as Readi-earth or Jiffy Mix, mulch the pot, and liquid feed weekly during summer. Zones 9–10.

Florists' chrysanthemums Fork in a balanced, general fertilizer one to two weeks before planting out the young or overwintered plants, and apply the same again as a top dressing about one month later. Do not mulch immediately after planting as newly planted border or florists' chrysanthemums are prone to damage from overwatering, but mulch in the usual way after about three weeks when the plants are well established. Zones 5–9.

Management *C. rubellum and shasta daisies* Cut back old flowered stems to soil level after flowering. Divide shasta daisies every two or three years (this is most important to maintain vigor), and *C. rubellum* every three or four years. The stems of shasta daisies easily kink and the entire plant can look open and unkempt, so stake them early in the season by placing several tiers of the criss-cross, trivet-style supports one above the other as the plant grows up.

Marguerites These are only hardy outdoors in very mild areas and are best grown in pots and taken into a cool greenhouse in late fall. They are most attractive when grown as standards by staking the strongest stem and pinching out any side-shoots that emerge low down.

Florists' chrysanthemums Plant out hardened-off plants in late spring each year – up to three weeks before the last frost is likely in your area. Insert a bamboo stake for each plant at planting time.

This type of chrysanthemum requires "stopping", that is, the growing tip of the main stem is removed as far as the uppermost fully developed leaves. The reasons for this are to encourage the development of side-shoots to make the plant bushier, to concen-trate its energies into producing better blooms, and to bring the flowering season forward, so there is less danger of the plant producing its best flowers just as the first frosts of fall begin.

Most gardeners would be safe stopping their chrysanthemums before the end of May, but for those growing plants to show, the time for stopping is rather critical, as it chiefly governs when the plants will flower. (On chrysanthemums, flowering is also related to temperature and day length: the longer the day, the later the plants will flower.) Each gardener will have to make his own decision about when to stop, for it will be different according to the variety, the age of the plants, and the soil conditions. In much of the north of the USA, and Canada, the best pinching or stopping time is early July.

Once the plant has been stopped, side shoots will develop. Some of these should also be removed for best results, so pinch them out one at a time as they emerge, until between six and eight remain. In due course the side-shoots produce their own side-shoots, and these should all be pinched out. As summer reaches its peak each side-shoot will be bearing a flower bud at its tip, with others surrounding it. On large-flowered varieties, these extra buds should be pinched out to leave just the terminal bud, which will produce good-sized blooms. On spray varieties, between five and seven buds should be left on each shoot to flower. Until the plants have flowered, shoots arising from the base of the plants should be pulled off; after the main flowering they can be allowed to develop to produce sprays of additional small blooms.

In late fall the plants should be lifted. Cut off any basal shoots, but leave about 2ft./60cm. of the main stem: this will produce shoots for cuttings in the spring. Shake off excess soil and plant the rootstocks (called stools) very shallowly in boxes of garden soil, synthetic soil mixes such as Jiffy Mix, or Readi-earth, or a mixture of slightly damp peat and sand. Water to make the mixture damp; but do not overwater. Store the stools in a well-ventilated cold frame, protected from more than one or two degrees of frost. Soon after midwinter the boxes should ideally be moved into a cool greenhouse offering a temperature of about 45°F/7°C, and given a little water; they can be left in the cold frame, but will start much later into growth in the next season. Many cultivars will overwinter outdoors successfully.

The overwintered stools should be hardened off over about a week before planting out in the border. They can be left entire, or divided first, but flower quality will deteriorate after a few years. The best course is to renew the stock from cuttings at least every two years.

COMMON PROBLEMS *C. RUBELLUM*, SHASTA DAISIES AND MARGUERITES Normally none.

FLORISTS' CHRYSANTHEMUMS Mildew; rust; gray mold; virus; leaf miners; aphids; slugs; eelworm.

PROPAGATION *C. RUBELLUM* AND SHASTA DAISIES Division in spring (important to maintain vigor anyway).

MARGUERITES Semi-ripe cuttings in fall or softwood cuttings in spring.

FLORISTS' CHRYSANTHEMUMS Division in spring or basal cuttings in spring. If few or no basal cuttings form, shoots arising from the old main stem may be used instead. Root the cuttings in trays of synthetic soil mixes such as Jiffy Mix, then move them onto

Chrysanthemum – Digitalis

Coreopsis verticillata

Delphinium 'Pacific Giant'

individual 3½in./9cm. diameter pots, subsequently hardening off the plants.

TROUBLESHOOTING Not likely to be necessary if plants are renewed as described. Any florists' chrysanthemums showing abnormal flower or leaf development are probably affected with virus and should be destroyed.

SIZE Shasta daisy 3 × 2ft./1m. × 60cm. after three years. *C. rubellum* 2½ × 1½ft./80 × 50cm. in two years. Marguerite 3–4 × 3ft./ 1–1.2 × 1m. within a year. Most varieties of florists' chrysanthemum will attain about 3–5 × 2–3ft./1–1.5m. × 60–90cm. within a year.

Coreopsis

An attractive group of yellow, daisy-flowered perennials, with most forms being lower growing and more compact than many other similar flowers. They are hardy but benefit from some extra winter protection in all except the mildest areas. The dainty-flowered *C. verticillata* has a long flowering period.

SOIL Any free draining, including lean types.

SITUATION Full sun. Zones 3–9.

WATERING AND FEEDING Mulch in fall (which will give that important winter protection), and again in spring. Feed with a balanced, general-purpose fertilizer in mid-spring, and lightly in midsummer. Too much fertilizer makes ungainly plants.

MANAGEMENT Cut back all growth above ground to soil level in fall. No staking is needed. Divide every three years in spring.

COMMON PROBLEMS None.

PROPAGATION By division (all varieties); some from cuttings.

TROUBLESHOOTING None should be necessary, but the plants tend to be short-lived and may decline after five or six years, especially if not divided regularly.

SIZE Most varieties will reach about 1½–2ft. × 8in. –1½ft./45–60 × 20–45cm. in two years.

Delphinium

These are among the classic border perennials, and some, such as the giant Pacific hybrids at 5–6ft./1.5–1.8m., are probably the tallest, but they are not the easiest to grow. They require more than the average amount of attention if they are to be successful.

SOIL Rich, well drained organic loams are ideal. They will not succeed in heavy cold clays or in very dry or poor soils, and respond well to applications of ground limestone.

SITUATION Full sun to light shade; shelter from strong winds is essential for the taller varieties – while the Blue Fountains, Blue Magic hybrids are much shorter, they lack much of the stateliness of the classic, tall delphinium and even they require some wind protection. Zones 3–7.

WATERING AND FEEDING Mulch in fall and spring. Feed with a balanced fertilizer in mid-spring, and again in midsummer.

MANAGEMENT Staking is most important and should be done early. To avoid having the border decorated with 10ft./3m. tall canes from the beginning of the season, when the vegetation around them is only knee high, I prefer to do a little extra work and replace short with medium length and then, finally, long supports as the plants grow. Although it is not essential, the best results will be obtained if the flowering stems are thinned out as they emerge, to leave no more than the five or six strongest, well spaced. Cut down old flowering spikes promptly after the flowers fade. Divide every four or five years in spring.

COMMON PROBLEMS Slugs; mildew; crown rot; cyclamen mites.
PROPAGATION Division in spring, and seed sown indoors in winter or outdoors in spring.
TROUBLESHOOTING Not likely to be necessary.
SIZE The taller varieties may attain $10 \times 2\frac{1}{2}$ft./3m. $\times$ 75cm. in a season, the dwarf types no more than a third of this.

Dicentra BLEEDING HEART

These are relatives of the poppies but are quite unlike them, having long stems of pendant, almost bell-like flowers in the case of *D. spectabilis* and shorter stems on *D. eximia* and *D. formosa*.
SOIL Rich and organic, moist but well drained.
SITUATION Always best in cool positions in light shade. Zones 4–8.
WATERING AND FEEDING Mulch in fall and spring. Feed with a balanced, general-purpose fertilizer in mid-spring. The foliage of *D. spectabilis* dies down after spring; both *D. eximia* and *D. formosa* and its hybrids often flower all summer.
MANAGEMENT *D. spectabilis* is difficult to stake. Plant where its somewhat spreading habit can be allowed full rein. Divide every three or four years in spring, but do so carefully for the fleshy roots are very brittle and easily damaged.
COMMON PROBLEMS Slugs.
PROPAGATION Division in spring.
TROUBLESHOOTING Not likely to be necessary.
SIZE Up to $3 \times 1\frac{1}{2}$ft./1m. $\times$ 50cm. within two years for *D. spectabilis*; up to about $1\frac{1}{2}$–2ft./45–60cm. for *D. eximia* and *D. formosa*.

Digitalis FOXGLOVE

The pink or white, fully hardy foxglove (*D. purpurea*) is known to every gardener. It may not be reliably perennial in most gardens, but this is not true of some of its less well-known relatives, which come in a range of colors and are equally easy to grow.
SOIL Tolerates most, but best in moist, organic soil with no tendency to water-logging.
SITUATION Foxgloves are always best in cool positions, in light to moderate shade. Most, Zones 4–9.
WATERING AND FEEDING Mulch in fall and spring. Feed with a balanced, general-purpose fertilizer in mid-spring, and again in midsummer.
MANAGEMENT Staking is barely necessary for *D. purpurea* but related species may need light support. *D. purpurea* tends to be biennial so maintain a few self-sown seedlings (of which there will

Dicentra spectabilis

Digitalis ambigua

Doronicum 'Spring Beauty'

be plenty). To be certain that a population of white-flowered plants remains white, pull out any seedlings in the vicinity whose flowers show any pink in the buds; if such plants are allowed to remain until the flowers are fully open, pollen will be transferred and the offspring will also be pink. Truly perennial species should be divided every four or five years in fall or spring.

COMMON PROBLEMS None.

PROPAGATION It may be possible to take offsets or basal cuttings in spring but from seed is the more reliable method.

TROUBLESHOOTING Not likely to be necessary.

SIZE Varies with species from about $2\frac{1}{2} \times 1$ft. to $5 \times 1\frac{1}{2}$ft./75 × 30cm. to 1.5m. × 50cm. in two years.

Doronicum LEOPARD'S BANE

These early-flowering, hardy yellow border daisies are useful and easy fillers, especially among drifts of tulips.

SOIL Tolerates most, but tends to suffer even worse than other daisy-like plants from mildew in dry sites.

SITUATION Full sun to light shade. Zones 4–8.

WATERING AND FEEDING Mulch in fall and spring. Feed with a balanced, general-purpose fertilizer in mid-spring. The foliage usually disappears in summer.

MANAGEMENT Staking is barely necessary other than in windy sites, as the stems are relatively stiff. Cut down dead flower stems immediately after the blooms have faded, and cut down the foliage as soon as it yellows with mildew. Divide every four or five years in fall or spring.

COMMON PROBLEMS Mildew.

PROPAGATION Division in fall or spring.

TROUBLESHOOTING Not likely to be necessary; even plants severely affected with mildew will regrow in the following year.

SIZE The common varieties will attain about 3ft. × 16in./1m. × 40cm. after two or three years.

Echinacea PURPLE CONE FLOWER

Another genus in that large and valuable group of perennial daisies that have a prominent raised center to the flowers, but these are unusual in having pink, red, or white colors.

SOIL Tolerates most, but best in free draining, moist, rich soils.

SITUATION Full sun. Zones 3–9.

WATERING AND FEEDING Mulch in fall and spring. Feed with a balanced fertilizer in mid-spring, and again in midsummer.

MANAGEMENT Cut back all growth above ground to soil level in fall. Many of the common cultivars of *E. purpurea* are tall and will require individual canes or wrap-around staking.

COMMON PROBLEMS None.

PROPAGATION Division in fall or spring every three or four years. Also easy to grow from seed in spring.

TROUBLESHOOTING None normally necessary.

SIZE *E. purpurea* will reach $3 \times 1\frac{1}{2}$ft./1m. × 50cm. after three years. The plants are often short-lived.

Echinacea purpurea

Echinops GLOBE THISTLE

As part of a mixed planting the characteristic spikes of the echinops thistles are most effective. They are fully hardy but a little difficult to grow to their best because most gardens have border soil that is too good for them.

SOIL Most, but best in rather poor conditions.

SITUATION Full sun to very light shade. Zones 3–8.

WATERING AND FEEDING Mulch in fall and spring. Feed with a very light dressing of balanced, general-purpose fertilizer in mid-spring, and again in midsummer.

MANAGEMENT Staking is barely necessary but the heavy stems tend to spread if they are not at least loosely tied. Cut down dead flower stems as soon as the flowers have faded and cut back the foliage as it browns and shrivels with mildew. Divide every four years in spring.

COMMON PROBLEMS Mildew, earwigs; four-lined plant bug can cause leaf damage.

PROPAGATION Division in fall or spring, or from seed.

TROUBLESHOOTING Not likely to be necessary.

SIZE The commonest form is *E. ritro*, which will reach 5 × 3ft./ 1.5 × 1m. in three years, although there are other, smaller and larger species and a few cultivars such as 'Taplow Blue'.

Echinops ritro

Epimedium BISHOP'S HAT

Epimediums are fairly low-growing, clump-forming, and more or less evergreen plants that have a special merit in their tolerance of shady, difficult conditions in which many other plants fail. I find they make excellent companions to *Omphalodes verna*, the forget-me-not-like plant known as blue-eyed Mary.

SOIL Tolerates most, including dry soils where the plants will perform adequately, but they produce their most luxuriant and attractive foliage in moist, rich conditions.

SITUATION Light to moderate or even deep shade. Zones 5–8.

WATERING AND FEEDING Mulch in fall and spring. Feed with a balanced, general-purpose fertilizer in mid-spring.

MANAGEMENT Trim back browned or dead leaves as appropriate but do not cut them back to soil level unless they are completely browned by cold weather. The plants may be left undisturbed as ground cover or divided every four or five years.

COMMON PROBLEMS None.

PROPAGATION Division in fall or spring.

TROUBLESHOOTING None normally necessary.

SIZE Most forms will reach $1-1\frac{1}{2} \times 1-1\frac{1}{2}$ft./30–45 × 30–45cm. after three or four years, depending on soil conditions.

Eryngium SEA HOLLY

The spiky sea holly often looks best grown as an individual specimen, with its glaucous foliage contributing to its overall appeal. Coastal gardens generally offer the best conditions.

SOIL Light, free draining, but fertile.

Epimedium × rubrum

Eryngium – Geranium

Eryngium alpinum

SITUATION Full sun to very light shade. Sea holly is intolerant of cold wind but is very reliable in coastal gardens as it is unaffected by salt spray. Hardiness zones vary according to species but mostly Zones 5–8.

WATERING AND FEEDING Mulch in fall and spring. Feed with a balanced, general-purpose fertilizer in mid-spring.

MANAGEMENT Should not need staking and apart from taking off dead flower heads, little attention is needed. Divide every four or five years in spring. *E. giganteum* is grown as a biennial.

COMMON PROBLEMS None.

PROPAGATION Division and root cuttings in spring, the species from seed.

TROUBLESHOOTING Not likely to be necessary.

SIZE One of the most popular species is also the largest, *E. giganteum*, which attains $4–5 \times 2\frac{1}{2}$ft./1.2–1.5m. $\times$ 75cm. in two years. *E. bourgatii* is longer-lived and will reach 2ft. $\times$ 8in./60 $\times$ 20cm.

Erysimum

Popularly called Siberian wallflowers, the low-growing erysimums have recently returned to favor. Though easy to grow (from seed sown in late fall or early spring where the plants are to bloom), their yellow or orange flowers bloom for only a short period. Try also the related, and taller, better-known *Cheiranthus cheiri*.

SOIL Most, provided it is well drained and fairly fertile; erysimum will not succeed in clay.

SITUATION Full sun to light shade. Zones 5–9.

WATERING AND FEEDING Mulch in fall and spring. Feed with a balanced, general-purpose fertilizer in mid-spring.

MANAGEMENT In the North, erysimum acts like an annual. Sow seeds in late fall or very early spring.

COMMON PROBLEMS None.

PROPAGATION Semi-ripe cuttings in early summer, or seed.

TROUBLESHOOTING Not likely to be necessary.

SIZE May spread to about $1 \times 1\frac{1}{2}$ft./30 $\times$ 45cm. in three years.

Euphorbia SPURGE

One of the most versatile genera of garden plants with deciduous and evergreen, winter- and summer-flowering species, but not all hardy in cold regions. One of the hardiest (Zones 4–10) and most distinctive is the mound-forming, yellow-bracted *E. epithymoides*.

SOIL Varies with species; most of the large summer-flowering species will succeed best in fertile but light, free draining soils; the winter-flowering and shade-tolerant species require slightly wetter and heavier conditions.

SITUATION Full sun (most large, summer-flowering types) to light shade (most winter-flowering forms), or moderate to deep shade (*E. robbiae*, Zones 8–9).

WATERING AND FEEDING Mulch in fall and spring. Feed with a balanced fertilizer in mid-spring, and again in midsummer.

MANAGEMENT The very large-headed, summer-flowering

Erysimum 'Bowles' Mauve'

euphorbias may require light wrap-around staking to prevent them from flopping; other kinds should need none, and require little other attention. Most types do not divide very successfully.

COMMON PROBLEMS None.

PROPAGATION Tip or basal cuttings in spring, semi-ripe cuttings in late summer, or from seed.

TROUBLESHOOTING Not likely to be necessary.

SIZE Varies considerably among species. There are dwarf forms for the rock garden, such as E. *myrsinites* (Zones 5–8) which attains 2–4 × 6–8in./5–10 × 15–20cm. over three years. Most of the medium-sized herbaceous species will reach about 2½–3 × 1½ft./75cm.–1m. × 50cm. after two or three years, and some of the larger, summer-flowering types, such as *E. characias wulfenii* (Zones 7–10), will be larger.

Euphorbia characias wulfenii

Geranium CRANE'S BILL

Probably the easiest and, overall, most useful of all genera of herbaceous perennials. Given the wide range of species and varieties, and allowing only for their slightly limited color range, there must be a geranium to suit almost every garden.

SOIL Almost any, provided it is not very heavy or water-logged. The shade-loving species are mostly tolerant of drier conditions, too. All the geraniums are tolerant of moderate acidity and, in some cases, high alkalinity.

SITUATION Varies with species. Most are best in full sun to light shade, although there is a small group of species, ranging from the fairly tall *G. phaeum* to the ground-covering *G. macrorrhizum*, that is tolerant of deep shade. Zones 3–8 for most species.

WATERING AND FEEDING Mulch in fall and spring. Feed with a balanced fertilizer in mid-spring, and again in midsummer.

MANAGEMENT The lower-growing geraniums require no staking. The taller-growing forms, such as G. 'Johnson's Blue', *G. wallichianum* ('Buxton's Blue'), *G. ibericum* or *G. pratense*, may be staked, although their stems and leaf stalks are so soft and pliable, and also so numerous, that this cannot be done on an individual basis; the best plan is to use metal stakes or thin canes and carefully provide support around the whole of each clump. A few forms (the cultivar *G. × oxonianum* 'Claridge Druce' most notably) self-seed very freely and unless they are required as ground cover, these seedlings must be assiduously pulled out. Divide the more vigorous forms every two years in fall or spring; the remainder, every four or five years.

COMMON PROBLEMS None.

PROPAGATION Division in fall or spring, or from seed.

TROUBLESHOOTING Not likely to be necessary.

SIZE Varies between species and cultivars. As a guide, the smallest, such as *G. cinereum*, are really little more than rock garden plants, reaching perhaps 4 × 8in./10 × 20cm. in two years; the ground-covering *G. macrorrhizum* will reach 1 × 2ft./35 × 60cm. in two years; the upright forms such as G. 'Johnson's Blue' 1 × 2ft./30 × 60cm. in two years, and the more vigorous *G. × oxonianum* 'Claridge Druce' 2½ × 2½ft./75 × 75cm. in two years.

Geranium endressii 'Wargrave Pink'

Geum AVENS

Undistinguished but useful, these are easy and hardy plants that add to the overall impact of a large border.

SOIL Almost any, provided it is not very heavy or water-logged.

SITUATION Full sun to light shade. Zones 5–9.

WATERING AND FEEDING Mulch in fall and spring. Feed with a balanced, general-purpose fertilizer in mid-spring, and again after midsummer.

MANAGEMENT I find it unnecessary to stake geums, although the taller cultivars such as *G. chiloense* 'Mrs. Bradshaw' may require some support if growing in an exposed situation. Divide every four or five years in fall or spring.

COMMON PROBLEMS None.

PROPAGATION Division in fall or spring, or from seed.

TROUBLESHOOTING Not likely to be necessary.

SIZE Most varieties will attain about 1×1ft./30×30cm. in two years; *G. chiloense* 'Mrs. Bradshaw' and G. 'Lady Stratheden' will reach about $2–2\frac{1}{2} \times 1\frac{1}{2}$ft./$60–80 \times 45$cm. in the same time.

Geum 'Borisii'

Gypsophila BABY'S BREATH

There are two common garden gypsophilas of similar form: the annual varieties derived from *G. elegans*, and the short-lived perennial *G. paniculata*. The perennials are pretty but often disappointing plants, with rather strict requirements.

SOIL Deep, neutral or limy, free draining soils are best, but the plants are tolerant of more moist conditions. They are quite intolerant of heavy, clayey or cold soils.

SITUATION Full sun, with shelter from cold wind. Zones 4–9.

WATERING AND FEEDING Mulch in fall and spring. Feed with a balanced, general-purpose fertilizer in mid-spring, and again in midsummer.

MANAGEMENT The plants greatly resent any disturbance, and attempts at moving or dividing gypsophilas almost always end unsuccessfully.

COMMON PROBLEMS None, but voles (mice) may eat roots.

PROPAGATION Not reliable enough to be practical.

TROUBLESHOOTING When the plants begin to decline (they may rather suddenly wilt during the summer), it is not practical to rejuvenate them; these are fairly short-lived plants that will need replacing after five or six years, or even sooner.

SIZE The commonest and most popular cultivar, *G. paniculata* 'Bristol Fairy', should attain $2\frac{1}{2} \times 2\frac{1}{2}$ft./$80 \times 80$cm. in three years.

Helenium SNEEZEWEED

Among the easiest and most reliable of fall border perennials, heleniums belong to a large group of daisy-like plants distinguished by pronounced button-like centers to the flowers, rich red, gold, and yellow colors, and a rather appealing, spicy smell.

SOIL Tolerates most, but best in rather moist, rich, and free draining soils.

Gypsophila paniculata 'Bristol Fairy'

SITUATION Full sun. Zones 4–8.

WATERING AND FEEDING Mulch in fall and spring. Feed with a balanced, general-purpose fertilizer in mid-spring, and again in midsummer.

MANAGEMENT Stake early to prevent the rather weak flower stems from flopping. Divide every four or five years.

COMMON PROBLEMS None.

PROPAGATION Division in fall or spring.

TROUBLESHOOTING Not normally necessary.

SIZE Reaches $3–4 \times 2–2\frac{1}{2}$ft./1–1.2m. × 60–75cm. in three years.

Helleborus   HELLEBORE, CHRISTMAS ROSE

Although the range of species is small, hellebores are among the most useful of ornamental herbaceous perennials. They are shade-tolerant, provide color foliage interest through the winter, and have a considerable variation in flower and form.

SOIL Tolerates most, but will generally give best results in moist, organic loams that are neither strongly acid nor alkaline.

SITUATION Light to moderate shade, with some shelter; ideally placed in woodland conditions or in the partial shade beneath isolated trees. Zones 4–8 for the hardy species.

WATERING AND FEEDING Mulch in fall and spring. Feed with a balanced, general-purpose fertilizer in mid-spring, and again after midsummer.

MANAGEMENT Dead or tattered leaves should be cut off at soil level in spring, allowing the emerging flowers to be seen to best advantage. The faded flowers should be left until they set seeds, partly because they remain attractive but also because self-sown seedlings often produce interesting and attractive variations. The early-flowering, evergreen species *H. niger*, the so-called Christmas rose, will give better blooms if protected from rain and soil splash: place cloches over them in late fall as the flower buds swell, and leave them on until the flowers open. In borders, hellebores are best divided every four or five years; in woodland positions, they and plants of the Lenten-rose, *H. orientalis* and its hybrids, may be left undisturbed.

COMMON PROBLEMS Leaf spotting occurs on most hellebores but is rarely serious.

PROPAGATION Division in spring (some species); basal, preferably rooted cuttings in spring; or the species from seed.

TROUBLESHOOTING Unlikely to be necessary.

SIZE Varies slightly among species but is usually around $1–2 \times 1–1\frac{1}{2}$ft./30–60 × 30 45cm. in three years.

Hemerocallis   DAY LILY

The day lilies have come into prominence recently with a great increase in the sizes and colors available; many are much less invasive than some of the older forms. They are striking hardy plants for the mixed border, and other garden uses.

SOIL Tolerates many, but generally best in free draining, rich, moist conditions.

Helenium 'Moerheim Beauty'
Helleborus orientalis
Hemerocallis hybrid

Hemerocallis – Lamium

Heuchera micrantha 'Palace Purple'

SITUATION Full sun to light shade. Mostly Zones 4–9.

WATERING AND FEEDING Mulch in spring and early fall. Feed by top dressing with bonemeal or superphosphate or a proprietary bulb fertilizer in early spring.

MANAGEMENT Remove individual flowers, which last a day, as they fade or cut down the flower stems as the flowers fade and cut all growth above ground to soil level in winter. Divide every three years.

COMMON PROBLEMS Thrips; deer will eat buds and flowers.

PROPAGATION Division in fall or spring.

TROUBLESHOOTING Unlikely to be necessary.

SIZE Large cultivars may reach a height of about 3ft./1m. and will spread to about 2ft./60cm. within two or three years.

Heuchera   CORAL FLOWER

Heucheras have always had a following, and they are certainly undemanding and supply colorful and evergreen foliage for rather difficult situations.

SOIL Tolerates most soil types, although is less reliable in very heavy or wet soils.

SITUATION Light to moderate shade. Zones 4–8.

WATERING AND FEEDING Mulch in fall and spring. Feed with a balanced, general-purpose fertilizer in mid-spring, and again in midsummer.

MANAGEMENT Cut away dead or ragged foliage in fall and again in spring. No staking is necessary. Divide plants every four or five years.

COMMON PROBLEMS None.

PROPAGATION Division in fall or spring; also seeds for the very popular *H.* 'Palace Purple', which has purple leaves.

TROUBLESHOOTING Unlikely to be necessary.

SIZE Most varieties will reach about $2\frac{1}{2} \times 1\frac{1}{2}$ft./$75 \times 50$cm. in three years, although a few are slightly less vigorous.

Hosta   PLANTAIN LILY

Hostas are among the most popular of modern herbaceous perennials and the number of cultivars proliferates. They are relatively easy to grow, but are a great favorite with slugs and snails.

SOIL Tolerates most; although traditionally associated with wet, waterside beds, hostas are in fact highly tolerant of much drier conditions. When hostas are grown in borders their leaves can become completely tattered through the ravages of slugs and snails, so one option worth exploring is to grow the plants in containers of a good garden soil mixture, then standing the pots in the borders. The pests will be deterred to some degree, and if the containers are stood on small feet on a hard surface such as a paved terrace, the problem can be almost totally overcome.

SITUATION Full sun to moderate shade. Zones 3–9.

WATERING AND FEEDING Mulch in fall and spring. Feed with a balanced, general-purpose fertilizer in mid-spring, and again in midsummer.

Hosta 'Tall Boy'

MANAGEMENT Cut out the flower spikes immediately after flowering – they become very hard and woody if left – and cut down the foliage as it dies in the fall. Divide plants every four or five years in spring.
COMMON PROBLEMS Slugs and snails eat leaves; mice, roots.
PROPAGATION Division in spring.
TROUBLESHOOTING Unlikely to be necessary.
SIZE Varies considerably; most attain about 1½ × 1ft./45 × 30cm. in three years, but the more vigorous, such as some cultivars of *H. fortunei*, will reach 3 × 3ft./1 × 1m. in the same time.

Kniphofia   RED HOT POKER

Red hot pokers justify the large amount of space they take up when the soil is right and the climate mild; then, they are always spectacularly attractive.
SOIL Rich, deep, moist but well drained; quite intolerant of heavy, water-logged, or cold soils.
SITUATION Full sun to light shade. Zones 6–9.
WATERING AND FEEDING Mulch in fall and spring. Feed with a balanced, general-purpose fertilizer in mid-spring, and again in midsummer.
MANAGEMENT Cut out dead flower spikes after flowering. Do not cut down the foliage in fall, and in colder areas provide some protection from penetrating frost and water by loosely tying the leaves over the crown with raffia. Divide every five or six years in spring.
COMMON PROBLEMS None, apart from those caused by cold or frost damage.
PROPAGATION Division in spring; the species from seed.
TROUBLESHOOTING Unlikely to be necessary.
SIZE Generally 3–5 × 1–2½ft./1–1.5m. × 40–75cm. after three years, although there are a few modern dwarf forms that barely exceed 2ft./60cm. in height.

Lamium   DEAD NETTLE

Lamium is often dismissed as uninteresting but is, in fact, a very easy, useful and hardy group of more or less evergreen, ground-covering plants, tolerant of much poorer conditions than many grander things. Best known are *L. album* and *L. maculatum* 'Beacon Silver'.
SOIL Most, including fairly dry and poor conditions.
SITUATION Full sun to moderate shade. Zones 4–8.
WATERING AND FEEDING Mulch in fall and spring. Feed with a balanced, general-purpose fertilizer in mid-spring.
MANAGEMENT Trim back to soil level in early spring. Divide every five or six years if not required as ground cover.
COMMON PROBLEMS Leaf spotting, and leaf-feeding pests.
PROPAGATION Division in spring, or from semi-ripe cuttings in summer.
TROUBLESHOOTING Unlikely to be necessary.
SIZE 10in. × 3ft./25cm. × 1m. in three to four years.

Kniphofia rooperi

Lamium maculatum 'Beacon Silver'

Ligularia – Lychnis

Ligularia dentata

Ligularia

A fine group of tall border perennials of two major types; both have large, lush leaves, but one (*L. dentata*) has large, single, orange, daisy-like flowers, while the other (*L. przewalskii* and *L. stenocephala*) has smaller daisy flowers massed in elongated spikes. All are essentially water-loving but otherwise easy to grow.

SOIL Rich, preferably organic and moist. The huge leaves wilt very rapidly in dry conditions.

SITUATION Prefers light to part shade; ligularias are eminently suitable for waterside plantings. Zones 4–8.

WATERING AND FEEDING Mulch in fall and spring. Feed with a balanced, general-purpose fertilizer in mid-spring, and again in midsummer.

MANAGEMENT Cut down dead flower heads after flowering. Staking is essential in exposed sites. Divide every three or four years in spring.

COMMON PROBLEMS Snails and slugs.

PROPAGATION Division in spring; some species from seed.

TROUBLESHOOTING Not normally necessary.

SIZE Will reach 4–5 × 2½ft./1.2–1.5m. × 75cm. after three years.

Limonium   SEA LAVENDER, STATICE

As the common name suggests, the leathery leaved sea lavender with summer sprays of tiny lavender flowers thrives in salt marshes and on the sea shore, but adapts to rock gardens and borders. *L. latifolium* is the species offered by nurseries. It, and related species with larger, brightly colored flowers known as statice, are valued for their flowers when dried.

SOIL Light, free draining; tolerant of alkalinity.

SITUATION Full sun with some shelter from cold winds.

WATERING AND FEEDING Mulch in fall and spring. Feed with a balanced, general-purpose fertilizer in mid-spring.

MANAGEMENT Flower heads for drying should be cut when almost fully open. Leave on any heads not required for cutting, and trim back hard in spring. Divide every four years in spring.

COMMON PROBLEMS None.

PROPAGATION Division in spring, or from seed.

TROUBLESHOOTING The plants tend to become straggly after six to eight years and are then best replaced.

SIZE *L. latifolium* may reach 2¼ × 2ft./7560cm. in a few years.

Limonium latifolium

Lobelia

Although the most familiar lobelias are those dwarf forms grown as half-hardy annuals, there are two native American perennials, *L. cardinalis* with bright red flowers, and *L. siphilitica* with blue flowers. Both are striking plants for woodland gardens.

SOIL Rich, preferably organic, moist.

SITUATION Part shade to shady situations; these will actually grow in a few inches of water at a pool edge, or by a stream. *L. cardinalis*, (Zones 2–8); *L. siphilitica*, Zones 4–9.

WATERING AND FEEDING Mulch in fall and spring. Feed with a balanced, general-purpose fertilizer in mid-spring, and again in midsummer – unless the plants are growing in water, when no fertilizer should be given.

MANAGEMENT Cut down dead flower spikes after flowering, or allow some spikes to form seed. Both species self-sow freely in the wild. *L. cardinalis* may need staking where it is not supported by other plants. Divide every four or five years in spring.

COMMON PROBLEMS None.

PROPAGATION Division in spring, or from seed (see above).

TROUBLESHOOTING None should be necessary.

SIZE 3ft. × 10in./1m. × 25cm. in two years.

Lupinus LUPINES

Lupines, especially the Russell Hybrids, are among the most familiar standbys of the herbaceous border but they have always had more than their fair share of pest and disease problems. This is a state of affairs likely to become worse rather than better, for the huge lupine aphid from North America is more tolerant of insecticides than seems at all reasonable.

SOIL Will tolerate most, but always best in fairly fertile, well drained and slightly alkaline conditions.

SITUATION Full sun or very light shade. Zones 3–6.

WATERING AND FEEDING Mulch in fall and spring. Feed with a balanced, general-purpose fertilizer in mid-spring, and again after midsummer.

MANAGEMENT Cut down dead flower spikes immediately after flowering and cut back foliage as soon as it begins to discolor with mildew. The plants should not need staking unless growing in a very windy site. Lupines often do not divide very satisfactorily and are best replaced by new plants grown from seed.

COMMON PROBLEMS Slugs; mildew; root aphid.

PROPAGATION From seed.

TROUBLESHOOTING None should be necessary, but plants are often short-lived and need frequent replacement.

SIZE 3–4 × 1½ft./1–1.2m. × 50cm. in two years.

Lychnis CAMPION, CATCHFLY

A small genus of low-growing, summer-flowering perennials, with red, pink, or white flowers. The most popular is *L. coronaria*, known as dusty miller.

SOIL Light, free draining, not too rich, tolerant of alkalinity.

SITUATION Full sun to light shade. Zones 4–8.

WATERING AND FEEDING Mulch in fall and spring. Feed with a balanced, general-purpose fertilizer in mid–spring, and again in midsummer.

MANAGEMENT Cut down dead flower spikes immediately after flowering. Divide every four or five years in spring.

COMMON PROBLEMS Aphids.

PROPAGATION By division in spring or from seed. Plants will often self-sow.

Lobelia cardinalis

Lupinus 'Russell' hybrids

Lychnis chalcedonica

TROUBLESHOOTING None should be necessary.
SIZE Varies with species and cultivar but the largest, such as *L. coronaria* 'Abbotswood Rose' (*L. × walkeri* 'Abbotswood Rose'), will attain about 14 × 10in./35 × 25cm. after three years.

Meconopsis

A stunningly lovely genus of poppies which includes the yellow-flowered *M. cambrica* and a group of mainly blue-flowered and quite magnificent Asiatic species and hybrids. The former is easy to grow; the latter tend to be difficult in some gardens and require rather specific conditions, such as in the Pacific Northwest. For the best chance of success, it is best to choose a reliably perennial form, such as *M. grandis* or one of the many strains of *M. betonicifolia*.
SOIL Rich, moist, organic, fully tolerant of alkaline conditions but the rich blue color of most forms develops much more satisfactorily on acid soils.
SITUATION Light to moderate shade. Mostly Zones 7–8.
WATERING AND FEEDING Mulch in fall and spring. Feed with a balanced, general-purpose fertilizer in mid-spring, and again in midsummer.
MANAGEMENT Cut down dead flower spikes immediately after flowering. Divide every three or four years in spring. The flower stems are slender and difficult to stake effectively as individuals; where support is needed, the best method is to encircle the whole clump with interlocking metal stakes or canes and string.
COMMON PROBLEMS None.
PROPAGATION Division in spring, or some forms from seed.
TROUBLESHOOTING Many of the blue Asiatic species are notoriously short-lived and some are monocarpic (they die after flowering), especially if raised from seed. The best advice for success is to buy named and proven perennial forms from a reputable nursery.
SIZE Varies with species and cultivar, some being rock garden dwarfs, but the largest of the common border plants, such as *M. grandis* or *M. × sheldonii*, will attain about 5 × 2ft./1.5m. × 60cm. after three years.

Mentha   MINT

The mints are usually thought of as inhabitants of the herb or kitchen garden, where some undoubtedly have an important place. But there are also several attractive and fragrant varieties that are useful in ornamental situations, provided they are kept within bounds (which can be difficult).
SOIL Tolerates most, but best in rich, moist, organic soils (unlike most other herbs).
SITUATION Full sun to light shade; arguably the most shade-tolerant of culinary herbs. Hardiness zones vary; most Zones 3–9.
WATERING AND FEEDING Mulch in fall and spring. Feed with a balanced, general-purpose fertilizer in mid-spring, and again in midsummer.

Meconopsis grandis

MANAGEMENT Cut down dead flower spikes after flowering. To control the invasiveness of mint, grow the plants in humus-rich soil in 8–10in./20–25cm. diameter pots and sink the pots to just below their rims in the border. Each fall, lift the pot and trim away any shoots or rhizomes that threaten to escape. Every third year, replace the plants with divisions (provided the parent stock has remained healthy).

COMMON PROBLEMS None.

PROPAGATION Division in fall or spring, or rhizome cuttings in spring.

TROUBLESHOOTING None should be necessary.

SIZE Varies with species, varieties, and hybrids; the least vigorous common mint is probably the creeping pennyroyal (*M. pulegium*), which is a mat-forming species with upright summer shoots; it will reach about 6 × 10in./15 × 25cm. in three years. The most vigorous is horsemint (*M. longifolia*), which will attain 3 × 1½ft./ 1m. × 50cm. if its roots are unconfined.

Nepeta CATMINT

One of the easiest and commonest of all herbaceous perennials, this is a most useful plant for the front of the border, its soft lilac-blue flowers making a foil for hotter colors.

SOIL Tolerates most except heavy, cold, and water-logged soils.

SITUATION Full sun to light shade. Zones 4–8.

WATERING AND FEEDING Mulch in fall and spring. Feed with a balanced, general-purpose fertilizer in mid-spring, and again in midsummer.

MANAGEMENT Cut back to soil level at the end of summer. Divide every two years in fall or spring, unless it is being grown in a situation where its vigor can be allowed free rein.

COMMON PROBLEMS None.

PROPAGATION Division in fall or spring; the species can be propagated from seed.

TROUBLESHOOTING None should be necessary.

SIZE Will reach about 1½ × 1½ft./45 × 45cm. in two years.

Mentha spicata

Nepeta 'Six Hills Giant'

Oenothera – Papaver

Oenothera tetragona

Oenothera EVENING PRIMROSE

The evening primroses have a rather straggly appearance for such low-growing plants, and flowers that, individually, are very short-lived. They are nonetheless popular for the front of the border and are easy to grow in all except cold, damp sites.
SOIL Light, free draining, and preferably sandy.
SITUATION Full sun, shelter from cold winds. Zones 5–8.
WATERING AND FEEDING Mulch in fall and spring. Feed with a balanced, general-purpose fertilizer in mid-spring, and again in midsummer.
MANAGEMENT Cut back to soil level at the end of summer. Divide every three years in spring.
COMMON PROBLEMS None.
PROPAGATION Division in fall or spring, or from seed.
TROUBLESHOOTING Most have a tendency to be short-lived, and once they begin to look straggly should be replaced.
SIZE The commonest form is the low-growing, clump-forming *O. missouriensis*, which will reach about 6 × 14in./15 × 35cm. in two years; the taller forms such as *O. perennis* will reach about 2 × 1ft./60 × 30cm. in the same time.

Omphalodes

The best-known species in this genus, the low-growing, blue-eyed Mary *(O. verna)*, has truly stunning little electric-blue flowers. It is an easy, undemanding, and very versatile plant, although a little slow to establish.
SOIL Tolerates most, including moderately dry soils, but best in moist, free draining, organic soils.
SITUATION Light to moderate or almost deep shade. Zones 5–8.
WATERING AND FEEDING Mulch in fall and spring. Feed with a balanced, general-purpose fertilizer in mid-spring, and again in midsummer.
MANAGEMENT Dead head after flowering in spring to encourage a second flush of blooms in the fall. In the south of the USA, the plant remains more or less evergreen, although it will look more attractive in winter if dead leaves are trimmed away. It may be divided every five or six years in spring, but is best grown where it can be left undisturbed as ground cover.
COMMON PROBLEMS None.
PROPAGATION Division in spring, or from seed.
TROUBLESHOOTING None necessary.
SIZE Will reach about 8 × 12in./20 × 30cm. after three years.

Paeonia PEONY

Although many peonies, with their large and fleshy tubers, grow naturally almost at the soil surface on bare mountainsides, they benefit from much better growing conditions if they are to give of their best in gardens.
SOIL Almost any provided it is well drained, but the best blooms will come from rich, fairly organic soils. Tolerant of moderate

Omphalodes cappadocica

acidity and alkalinity. Plant the tubers with their tops at a depth of about 1–2in./2.5–5cm.

SITUATION Full sun to very light shade; peonies in east-facing beds sometimes suffer in late frosts because their ripe flower buds freeze, then thaw out damagingly quickly when struck by early morning sun.

WATERING AND FEEDING Mulch in spring and early fall. Top dress with blood, fish, and bone or a similar general-purpose fertilizer in early spring and again around midsummer.

MANAGEMENT Cut down old flower heads promptly after flowering and also cut off any damaged heads after heavy rain, as they will rapidly attract botrytis gray mold. Cut back all growth above ground to soil level in the fall and destroy. Most peonies benefit from staking, and interlocking metal stakes or other wrap-around support is the most satisfactory method. Peonies should be left undisturbed for as long as possible, and if they must be moved or divided, this is best done in mid-spring just as shoot growth is beginning, or in the fall after plants become dormant.

COMMON PROBLEMS Gray mold stem blight (botrytis).

PROPAGATION Division in fall; allow 3–5 buds per division.

TROUBLESHOOTING Not normally necessary.

SIZE Most cultivars will reach about 3 × 3ft./1 × 1m. within four or five years.

Paeonia lactiflora

Papaver POPPY

Many of the popular garden poppies are annuals but there are two important groups of perennials; the Iceland poppy (*P. nudicaule*), usually grown as a rock garden plant, and the large, showy, and popular Oriental poppies (*P. orientale*), whose flowers last for all too short a time even if the plants do compensate with attractive seed-heads later on. These are among the least tameable of herbaceous perennials, looking particularly untidy once flowering has finished; careful siting of other plants around can overcome this.

SOIL Fairly rich, moist, but free draining.

SITUATION Full sun to light shade. Zones 4–8.

WATERING AND FEEDING Mulch in fall and spring. Feed with a balanced, general-purpose fertilizer in mid-spring. The foliage dies down soon after flowering; mark the location and overplant with annuals.

MANAGEMENT I think that most gardeners who grow Oriental poppies are resigned to having a large, unruly bunch of vegetation with vivid and blowsy flowers in the middle of it: for these poppies flop uncontrollably and there is no border perennial that is more impossible to stake. They are best renewed from root cuttings every five or six years in late summer.

COMMON PROBLEMS Aphids; voles (mice) eat roots.

PROPAGATION Root cuttings in summer; *P. nudicaule*, short-lived and really a biennial, can be propagated by seed.

TROUBLESHOOTING None necessary.

SIZE Oriental poppies reach about 3 × 3ft./1 × 1m. after three years. Iceland poppies may grow to 2ft./60cm.

Papaver orientale

Penstemon 'Garnet'

Penstemon

This is a large genus that includes annuals and shrubby species, as well as some useful but often tender, predominantly white-, red- or pink-flowered, semi-evergreen perennials.

SOIL Well drained but moist, rich, and fertile; penstemons will be dismal in poor soils.

SITUATION Full sun or very light shade. Zones vary; many 5–9.

WATERING AND FEEDING Mulch in fall and spring. Feed with a balanced, general-purpose fertilizer in mid-spring, and again in midsummer.

MANAGEMENT Cut back dead flower spikes after flowering but do not cut foliage down to soil level unless it is browned by cold weather. Some staking may be needed: taller forms are best staked individually, whereas the lower-growing, more compact varieties are best supported with interlocking metal stakes or other wrap-around support.

COMMON PROBLEMS None.

PROPAGATION Semi-ripe cuttings in summer, division in spring, or the species from seed.

TROUBLESHOOTING None necessary.

SIZE Varies considerably among species. Most of the strictly herbaceous perennials, such as the popular *P.* 'Apple Blossom', will reach about $1\frac{1}{2} \times 1\frac{1}{2}$ft./45 × 45cm. by the second or third year, but there are many smaller and taller, such as *P. barbatus* 'Rose Elf', which reaches 18–22in./45–55cm.

Perovskia   RUSSIAN SAGE

A cross between a shrub and a herbaceous perennial, perovskia has flower spikes of a most appealing shade of blue that mixes particularly well with purples. It is not a plant for cold, damp gardens.

SOIL Fairly rich, but light and free draining.

SITUATION Full sun. Zones 4–9.

WATERING AND FEEDING Mulch in fall and spring. Feed with a balanced, general-purpose fertilizer in mid-spring, and again in midsummer.

MANAGEMENT Cut down to soil level either in the fall or in early spring. In a large mixed planting perovskias don't really need staking, but when grown in isolation some wrap-around support may be useful. Divide in the spring every four years.

COMMON PROBLEMS None.

PROPAGATION Division or softwood cuttings in spring.

TROUBLESHOOTING None necessary.

SIZE Will reach 1.2 × 1m./4 × 3ft after three years.

Phlox

Phlox are among the classic border perennials, and require little routine maintenance. Against this, however, must be set their frustrating susceptibility to disease.

SOIL Tolerates most, but generally best in light, free draining but fertile conditions.

Perovskia 'Blue Spire'

SITUATION Full sun to light or even moderate shade. Zones 4–8.
WATERING AND FEEDING Mulch in fall and spring. Feed with a balanced, general-purpose fertilizer in mid-spring, and again in midsummer.
MANAGEMENT Phlox should not require staking, but the stems should be cut back to soil level as soon as the almost unavoidable attacks of mildew begin to take their effect. The stems are rather tough and sharp, so take particular care not to poke yourself in the face when cutting them down. Divide the plants every three or four years.
COMMON PROBLEMS Mildew; phlox plant bug; nematodes.
PROPAGATION Division in spring, semi-ripe cuttings in summer, basal cuttings in spring, root cuttings in winter.
TROUBLESHOOTING None normally necessary, but root cuttings may be used to save valuable plants that display the leaf-narrowing symptoms of stem nematode attack, as the pest does not penetrate the roots. Cut back the stems in fall and destroy.
SIZE Most of the common border phlox will reach about 3–4 × 2–2½ft./1–1.2m. × 60–75cm. after three years.

Phlox paniculata 'Franz Schubert'

Phormium NEW ZEALAND FLAX

The phormiums are striking evergreen plants that can be useful in bold plant groupings. They succeed best where the mild, damp conditions of their native New Zealand can be provided, such as on the West Coast of the USA.
SOIL Not easy to satisfy, as it must be moist and fairly rich but also light and well drained.
SITUATION Full sun and shelter from cold wind; shelter is especially important for the variegated cultivars, which are appreciably less hardy. Zones 9–10.
WATERING AND FEEDING Mulch in fall and spring. Feed with a balanced fertilizer in mid-spring, and midsummer.
MANAGEMENT Phormiums do not require staking. In the fall cut or pull away (using strong gloves) dead foliage, and spring. The plants may be divided every five or six years, but given appropriate space and attention to feeding they will continue to thrive in the same position for considerably longer.
COMMON PROBLEMS None.
PROPAGATION Division in spring, or from seed.
TROUBLESHOOTING None normally necessary.
SIZE Most cultivars of *P. tenax* are huge plants, reaching 10 × 6½ft./3 × 2m. after four years. Cultivars of *P. cookianum* and many of the more decorative variegated forms tend to be smaller, about 3 × 1½ft./90 × 45cm. over the same timespan.

Platycodon BALLOON FLOWER

The balloon flower is a one-off, a one-species genus of a low-growing, summer-flowering perennial, distinguished by bell-shaped bluish flowers and balloon-like buds. Although said to be easy, I have always found *P. grandiflorus* to be fickle in its growing requirements.

Phormium tenax

Platycodon – Pulmonaria

Platycodon grandiflorus

SOIL Light, free draining; any tendency to cold and wet conditions will lead to failure.
SITUATION Full sun. Zones 4–9.
WATERING AND FEEDING Mulch in the fall and spring. Feed with a balanced, general-purpose fertilizer in mid-spring, and again in midsummer.
MANAGEMENT Cut down to soil level in late fall. No staking is needed unless in a very windy spot where some light, wrap-around support may be beneficial. Divide every four or five years.
COMMON PROBLEMS None.
PROPAGATION Division or basal cuttings in spring, or seed.
TROUBLESHOOTING Growth often slow in spring; label area.
SIZE Will reach $1\frac{1}{2} \times 1\frac{1}{2}$ft./$45 \times 45$cm. in four years.

Polygonatum SOLOMON'S SEAL

This is a wonderful arching foliage plant for difficult and shady corners; excellent in a woodland garden among ferns and other wild flowers. *P. odoratum* 'Variegatum' is the most artistic.
SOIL Rich, moist but well drained; intolerant both of dry and water-logged conditions.
SITUATION Light to deep shade. Zones 4–8.
WATERING AND FEEDING Mulch in fall and spring. Feed lightly with a balanced, general-purpose fertilizer in mid-spring.
MANAGEMENT Cut down to soil level in fall; no staking is needed, the arching habit of the stems being a major attraction. The plants may be divided every five years or left undisturbed.
COMMON PROBLEMS Slugs can disfigure foliage.
PROPAGATION Division in spring, or from seed.
TROUBLESHOOTING Cut back in the normal way if slugs attack and the plant will grow again the following year.
SIZE The largest species is *P. commutatum* (*P. biflorum*), which will reach 5×2ft./1.5m. $\times 60$cm. in three years, but there are several smaller species, particularly the widely grown *P. × hybridum*, attaining approximately three quarters of this height and spread. *P. odoratum* 'Variegatum' will reach about 2ft./60cm.

Polygonum KNOTWEED

Polygonums are a mixed bunch, including some invasive weeds and some astonishingly vigorous climbers, several useful ground-covering perennials, and one tall border species.
SOIL Tolerates most.
SITUATION Full sun to moderate shade. Zones 3–9 for most.
WATERING AND FEEDING Mulch in fall and spring. Feed with a balanced, general-purpose fertilizer in mid-spring, and again in midsummer.
MANAGEMENT Cut down deciduous species to soil level in fall; evergreen species such as *P. affine* should simply have the dead flower stems trimmed back. The plants may be divided every four or five years, although when grown as carpeting ground cover they may be left undisturbed for much longer. *P. amplexicaule* (Zones 5–9) will benefit from wrap-around support.

Polygonatum × hybridum

Polygonum affine

COMMON PROBLEMS None.
PROPAGATION Division in fall or spring, or from seed.
TROUBLESHOOTING None normally necessary.
SIZE The best of the ground covering forms is *P. affine* (*Persicaria affinis*), which will reach about 1 × 1ft./30 × 30cm. in two years. The upright border plant *P. amplexicaule* (*Persicaria amplexicaulis*) will attain 4 × 4ft./1.2 × 1.2m. in the same time.

Pulmonaria LUNGWORT

A lovely group of deciduous or semi-evergreen, ground-covering plants, grown for their bright blue, red, or white spring flowers and variegated leaves. Pulmonarias are easy to establish and easy to grow, provided attention is given to supplying them with the correct soil conditions.

SOIL Tolerant of many, but must be moist; a deep, rich, fertile loam will give the best results.
SITUATION Full sun to moderate shade; shade must be given on soils prone to any drying out. Zones 4–8 for most.
WATERING AND FEEDING Mulch in fall and spring. Feed with a balanced, general-purpose fertilizer in mid-spring, and again in midsummer.
MANAGEMENT Cut down to soil level in fall. Once the leaves begin to shrivel, they may be pulled away by hand.
COMMON PROBLEMS None; voles (mice) may eat roots.
PROPAGATION Division in fall or spring.
TROUBLESHOOTING None normally necessary.
SIZE Varies with species; the commonest of the ground-covering forms is *P. angustifolia*, which will attain about 8 × 8in./20 × 20cm. in two years. *P. saccharata* 'Mrs. Moon' will reach 1ft./30cm.

Pulmonaria angustifolia

Ranunculus – Salvia

Ranunculus acris 'Flore Pleno'

Ranunculus BUTTERCUP

This is the large genus that embraces the wild species of buttercup but also includes a number of annual and perennial species for the border. I find the most attractive, and certainly the easiest to grow, are the double-flowered forms of the wild species, but care is needed for some are invasive.

SOIL Tolerates most, but best in rich and slightly moist soils.

SITUATION Full sun to moderate shade. Zones 4–8 for most.

WATERING AND FEEDING Mulch in fall and spring. Feed with a balanced, general-purpose fertilizer in mid-spring.

MANAGEMENT Cut down to soil level in the fall. The taller-growing forms will need some wrap-around support. Divide most forms every four or five years; ground-covering types are best left undisturbed.

COMMON PROBLEMS None.

PROPAGATION Division in fall or spring, or from seed.

TROUBLESHOOTING None normally necessary.

SIZE Varies with species; two of the best are the double forms of the meadow buttercup, *R. acris* 'Flore Pleno', which will attain $2\frac{1}{2} \times 2\frac{1}{2}$ft./75 × 75cm. in three years, and the lesser celandine, *R. ficaria* 'Flore Pleno', which must only be planted where its invasiveness can be allowed free rein. Individual plants will reach 2×30in./5 × 75cm. in about four years but each multiplies rapidly to produce a ground-covering carpet.

Romneya TREE POPPY

The Californian tree poppies always arouse interest and comment when bearing their large, poppy-like flowers in late summer, but they are fickle both in their site requirements and their early establishment. They are reliable only in milder areas.

SOIL Prefer nearly dry and infertile; they are intolerant of water-logging.

SITUATION Full sun; intolerant of exposure to cold winds. Zones 8–9, but some success can be expected in Zones 6–7 if plants are heavily mulched over winter.

WATERING AND FEEDING Mulch in fall and spring.

MANAGEMENT The old shoots should be left on over the winter to provide protection, and in mild areas they may all survive until the spring, when the oldest half of them should be cut back to soil level. Usually, however, there will be considerable frost damage and all shoots should then be cut down to soil level in spring – the flowers will be borne on the new shoots. As the plants greatly resent disturbance once established, they are best not moved unless absolutely necessary. They will require some staking to give the best display.

COMMON PROBLEMS None.

PROPAGATION Root cuttings in winter; some forms from seed.

TROUBLESHOOTING None normally necessary.

SIZE In good growing conditions, the shoots will attain about $5-6\frac{1}{2}$ft./1.5–2m. within a year, and the plant will spread to about $6\frac{1}{2}$ft./2m. after three or four years.

Romneya coulteri

Rudbeckia   CONEFLOWER

Belonging to a group of very easily grown and rather similar border perennials in the daisy family, these are especially useful for their mainly yellow and golden flowers in summer and fall.

SOIL Tolerates almost any, but always best in fairly rich and moist but free draining soils.

SITUATION Full sun or light shade. Zones 3–9.

WATERING AND FEEDING Mulch in fall and spring. Feed with a balanced, general-purpose fertilizer in mid-spring, and again in midsummer.

MANAGEMENT Cut down to soil level after flowering in fall, or in spring. They often require staking. Divide every four or five years in fall or spring.

COMMON PROBLEMS None.

PROPAGATION Division in fall or spring, or from seed.

TROUBLESHOOTING None normally necessary.

SIZE Varies with species; the common black-eyed Susan, *R. fulgida* 'Goldsturm', attains 3 × 2ft./1m. × 60cm. after three years, the more vigorous *R. laciniata* at least double this.

Rudbeckia fulgida

Ruta   RUE

A small group of rather woody perennials verging on the shrubby, the best known being the glaucous-leaved *R. graveolens* 'Jackman's Blue'. They are aromatic herbs at home both in the herb garden and the herbaceous border.

SOIL Light, well drained, not very rich.

SITUATION Full sun or very light shade. Zones 5–9.

WATERING AND FEEDING Mulch in fall and spring. Feed with a balanced, general-purpose fertilizer in mid-spring, and again in midsummer.

MANAGEMENT For the bushiest plants, cut back all stems hard to new growth annually in spring, or at least cut back dead flower spikes to their woody base. No staking is needed.

COMMON PROBLEMS None.

PROPAGATION Semi-ripe cuttings in summer, or from seed.

TROUBLESHOOTING Leggy plants can be cut hard back into old wood in spring, and will rejuvenate.

SIZE *R. graveolens* 'Jackman's Blue' will reach about 2½ × 2ft./75 × 60cm. after two or three years. 'Blue Beauty', at 1½ft./45cm. is lower.

Salvia

It is unfortunate that the best known salvias are the strident red ones only perennial in very warm climates; for there are also some easy and interesting hardy forms. There are the rosette-forming perennials derived from such species as *S. bulleyana*, the semi-shrubby types including the common sage, *S. officinalis*, and a number of more-tender forms, such as *S. microphylla*.

SOIL Most forms tolerate most soils, but are best in well drained, fairly rich conditions.

Ruta graveolens 'Jackman's Blue'

Salvia – Verbascum

Salvia microphylla

Sanguinaria canadensis 'Plena'

SITUATION Full sun. Zones vary among species, *S. argentea*, 5–9; *S. farinacea*, 8–10; *S. nemerosa*, 5–9; *S.* × 'Superba', 5–8.
WATERING AND FEEDING Mulch in fall and spring. Feed with a balanced fertilizer in mid-spring, and in midsummer.
MANAGEMENT TRUE HERBACEOUS FORMS Cut back dead flower stems after flowering and cut all growth above ground back to soil level in fall. Divide every four or five years.
SEMI-SHRUBS For most, cut out any frost-damaged shoots in spring; otherwise, no treatment is needed, although the common sage is best cut back hard in spring to its woody base.
COMMON PROBLEMS None.
PROPAGATION TRUE HERBACEOUS FORMS Division in spring.
SEMI-SHRUBS Softwood or semi-ripe cuttings in early summer.
TROUBLESHOOTING Semi-shrub forms will usually regenerate if cut back hard into old wood in spring.
SIZE The rosette-forming herbaceous types will reach about 2 × 2ft./60 × 60cm. in two or three years. Most of the semi-shrubs attain 2–3 × 1½–3ft./60cm.–1m. × 50cm.–1m. in the same time.

Sanguinaria   BLOODROOT

A one-species genus but nonetheless a valuable low-growing, spring-flowering plant for mostly woodland conditions. The double white-flowered *S. canadensis* 'Plena' is best.
SOIL Must be moist, but well drained, organic, and nutrient rich if the plant is to give anything approaching its true potential.
SITUATION Full sun or light to moderate shade. Zones 5–8.
WATERING AND FEEDING Mulch in fall and spring. Feed with a balanced fertilizer in mid-spring. In the ideal woodland garden enriched with decaying leaves, feeding is rarely needed.
MANAGEMENT Little is needed; the foliage and flowers wither away and vanish by early summer and the only important consideration is to be sure that the position is well marked, as it is very easy to damage the clumps when planting bulbs. In most situations the plants may be left undisturbed for many years.
COMMON PROBLEMS None, but voles (mice) may destroy roots.
PROPAGATION Division in late summer.
TROUBLESHOOTING None normally necessary.
SIZE Will attain about 6in. × 1½ft./15 × 50cm. after four years.

Stachys

Among the common and popular species of this genus, *S. byzantina*, lamb's ears, has attractive woolly leaves, while *S. macrantha* features lush and richly colored flower spikes. They are versatile plants, but not suitable for cold and wet gardens.
SOIL Tolerates most, provided it is well drained; will tolerate fairly dry and impoverished soils.
SITUATION Full sun; there are a few common wild species that are woodland plants, such as *S. officinalis*, wood betony, which will grow in some shade as well as sun. Zones 4–9.
WATERING AND FEEDING Mulch in fall and spring. Feed with a balanced fertilizer in mid-spring, and in midsummer.

MANAGEMENT Cut back dead flower stems after flowering and cut all growth above ground back to soil level in the fall on all species except the grayish, woolly-leaved *S. byzantina*: this form is evergreen and should simply have dead or browned shoots cut back. Divide all species every three or four years.

COMMON PROBLEMS None.

PROPAGATION Division in spring.

TROUBLESHOOTING None normally necessary.

SIZE Most will reach about $1\frac{1}{2}$–2×1–$1\frac{1}{2}$ft./45–60 × 30–45cm. in two or three years, but *S. byzantina* is a ground-covering plant attaining about 4–6in. × $1\frac{1}{2}$–$2\frac{1}{2}$ft./12–15 × 50–75cm. in the same time.

Stachys byzantina

Thalictrum   MEADOW-RUE

These are graceful and under-appreciated plants for lightly shaded situations, particularly useful for borders that do not receive full sun for the whole of the day; they can disappoint if their roots are allowed to dry out. The flowers are not spectacular but light, tiny, and feathery with rather an individual appeal.

SOIL All of the commonly grown species require moist, fairly rich soils.

SITUATION Thalictrum tolerates full sun but always performs better in light or moderate shade. Zones mostly 5–9.

WATERING AND FEEDING Mulch in fall and spring. Feed with a balanced, general-purpose fertilizer in mid-spring, and again in midsummer.

MANAGEMENT Cut down to soil level in the fall; the stems are too feeble to leave, and as soon as the winter weather arrives they look a mess. With luck and careful planting among other tall plants, you may find no staking is needed; otherwise, some wrap-around support will be essential. Divide every three or four years.

COMMON PROBLEMS None.

PROPAGATION Division in fall or spring, or from seed.

TROUBLESHOOTING None normally necessary.

SIZE Most of the popular true border species, such as *T. delavayi* and *T. aquilegiifolium*, will reach heights of 3–5ft./1–1.5m. and a spread of about 2ft./60cm. in two or three years; but there are also some lower-growing forms, and a rather useful ground-covering species for a woodland garden is *T. minus*, which has flower stems about 2ft./60cm. tall and will spread fairly vigorously.

Verbascum   MULLEIN

Some of the best mulleins are biennials or monocarpic perennials (they die after flowering), but there are a few reliably perennial species that can form majestic components to any border, especially in gentler conditions.

SOIL Tolerates most unless cold, heavy, and water-logged, but always best on slightly alkaline, free draining but fairly rich soils.

SITUATION Full sun to light shade. Zones 5–9.

WATERING AND FEEDING Mulch in fall and spring. Feed with a balanced fertilizer in mid-spring, and again in midsummer.

Thalictrum aquilegiifolium 'Thundercloud'

Verbascum olympicum

MANAGEMENT Cut down the flower spike after flowering; I prefer to leave some of the old foliage until the spring and then cut it down to soil level. The tall flower spikes are stout and should not require support if protected by other plants nearby. Verbascums do not divide satisfactorily and are best renewed every four or five years.

COMMON PROBLEMS Leaf-eating insects are common but rarely very damaging. Mildew can be serious but not usually until late in the season.

PROPAGATION Root cuttings in spring, or seeds. Plants will self-sow.

TROUBLESHOOTING None normally necessary.

SIZE Varies with species but as a rough indication the most imposing of the perennial forms, such as *V. densiflorum*, will attain $5 \times 2\frac{1}{2}$ft./1.5m. $\times$ 75cm. in two years. *V. chaixii* and *vophownixlum* cultivars remain at 3–4ft./1–1.2m.

Veronica   SPEEDWELL

The various veronicas are a fine group of hardy perennials with mostly blue or purple flower spikes in late spring or summer. Some, including *V. gentianoides*, are mat-forming and belong in rock gardens, but most species and their cultivars, are excellent border subjects in groups of three to five.

SOIL Tolerates most, but must be well drained.

SITUATION Full sun to very light shade. Zones 4–8.

WATERING AND FEEDING Mulch in fall and spring. Feed with a balanced fertilizer in mid-spring, and in midsummer.

MANAGEMENT Cut down to soil level in the fall, and protect the crown over the winter by mounding a few inches of organic mulch over it. The flower spikes of some varieties tend to flop and kink but are not easily supported in an attractive manner; the best answer is to use some wrap-around support or possibly to place wide mesh netting over the top through which the stems can grow. Divide every three or four years.

COMMON PROBLEMS None.

PROPAGATION Division in spring.

TROUBLESHOOTING None normally necessary.

SIZE Species, such as *V. gentianoides* reach several inches when in bloom. *V. incana* reaches 1×1ft./30×30cm.; *V. longifolia*, 3ft./1m.

Yucca

Yuccas are among the very few large, spiky-leaved monocotyledons to be really hardy, a fact that makes them useful as garden features or, as garden designers call them, "architectural plants". They benefit from some protection in other than very mild areas, and are often put in containers and moved indoors. Two hardy species for the North are *Y. filamentosa*, and *Y. glauca*.

SOIL Must be well drained and preferably fairly rich; tolerant of alkalinity. In containers use good garden soil, or use part soil and part Jiffy Mix or Redi-Earth.

SITUATION Full sun. Hardy species, Zones 5–10.

Veronica gentianoides

WATERING AND FEEDING Mulch in fall and spring. Feed with a balanced, general-purpose fertilizer in mid-spring, and again in midsummer. Take care that plants in containers are not allowed to become very dry in summer.

MANAGEMENT Cut down old flower spikes as flowers fade; carefully cut away dead leaves from around the sides of the clump in late fall. When in flower, the spike may need some improvised support although this is difficult to do unobtrusively. Less hardy species in colder areas are best protected by loosely wrapping burlap or a similar porous material (but not plastic sheet) around them during the coldest weather. Hardy yuccas may be left undisturbed or divided every five or six years.

COMMON PROBLEMS Fungal leaf spotting.

PROPAGATION Division in spring, root cuttings in winter, or offsets in spring, and seeds.

TROUBLESHOOTING None normally necessary; if severely damaged by frost, plants may regenerate when cut back into healthy tissue.

SIZE The hardy forms will reach up to $6\frac{1}{2} \times 6\frac{1}{2}$ft./$2 \times 2$m. after about eight or ten years. *Y. glauca* remains at a modest 3ft./1m.

Yucca gloriosa

Ferns

Hardy ferns have waxed and waned in gardening popularity and are passing through a well-justified revival. The species, and cultivars offer a pleasing contrast to flowering plants, while the evergreen types are particularly valuable. Provided their basic site requirements can be met, there are few garden plants that need so little attention.

SOIL With very few exceptions, ferns require a moist, organic, and fairly rich soil. Among common species, only the European fern *Polypodium vulgare* is tolerant of dry conditions; it is also one of the few that is tolerant of high alkalinity.

SITUATION Although most ferns, other than those with very fragile foliage, will survive in full sun provided the soil is very moist, they are much more successful in light to deep shade. A few of the exotic evergreen species are slightly tender and must be planted in sheltered positions and well away from winter winds. Hardiness zones vary, but Zones 3–8 for many.

WATERING AND FEEDING Mulch in fall and spring. Apply a light dressing of balanced, general-purpose fertilizer in mid-spring, and again in midsummer.

MANAGEMENT Ferns require no staking and most will not require division more than every six or seven years in spring. Indeed, many can be left more or less indefinitely without disturbance. The dead fronds of deciduous species are best cut away (not pulled, for they may cut your hands) in late fall. The old fronds of evergreen types may be left until they become frayed and tattered, then cut away.

COMMON PROBLEMS None.

PROPAGATION From spores, by division, or by offsets (where produced) in spring.

TROUBLESHOOTING Not likely to be necessary.

Phyllitis scolopendrium

SIZE Varies among species, so read label information carefully. The smallest forms suitable for growing in wall crevices, such as some of the *Adiantum* species, will only attain 6 × 8in./15 × 20cm. in two or three years, whereas the largest of the hardy species, *Osmunda regalis*, the royal fern, will reach 6½ × 3ft./2 × 1m. in the same time.

Grasses

The days when the lawn was considered the only place in the garden in which to grow grasses have now passed. Apart from the many annual species and the perennial bamboos, there are numerous ornamental herbaceous species that can be used effectively in the border or as isolated clumps. Most are fully hardy and easy to grow, although a few can be invasive. (Some so-called grasses are actually sedges or rushes, and are discussed separately.)

Grasses

SOIL Almost any, provided it is not very heavy or water-logged. There are a few species, including the popular and rather invasive *Glyceria maxima* 'Variegata', which must have wet soil and are suitable for waterside plantings or bog gardens.

SITUATION Full sun to moderate shade, depending on species. It is important to buy named varieties of plants from a reputable nursery that will supply accurate information, because shade tolerance ranges from such species as the woodland grass *Millium effusum*, which is a deep-shade plant, to the many sun-loving species of *Cortaderia* (pampas grass). Zones 4–9 for many.

WATERING AND FEEDING Mulch in fall and spring. Feed with a balanced, general-purpose fertilizer in mid-spring, and again in midsummer.

MANAGEMENT Grasses require no staking and the clump-forming species should be divided very infrequently – in spring, once every ten years may be adequate. Where space allows you to grow the more invasive stoloniferous forms, such as *Phalaris arundinacea*, they should be divided every three or four years. The soft-leaved forms are best cut down to soil level in the fall, but those with stiff stems and attractive dead seed-heads should be left over the winter and then cut down in early spring. There is a belief that the best way to deal with pampas grass (*Cortaderia*) is to set fire to the clump at the end of the winter. Don't try it; you stand a good chance of killing the plant. Equip yourself with a pair of very strong gloves and pull out the dead material from the center.

COMMON PROBLEMS None.

PROPAGATION Division in fall or spring; some from seed.

TROUBLESHOOTING Not likely to be necessary but a common complaint is that pampas grasses fail to flower. This is almost invariably due to the plants having been raised from seed; always buy named, selected forms that flower reliably.

SIZE Varies, so read label information carefully. The smaller, clump-forming species such as *Festuca glauca* will not exceed $1\frac{1}{2} \times 1\frac{1}{2}$ft./45 × 45cm. in five years, while the very vigorous *Leymus arenarius* will reach 5 × 10–13ft./1.5 × 3–4m. in the same time.

Sedges and rushes

Although fewer in number and generally less important than grasses as garden ornamentals, the evergreen sedge and rush families include several valuable attractive species. All are easily grown, although individual requirements vary widely.

SOIL Varies with type; among rushes, *Luzula* species require dry, more or less sandy soils, while *Juncus*, in general, need wetter conditions and several make very useful waterside plants. Sedges generally tend to thrive in moist soils; and included among these are several species that are best grown in the water garden; check label information carefully.

SITUATION Full sun or light shade. Many in Zones 5–9.

WATERING AND FEEDING Mulch in fall and spring where practical – clearly this is not feasible in a bog garden. Feed with a balanced, general-purpose fertilizer in mid-spring, and again in midsummer where the plants are growing in a conventional border; do not use fertilizer close to pools.

MANAGEMENT Little is needed; even for the kinds with very tall flower stems staking is never really successful or aesthetically pleasing. Allow dead flower stems to remain over winter and then cut them back in spring, or when they become very damaged by rain and wind. Trim back foliage lightly in spring but do not cut right back to soil level.

COMMON PROBLEMS None.

PROPAGATION Division in fall or spring; some from seed.

TROUBLESHOOTING None normally necessary.

SIZE Varies greatly, so check label information; some of the more vigorous forms such as *Carex riparia*, the pond sedge, will attain a height of about 3–4ft./1–1.2m. and spread invasively.

Carex pendula

BULBOUS PLANTS

Agapanthus	*Gagea*
Allium	*Galanthus*
Alstroemeria	*Gladiolus*
Amaryllis	*Hyacinthoides*
Anemone	*Hyacinthus*
Arum	*Iris*
Bulbocodium	*Leucojum*
Chionodoxa	*Lilium*
Colchicum	*Muscari*
Convallaria	*Narcissus*
Corydalis	*Nerine*
Crocosmia	*Ornithogalum*
Crocus	*Schizostylis*
Cyclamen	*Scilla*
Dahlia	*Sisyrinchium*
Eranthis	*Sternbergia*
Eremurus	*Trillium*
Erythronium	*Tulipa*
Fritillaria	*Zantesdeschia*

Principles of care

I use the term bulbous plants here to describe all those deciduous or evergreen herbaceous perennials that have a swollen underground food storage structure, whether in the form of a bulb, a corm, a tuber, or a rhizome. They offer gardeners a rapid source of satisfaction, the stored food reserves virtually guaranteeing strong growth and a fine display of flowers in the first season after planting. Given the modest proviso that only high-quality, plump bulbs are bought and that "job lots" of cut-price, end-of-season mixtures are avoided, it is hard to go wrong. The only real problems with them arise in subsequent years.

PLANTING

Most bulbs require well drained soils and most are tolerant of moderate acidity and alkalinity. The need for good drainage is particularly important from early summer onward: although many spring-flowering bulbous plants grow in rather wet conditions in the wild, when these conditions continue throughout the year problems are likely to arise from fungal decay. Either do not plant bulbs in soil that is very soggy, or improve the area's drainage: really wet soil can be drained by laying underground pipes; moist clay soils can be improved by incorporating coarse sand and/or gravel and

quantities of organic matter (rotted leaves, compost); or plant bulbs in raised beds. The advice often given to add a handful of sand to the bottom of each bulb's hole is time consuming and of dubious value.

Almost all bulbous plants make good subjects for containers as temporary or permanent plantings, preferably in a soil-based mixture. If they are fed as I recommend, hardy bulbs can usually give a good display for a few years.

In general, bulbous plants should be planted as soon as possible after purchase and before shoot growth begins. This will give them the best opportunity to develop a strong root system; there is no advantage in planting them more shallowly than normal toward the end of the planting period, as is sometimes supposed. A few types, such as snowdrops, are often slow to become established. If the ground isn't frozen, it is often possible to lift clumps in leaf from a neighbor's planting.

Although in the following descriptions I have indicated the approximate distances to which individual plants will spread, this is fairly academic information as most bulbs are best planted in groups of six to twelve or more (depending on size), with a space between each bulb equivalent to at least three times its diameter if the bulbs are intended as long-term plantings. You can achieve a good display, especially in containers, by planting more closely, and treating the bulbs as annuals.

Planting depths for bulbs

PLANTING DEPTHS In general, bulbs should be planted with their bases at a depth equal to about $2\frac{1}{2}$ to 3 times their average diameter, with the notable exceptions of *Lilium candidum* and cyclamen; *Fritillaria imperialis* should be planted on its side. It is better to err on the deep rather than the shallow side, but on heavier soils, where success is less certain, it may be better to plant the bulbs about thirty per cent nearer the surface.

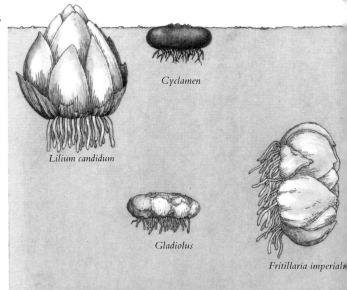

Cyclamen

Lilium candidum

Gladiolus

Fritillaria imperialis

GENERAL MANAGEMENT

Non-hardy bulbs should always be lifted at the end of the growing season and stored in a frost-free place, but most hardy types (the most significant exception to this being hybrid tulips) are best left to "naturalize" or multiply in situ. If they are fed with bonemeal or a bulb fertilizer early in the season, when growth begins, and then given liquid feed after flowering, most bulbs should naturalize satisfactorily. Don't underestimate the importance of the foliage in producing food to build up the bulb's strength for flowering the following year.

PROPAGATION

Natural multiplication of the bulbous structure is the most reliable method of propagation, and in most cases established clumps benefit from being lifted and split up every four or five years. Most bulbous plants may also be propagated from seed sown in pans of gritty soil-based mixtures, but they will take from two to seven years to flower. In a few instances, as with lilies, the plant will produce bulbils or bulb scales, which can be removed and grown on.

TROUBLESHOOTING

The most frequent reasons for the failure of bulbs are often shallow planting – bulbs are more accessible to mice and freezing – a lack of feeding in lean soils; some kinds, however, are not suitable for planting under turf as they are unable to compete effectively with the grass, and label information on individual species should be carefully checked. The commonest problem by far is blindness – a failure to form flowers. This is rare in the first year but thereafter can result from a variety of causes: a lack of feeding or overfeeding with nitrogen and competition among bulbs that have multiplied and are crowded. Lifting, dividing, and replanting is the remedy, but a bulb that has become enfeebled through lack of feeding will require a few seasons of attention, with regular feeding while in leaf, before it flowers again.

Sometimes blindness arises from damage to the growing point caused by the larvae of insects such as the narcissus fly, or from damage to the whole bulb by fungal decay. If the bulbs are dug up and found to be decaying, they are best discarded.

Shallowly planted bulbs or corms, such as crocus, can occasionally suffer from a condition known as frost heave, in which they are forced to the surface of frozen soil. They will generally survive if replanted rather more deeply. Mice and voles will also dig up and eat crocus in particular, but this problem can be circumvented by planting the corms slightly more deeply and placing chicken wire over them before replacing the soil. Tulip and lily bulbs are also targets of mice. Planting several bulbs in open-top baskets may help.

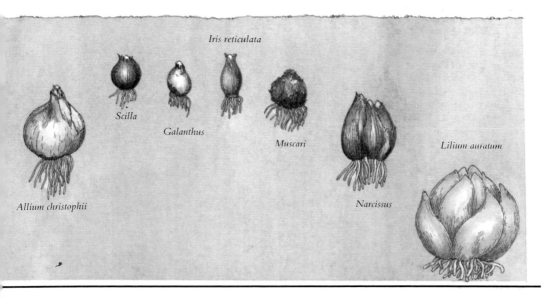

Iris reticulata

Scilla

Galanthus

Muscari

Lilium auratum

Allium christophii

Narcissus

Agapanthus – Anemone

Agapanthus 'Castle of Mey'

Agapanthus   AFRICAN LILY

In a mild situation the massed blue or white flowers of agapanthus are magnificent in borders, but in cold climates they make a fine summer display in tubs on a terrace.

SOIL AND PLANTING Moist, well drained, rich, organic soil; intolerant of very light or poor soils or of water-logging. The roots should be planted with their tops covered by about 2in./5cm. of soil. Agapanthus can be grown successfully in large containers of rich garden soil, and this is useful in cold areas where the tubs can be moved into some shelter from frost in winter.

SITUATION Full sun to light shade, shelter from cold winds. Always most successful in mild, coastal gardens, although the 'Headbourne Hybrids' are hardy enough to overwinter in gardens in Zones 6–10. *A. orientalis* and others: Zones 8–10.

WATERING AND FEEDING Mulch in fall and spring. Feed with a balanced, general-purpose fertilizer in mid-spring, and again around midsummer. The fall mulch should be mounded around the crowns to provide protection from winter freezing.

MANAGEMENT Cut off dead flower spikes after flowering; divide every eight or ten years, and certainly no more frequently than about once every five or six years.

COMMON PROBLEMS None.

SIZE The forms most commonly seen are the 'Headbourne Hybrids', which will reach about $3 \times 1\frac{1}{2}$ft./90cm.–1m. $\times$ 50cm. after five years, but can eventually spread considerably more.

Allium   FLOWERING ONION

A very useful group of summer-flowering bulbs with white, pink, red, mauve, blue, or yellow flowers, growing to a wide range of sizes. They are related to the onion, and it is possibly the thought of an onion smell that explains why they are not more widely grown; yet, in practice, any smell is rare. Alliums will be more popular in the future as their value for summer flowering becomes more widely appreciated. They have a further advantage in making excellent dried heads for flower arrangements.

SOIL AND PLANTING Light, rich, fairly free draining; tolerant of alkalinity. The bulb bases should be planted at a depth of $2\frac{1}{2}$ times their average diameter.

SITUATION Always best in full sun. Zones 4–10 for most.

WATERING AND FEEDING Mulch in fall and apply a top dressing of bonemeal or a proprietary bulb fertilizer in early spring. Feed with a fertilizer high in potash once a week after blooming until the leaves turn yellow.

MANAGEMENT Do not lift annually but divide the clumps every five or six years. Remove the flower heads after blooming, and trim back the leaves to soil level as soon as they turn yellow.

COMMON PROBLEMS None.

SIZE The range in size among many species is probably greater than for any other bulb genus. At the two extremes are *A. moly* with a height and spread of 4–12×4–5in./10–30×10–12cm., and *A. giganteum* at 5×1ft./1.5m. $\times 30$cm.

Allium aflatunense

Alstroemeria PERUVIAN LILY

These summer-flowering, tuberous perennials come in a wide range of usually mixed colors, and are popular as cut flowers in the North. *A. aurantiaca* can remain in gardens all year (Zones 5–10) if protected over winter (see below). Other kinds must be grown in 12in./30cm. pots and wintered in frost-free shelter.

SOIL AND PLANTING Light, rich, fairly free draining. The tuber bases should be at a depth of $2\frac{1}{2}$ times their average diameter.

SITUATION Always best in full sun, but with some shelter from cold winds. For most, Zones 8–10.

WATERING AND FEEDING Mulch in fall. Top dress with bonemeal or a proprietary bulb fertilizer in early spring.

MANAGEMENT Divide the clumps every five or six years. There is a temptation in cold areas to lift the plants annually but, because they often take at least two years to establish, this is unwise and in cold gardens it is better to mound a protective mulch over the plants in late fall. Remove flower heads after flowering and trim back leaves to soil level when they turn yellow.

COMMON PROBLEMS None.

SIZE Most forms will reach 3×2ft./1m. $\times$ 60cm.

Alstroemeria hybrid

Amaryllis

To many gardeners, the name amaryllis conjures up an image of the huge flowering bulb more correctly called *Hippeastrum*, but most experts use the name for a single species, *A. belladonna*. It bears a group of fairly small flowers on a tall stem in late summer, and is hardy in some northern areas if mulched over winter.

SOIL AND PLANTING Light and free draining, but not impoverished. The bulbs must be planted deeply, with the bases at a depth of about 8in./20cm.

SITUATION Full sun or light shade, with shelter from cold winds; close to a south- or south-west-facing wall is ideal. Zones 5–8.

WATERING AND FEEDING Mulch in fall. Top dress with bonemeal or a proprietary bulb fertilizer in early summer, and feed with a liquid fertilizer high in potash once a week after blooming and until the leaves turn yellow.

MANAGEMENT The bulbs must not be lifted or disturbed, for flowering may be disrupted for two or three years.

COMMON PROBLEMS None.

SIZE Up to 2ft./60cm. in height, and spreading as the bulbs multiply to reach perhaps 12in./30cm. after five years.

Anemone WINDFLOWER

There are several groups of garden anemone, not superficially very similar. The rhizomatous forms are of two main types: the hardy, small, spring-flowering species such as *A. blanda*, in turn related to the native wood anemone *A. nemorosa*; and the 'De Caen' strain of *A. coronaria*, which are less hardy in the North (Zones 7–10). *A. × hybrida* is fibrous-rooted, and is discussed on page 106.

Amaryllis belladonna

Anemone – Colchicum

Anemone 'De Caen'

Soil and planting Moist, fairly rich but free draining soils suit all types, although *A. nemorosa* is better in free draining organic soils. The tuber or bulb bases should be at a depth of 2½ times their average diameter.

Situation All are best in full sun or light shade, except *A. nemorosa*, which prefers light to moderate or even deep shade, and is a good plant for a woodland garden. Zones 4–8.

Watering and feeding SMALL PERENNIAL BULBS Mulch in fall. Top dress with bonemeal or a proprietary bulb fertilizer in early spring, and feed with a liquid fertilizer high in potash once a week after blooming and until the leaves turn yellow.

'DE CAEN' STRAIN Top dress the soil with bonemeal before planting. Feed with a liquid fertilizer as the flower buds form, and, if experience suggests they are perennial in your area, feed again after the flowers fade and until the foliage turns yellow.

Management The small perennial bulbs should not be lifted and seldom, if ever, require dividing.

Common problems None.

Size The small perennial forms reach a height of 6–8in./ 15–20cm. and a spread of about 3–4in./8–10cm., with each plant multiplying to form a clump perhaps 8in./20cm. in diameter after five years. 'De Caen' and similar strains grow up to 12in./30cm. tall and spread to 2–3in./5–8cm. within their first year.

Arum

The most familiar arum is the cuckoo pint or lords and ladies, *A. maculatum*, but there is also a related species, *A. italicum*, which is almost as hardy and whose handsome variegated leaves in the cultivars 'Pictum' and 'Marmorata' can, given the correct conditions, provide interest for much of the year.

Soil and planting Moist, rich, organic soils always provide the best results. The tubers are horizontal and should be planted at a depth of about 2–3in./5–7cm.

Situation These are plants for the woodland garden and require light to moderate shade; some gardeners claim their variegation is less pronounced in deep shade. Zones 6–9.

Watering and feeding Mulch in fall. Top dress with bonemeal or a proprietary bulb fertilizer in early spring, and again in midsummer, although the foliage may have died down.

Management Leave the plants undisturbed; do not even cut down the dead flower spikes, as bright red fruits will follow.

Common problems None.

Size Depending on the richness of the soil, arums will reach a height of 6–10in./15–25cm., and a similar spread.

Bulbocodium   RED CROCUS

The spring-flowering red crocus is more closely related to colchicums than true crocuses, and their requirements are similarly best satisfied in the rock garden. Of the only two species, *B. vernum*, commonly known as spring meadow saffron, is the one likely to be seen.

Arum italicum

SOIL AND PLANTING Light, preferably gritty, and free draining; tolerant of moderate acidity and alkalinity. The bulb bases should be at a depth of $2\frac{1}{2}$ times their average diameter. Plant in the fall.

SITUATION Full sun to very light shade. Zones 3–9.

WATERING AND FEEDING In early spring, mulch very lightly and top dress with bonemeal or a proprietary bulb fertilizer.

MANAGEMENT Almost none needed. Do not lift the bulbs annually and leave them undisturbed for as long as possible.

COMMON PROBLEMS None.

SIZE *B. vernum* will reach $1\frac{1}{2} \times 1\frac{1}{2}$ in./4×4cm. in two or three years.

Bulbocodium vernum

Chionodoxa GLORY OF THE SNOW

These are among my favorite small spring–flowering bulbs; they are easy to grow and have the advantages of producing their usually blue flowers early, even after severe winters, and of tolerating more shade than many similar species.

SOIL AND PLANTING Light, free draining; tolerant of moderate acidity and alkalinity. The bulb bases should be at a depth of $2\frac{1}{2}$ times their average diameter.

SITUATION Full sun to light or even moderate shade.

WATERING AND FEEDING Mulch very lightly in early spring. Top dress with bonemeal or a proprietary bulb fertilizer in early spring; liquid feed can be applied until the foliage turns yellow.

MANAGEMENT Do not lift the bulbs annually and leave them undisturbed for as long as possible – they will self seed freely.

COMMON PROBLEMS None.

SIZE There is some variation among species but the commonest, *C. luciliae*, will reach 4×2 in./10×5cm. after two years; some strains of the same species are smaller.

Chionodoxa luciliae

Colchicum

Sometimes confusingly called fall crocuses, colchicums are quite distinct in their large, goblet-shaped flowers produced on bare stems before the leaves emerge. They are most attractive if well grown, but I never find them easy plants to manage.

SOIL AND PLANTING Will tolerate many but always best in moist, rich, organic soils. The bulb bases should be at a depth of $2\frac{1}{2}$ times their average diameter.

SITUATION Full sun to light or moderate shade. Zones 5–9.

WATERING AND FEEDING Mulch in early spring. Top dress with bonemeal or a proprietary bulb fertilizer in early spring; liquid feed can be applied until the foliage turns yellow.

MANAGEMENT The tall, leafless flower stems are feeble and very readily pushed over and broken by winds and rain. I find the answer is to grow them in tall, unmown grass, which provides support. Leave the bulbs undisturbed for as long as possible.

COMMON PROBLEMS None.

SIZE The largest hybrids, such as *C.* 'The Giant', will reach a height and spread of 8in./20cm. within three years; smaller species will barely reach half this size in the same time.

Colchicum autumnale

Convallaria majalis

Convallaria   LILY OF THE VALLEY

One of the classic garden plants, but also one of gardening's enigmas: on some sites it becomes an ineradicable weed, while in others it obstinately refuses to establish. Not for warm climates.
SOIL AND PLANTING Tolerant of many but always best in moist, rich, organic soils. Where it is difficult to establish, try digging up and transplanting in late winter or early spring a clump that is growing well, with as much soil as possible. The horizontal rhizomes should be at a depth of about 2in./5cm.
SITUATION Best in light to moderate shade. Zones 3–7.
WATERING AND FEEDING Mulch in fall. Top dress with bonemeal or a proprietary bulb fertilizer in early spring.
MANAGEMENT Do not lift the bulbs annually, but divide the clumps every five or six years in late winter or very early spring, unless they are growing in a semi-wild situation when they may be left undisturbed.
COMMON PROBLEMS None; if the bulbs become too invasive they may be controlled with glyphosate weedkiller.
SIZE Reaches a height of about 12in./30cm. in good soils and will spread to a similar extent within three years.

Corydalis

This is a large genus of plants in the fumitory family (has been listed in the poppy family), and includes many with tuberous roots. Some can become weedy, but there are a few choice and easy species, particularly *C. bulbosa* and the fibrous-rooted, blue-flowered *C. cashmeriana*.
SOIL AND PLANTING Tolerates most provided the soil is well drained. Plant with the roots about 2in./5cm. deep.
SITUATION Full sun to moderate shade; some forms are good plants for growing between paving slabs. Zones 5–8 for most.
WATERING AND FEEDING Apply a light mulch where feasible in spring and fall. Top dress with bonemeal or a proprietary bulb fertilizer in early spring, and again in midsummer.
MANAGEMENT Do not lift annually but divide clumps every five or six years in late winter or early spring, unless they are growing in a semi-wild situation when they may be left undisturbed.
COMMON PROBLEMS None.
SIZE Varies with species; most of the commoner forms will reach about 8 × 4in./20 × 10cm. in two or three years.

Crocosmia   MONBRETIA

The montbretia is an undervalued plant, largely because the older orange-flowered forms can be invasive. Modern hybrids are more compact and come in a good range of colors, so this most adaptable plant could be considered more seriously.
SOIL AND PLANTING Almost any; I have seen successful plantings on soil that resembled beach sand and others on a waterlogged stream bank. Plant the corms or horizontal stolons at a depth of about 2in./5cm.

Corydalis bulbosa

SITUATION Full sun to light shade, with shelter from cold winds. Zones 6–9 for most.

WATERING AND FEEDING Mulch in fall. Top dress with bonemeal or a proprietary bulb fertilizer in early spring.

MANAGEMENT Cut down the foliage as it discolors. Do not lift annually but divide clumps every five or six years. Above Zone 6, corms must be lifted in the fall and handled like gladiolus (page 157) over winter.

COMMON PROBLEMS None.

SIZE The modern hybrids reach a height of about $2\frac{1}{2}$–3ft./ 80cm.–1m. and will spread to about 1ft./30cm. within three years; the old, orange-flowered *C.* × *crocosmiiflora* reaches a similar height but spreads twice as far and continues to do so invasively.

Crocus

Of all the small bulbous plants, the crocus is one of the most useful and easy to grow. Most crocuses are spring-flowering, although by careful selection of species it would be possible to have a crocus in flower for almost every month of the year.

SOIL AND PLANTING Tolerates most, provided neither heavy nor water-logged. The corm bases should be at a depth of 3–$3\frac{1}{2}$ times their average diameter.

SITUATION Full sun to light shade; some species only open completely in full sun. The large-flowered Dutch crocuses are very effective if planted in grass, especially close to deciduous trees where they will flower before the trees come into leaf. Zones 3–9.

WATERING AND FEEDING Where growing in bare soil, mulch in spring and early fall; top dress with bonemeal or a proprietary bulb fertilizer in early spring; and, if possible, liquid feed two or three times while in full leaf. Where established in grass, mulching is neither necessary nor practicable, but apply a fertilizer in early spring if possible. Do not cut grass until bulb leaves have dried.

MANAGEMENT Almost none required, but shriveled foliage can be pulled away about six weeks after flowering. The blooms of winter-flowering species can be knocked about by rain, so protect with cloches when bad weather threatens. Do not lift the corms unless they are growing in containers, when they should be carefully dried off and stored until the fall; otherwise, leave plants undisturbed for as long as possible. Small species growing in beds may be divided after about six years. Crocuses growing in grass at lawn edges or under trees may have their foliage mown off six weeks after the flowers have faded; then it will be perfectly safe to apply weedkiller to the turf.

COMMON PROBLEMS Voles, birds, squirrels, and mice will all eat crocus corms. Corms that appear above the soil can be left alone, as their contractile roots pull them under again.

SIZE Varies with species and cultivar; the large Dutch crocus will reach a height of 5–6in./12–15cm. and spread to about 2in./5cm. within two years – although these spread figures are really academic because the corms will always be planted in groups. The smaller flowered species typically reach about 3–4in./8–10cm. in height and a spread of 1–$1\frac{1}{2}$in./3–4cm. in the same time.

Crocosmia 'Lucifer'

Crocus chrysanthus

Cyclamen – Eranthis

Cyclamen hederifolium

Cyclamen

Cyclamens are fairly unusual among common bulblike plants in being dicotyledonous and members of the primrose family, but they are very valuable in the garden because their surface-living tubers will thrive in conditions where most true bulbs will not. In many forms, the ornamental foliage is almost as important as the flowers.

SOIL AND PLANTING Although always best in moist, organic soils, cyclamen will thrive in the thin soil beneath deciduous trees, provided some organic mulch or top dressing is applied. They are tolerant of acidity and moderate alkalinity. If planting directly into the soil, place the corms with the top just showing through the soil surface; but those species with large corms are best grown for their first season in pots of good garden soil enriched with compost or leaf mold, as corms may remain dormant for months.

SITUATION Full sun to moderate shade. Zones 5–8.

WATERING AND FEEDING Mulch in spring and early fall. Top dress with bonemeal or a bulb fertilizer in early spring. If possible, liquid feed two or three times while corms are in full leaf.

MANAGEMENT Almost none required, although plants growing in thin soil must be mulched as described above: as well as preventing them from drying out, this will also encourage self-sown seedlings. Do not lift annually but separate corms of very overcrowded clumps every five or six years.

COMMON PROBLEMS None.

SIZE Most of the hardy forms, including the commonest, *C. hederifolium*, will reach 4 × 4in./10 × 10cm. in two or three years.

Dahlia

The most important of the half-hardy, tuber-forming perennials. Loved or loathed by gardeners, they certainly require some management if they are to give of their best. For those not willing to devote the necessary time and energy, and who perhaps dislike the large-flowered cultivars, the smaller-flowered bedding dahlias, grown as annuals from seed, can be very pretty and rewarding.

SOIL AND PLANTING Nutrient rich, moist but free draining; intolerant of extremes of acidity and alkalinity. If planted as tubers, rather than young plants, they should be planted about three weeks before the last frost is likely, and with the tuber base at a depth of 6–8in./15–20cm.

SITUATION Full sun to light shade. Zones 3–9.

WATERING AND FEEDING Top dress the planting bed with bonemeal about two weeks before planting. Mulch soon after planting and again halfway through the summer, ensuring that the soil around the plants is not allowed to dry out. Liquid feed with fertilizer high in potash every week during the growing season.

MANAGEMENT Stake at planting time with a single, firm stake and tie the plant onto this as it grows. Dahlias should be pruned by having the growing tip removed about four to six weeks after growth first emerges; this will encourage the formation of side-shoots and more flowers. If the very best large blooms are required, disbud by removing all flower buds except that at the tip of each shoot, as with chrysanthemums (page 112); but most gardeners will prefer a bushy plant with more, if smaller, flowers.

In all but the mildest climates, dahlias need to be lifted and stored over winter. Once the fall frost has blackened the foliage, cut the stems down to leave about 6in./15cm. Lift the tubers very carefully with a fork, taking care not to spear them. Carefully poke away any excess soil caught in them with a small cane, and stand them upside down for about a week to drain. Dust them with sulphur fungicide and store them in a frost-free place for the winter, either in envelopes made from layers of newspaper, or, better still, in boxes packed with old, almost dry peat moss or similar organic material; leave the tops of the tubers uncovered.

Every three or four years the stock should be renewed from cuttings taken in the spring, instead of planting out the old tubers. You will require a greenhouse or other facility where the temperature will not drop below 50°F/10°C. About three months before the last frost is likely, place the tubers in boxes of well-watered synthetic soil mixtures, such as Jiffy Mix, the mix to come only to the point where the roots join the tubers. Green shoots will soon emerge and are suitable for cuttings when about 4in./10cm. long. They are best removed by bending them until they just break away from the tuber, but they may also be severed with a razor blade. Dip the cuttings in rooting powder and plant them in 3½in./9cm. diameter pots filled with a mixture of equal parts by volume of peat and sand. Place in propagator trays. The cuttings will root in about two weeks, and should be hardened off for planting out once the danger of frost has passed.

COMMON PROBLEMS Plants may be affected by aphids; slugs; red spider mite; earwigs; virus; voles (mice) may eat tubers.

SIZE A cutting should attain about 3 × 2ft./1m. × 60cm. in its first year; a mature plant grown from tubers may range from 3 × 3ft./ 1 × 1m. to 6½ × 5ft./2 × 1.5m. depending on the variety.

Dahlia 'Preference' and 'Doris Day'

Eranthis   WINTER ACONITE

One of the joys of early spring is the first appearance of these cheerful yellow flowers. They resemble their close relation the buttercup, but unlike them seldom become seriously invasive.

SOIL AND PLANTING Tolerates most, provided the soil doesn't dry out, but always most successful in organic, woodland soils. The tubers should be approximately 2in./5cm. deep. If they seem difficult to establish, try transplanting a clump from a mature colony in full leaf, taking as much soil as possible with them. Soak new tubers overnight before planting.

SITUATION Will tolerate full sun but much better in light to moderate shade. Zones 4–9.

WATERING AND FEEDING Where growing in bare soil, mulch in spring and early fall. Top dress with bonemeal or a proprietary bulb fertilizer in early spring; and, if possible, give a liquid feed two or three times while in full leaf. Where established in grass, mulching is neither necessary nor practicable, but apply a fertilizer in early spring if possible.

Eranthis hyemalis

Eranthis – Gagea

Eremurus elwesii

MANAGEMENT Plants growing in bare soil will benefit from mulching. Leave the tubers undisturbed for as long as possible.
COMMON PROBLEMS None.
SIZE Attains a height of about 4in./10cm. within the first year and a spread of about 4in./10cm. with two years – although almost invariably planted in clumps.

Eremurus   FOXTAIL LILY

These must be among the tallest of all bulbous-rooted garden plants, forming elongated root tubers which are remarkably easy to break off. When well grown, these are wonderful plants but I find their conditions difficult to satisfy.
SOIL AND PLANTING Very well drained but also rich and preferably organic. Tubers should be planted carefully, roots spread out, and at a depth of about 3–4in./8–10cm.
SITUATION Full sun to very light shade with plenty of shelter from strong winds. Zones 5–8.
WATERING AND FEEDING It is very important to mulch in spring and early fall to provide frost protection for the young shoots, which can emerge very early in mild seasons. Feed with a balanced, general-purpose fertilizer in early spring, and again in midsummer.
MANAGEMENT They must be staked carefully, either with wraparound support if the clump is large enough, or with individual canes. Cut down flower spikes as the flowers fade and cut all growth down to soil level after the fall frosts.
COMMON PROBLEMS None.
SIZE This varies among species and hybrids but can reach up to $6\frac{1}{2}$–10 × 3ft./2–3 × 1m. so only plant them where they really do have room to grow.

Erythronium   DOG'S TOOTH VIOLET

Erythroniums are among the great under-appreciated delights of the bulbous plant world, principally, I think, because they are fairly expensive, but also because they tend to be disappointingly short-lived. One of the more durable species is *E. americanum*.
SOIL AND PLANTING Moist, rich, organic, and preferably slightly acidic. Plant tubers approximately 2in./5cm. deep.
SITUATION They are intolerant of full sun and require light to moderate shade. Zones 3–9.
WATERING AND FEEDING Mulch in spring and early fall and top dress with bonemeal or bulb fertilizer in early spring; if possible, liquid feed two or three times while in full leaf.
MANAGEMENT None required; ideally, erythroniums should be grown in an undisturbed woodland garden or shady bed. I think they tend to be shorter-lived when they have been disturbed and where the soil is not naturally organic and rich in leaf mold.
COMMON PROBLEMS None.
SIZE This varies slightly but most forms will reach a height of about 8–10in./20–25cm. within two years and spread to 4–6in./10–15cm. in the same time.

Erythronium dens-canis

Fritillaria

Although the genus *Fritillaria* is a very large one with over one hundred species, two rather contrasting types far outweigh all others in garden importance. The small snake's head fritillary (*F. meleagris*) is a rare European native plant of damp pastures, whereas the tall and very distinctive crown imperials (*F. imperialis*) are most at home in the herbaceous border; both share certain important cultivation features. Cultivation details about the relatively few other species commonly offered should be checked at the time of purchase.

SOIL AND PLANTING Moist but free draining and fairly rich for *F. imperialis*, wetter although not quite water-logged for *F. meleagris*. Snake's head bulbs should be planted approximately 2in./ 5cm. deep; crown imperial bulbs should be planted approximately 6in./15cm. deep on their sides: this is important to prevent water from collecting in the hollow where the stem emerges.

SITUATION Full sun to light shade. Zones 5–9.

WATERING AND FEEDING Mulch in spring and early fall (except where snake's heads are growing in grass, making this impossible). Top dress with bonemeal or a proprietary bulb fertilizer in early spring; if possible, give all types a liquid feed two or three times after blooming and while in full leaf.

MANAGEMENT Crown imperials may require light, wrap-around support if grown in an exposed site; their fleshy stems may be cut back six weeks after the flowers have faded, although by this time they will generally be rotting at the base and can easily be pulled away from below soil level. Snake's heads are best grown in fairly long grass which should not be mown until at least six weeks after the flowers fade. Fritillarias should not be moved once established because they will take several years to flower fully again, but old, non-flowering clumps eventually need dividing.

COMMON PROBLEMS None.

SIZE The snake's head fritillary will reach about 12in./30cm. in height after two years and spreads slowly to reach perhaps 8in./ 20cm. after seven or eight years. Crown imperials will reach a height of 3–5ft./1–1.5m. after two years and spread to around 1ft./30cm. after four or five years.

Fritillaria imperialis

Gagea

Small, spring-flowering bulbs with bright yellow, star-shaped flowers. Their growing conditions can be met by growing them in a rock garden or alpine bed. (These little bulbs are unknown to most American gardeners.)

SOIL AND PLANTING Light, preferably gritty, and free draining; tolerant of moderate acidity and alkalinity. The bulb bases should be at a depth equal to 2½ times their average diameter.

SITUATION Full sun but not too hot; they are best planted with the shelter of a large rock or larger plant nearby. Zones 4–9.

WATERING AND FEEDING Apply a very light mulch in spring and early fall. Top dress with bonemeal or a proprietary bulb fertilizer in early spring; if possible, give a liquid feed two or three

Gagea lutea

Galanthus nivalis

times after blooming and while in full leaf.

MANAGEMENT Allow foliage to die down naturally. The bulbs should not be lifted annually and are best left undisturbed.

COMMON PROBLEMS None.

SIZE They will reach 2–6 × 1–2in./5–15 × 2.5–5cm. after three or four years, depending on the species.

Galanthus SNOWDROP

Among the top half-dozen bulbous plants by almost anyone's reckoning, snowdrops are undemanding in their requirements and easy to grow once they are over the initial, slightly tricky, phase of establishment.

SOIL AND PLANTING Tolerant of most, but always best in moist but free draining and fairly rich organic soils. The bulbs should be planted with their bases at a depth equal to 2½–3 times their average diameter, but they may be difficult to establish from dormant bulbs and are better planted while in full leaf. Nurseries may sell snowdrops in this way, referred to as "in the green".

SITUATION They will tolerate full sun but are better in light to moderate or even deep shade. Zones 2–9.

WATERING AND FEEDING Mulch in spring and early fall. Top dress with bonemeal or a proprietary bulb fertilizer in early spring; if possible, give a liquid feed two or three times after blooming and while still in full leaf.

MANAGEMENT Do not cut back the foliage until at least six weeks after the flowers have faded, by which time it will be beginning to shrivel and before long can be pulled away like straw. In semi-natural situations, the foliage may simply be left to die away. The bulbs should not be lifted annually.

COMMON PROBLEMS None.

SIZE Height and vigor vary considerably between species. The commonest, *G. nivalis*, will attain about 6 × 3–4in./15 × 8–10cm. after four years, but some forms are shorter and others, most notably *G.* 'Atkinsii' and *G.* 'Sam Arnott', are much taller, reaching 14 × 3–4in./35 × 8–10cm. within two years.

Gladiolus

A plant that possibly divides the passions even more than the dahlia, but still almost certainly the most important non-hardy, corm-forming garden genus. There is nothing difficult about growing gladioli and in most gardens they will thrive and give a good display, in return for relatively little effort.

SOIL AND PLANTING Tolerant of most, provided it is not heavy and clayey, but always best in a fairly rich but free draining soil. Plant the corms with their bases at a depth equal to about 3 times their average diameter, and in succession from about ten to six weeks before the likelihood of the last frost. This will result in a succession of blooms.

SITUATION Full sun to very light shade, preferably with some shelter from cold winds. Two fairly hardy species, *G. byzantinus* and *G. covillei*, can stay in the garden all year in Zones 5–10.

WATERING AND FEEDING Work in a dressing of bonemeal or a proprietary bulb fertilizer about one week before planting, then mulch lightly over the corms after planting. Give a liquid feed high in potash every two weeks before and after flowering.

MANAGEMENT In all but the mildest areas (Zones 9–10), gladioli should be lifted and overwintered indoors. Around the time of the first fall frosts is safest, but it is also important to leave the corms in place for about six weeks after the flowers have been cut. If the first frosts are not too severe and mild weather returns, it may therefore be advantageous to leave the later-flowering plants in the ground for a few more weeks before lifting them. Once lifted, cut back the foliage to about 4in./10cm. above the corms and allow them to dry in a warm but airy place, out of full sun. Peel away the dead leaves and carefully remove any small daughter cormlets. Store corms and cormlets in separate paper bags in a frost-free place. In the spring, pot up the cormlets into pots of Jiffy Mix or good potting soil. Gladioli will require staking and this is done most neatly and effectively by tying them individually to slender canes, inserted close to each plant.

COMMON PROBLEMS Fungal corm rots; virus; thrips; slugs; voles (mice) may eat corms.

SIZE There are many dwarf species of gladioli suitable for the alpine garden but these tend to be grown only by specialists. The common, large-flowered garden hybrids will mostly attain 3–5ft. × 6–12in./1–1.5m. × 15–30cm. within the season, depending on variety. The smaller-flowered butterfly hybrids will reach about half to two thirds of these sizes.

Gladiolus Butterfly hybrid

Hyacinthoides   BLUEBELL

This is the name now used to describe the genus that was formerly *Endymion* and *Scilla*, but long known best as bluebells or wood hyacinth. Most bulb catalogues still list it as *Endymion* and offer two species, *E. hispanicus* (Spanish bluebells), and *E. non-scriptus* (English bluebells). They can be invasive in small gardens.

SOIL AND PLANTING Tolerates most, but, unlike the majority of bulbs, performs best in heavy soil and is a valuable carpeting species on clayey sites. Ideally, the bulbs should be planted with their bases at a depth equal to about 2½ times their average diameter, but will establish well even if planted carelessly.

SITUATION Tolerates full sun but performs much better in light to fairly deep shade; it is a plant of woodland glades. Zones 4–9.

WATERING AND FEEDING If practical, mulch in spring and early fall. Top dress with bonemeal or a proprietary bulb fertilizer in early spring.

MANAGEMENT Very little is required. The dead foliage and flower stems may be pulled away as they discolor, but in a semi-natural planting they will fade away of their own accord and self-mulch the bulbs.

COMMON PROBLEMS Rust.

SIZE Will attain a height of about 8in./20cm. and spread to about 4in./10cm. individually within two or three years; the groups will spread continuously to form a ground-covering carpet.

Hyacinthoides non-scripta

Hyacinthus 'Delft Blue'

Hyacinthus   HYACINTH

Perhaps because the hyacinth is best known as an indoor pot plant it is often neglected as a garden bulb; it is, however, a useful subject for a formal planting, and is attractive in large containers.

SOIL AND PLANTING Intolerant of water-logging and requires a fairly rich but free draining soil. In containers, use either a soil-less mixture, such as Jiffy Mix, or potting soil. The bulbs should be planted with their bases at a depth equal to $2\frac{1}{2}$ times their average diameter.

SITUATION Full sun; the plants will soon deteriorate in anything deeper than very light shade. Zones 4–9.

WATERING AND FEEDING Mulch in spring and early fall. Top dress with bonemeal or a proprietary bulb fertilizer in early spring; if possible, give a liquid feed two or three times after blooming and while still in full leaf.

MANAGEMENT Pull away the dead foliage and flower stems as they discolor. Once the top growth has died down, the bulbs may be lifted, dried off, and stored for replanting, or left in situ; in my experience, there is little difference in the results. Plants grown in containers can be lifted to make room for summer-flowering subjects. After indoor plants have finished flowering, cut down the old flower stems and continue to give a liquid feed until the leaves turn yellow. Then stop feeding, allow them to dry off, and remove them from the medium; they can be planted outdoors in the fall, but will not achieve the same quality of bloom, nor flower so early.

COMMON PROBLEMS Fungal bulb rots; slugs; mice eat bulbs.

SIZE About 8–10 × 4in./20–25 × 10cm. within the first year.

Iris

Iris is a large genus of about 250 species and many garden hybrids. Water-loving and alpine kinds are described on pages 186 and 173–4, but the most important group comprises the bearded irises and one or two slightly lesser-known groups grown as border perennials, such as *I. foetidissima* and the popular *I. sibirica*, Siberian iris. All are easy to grow if a few guidelines are adhered to.

SOIL AND PLANTING Rich, fairly moist but must be free draining; tolerant of alkalinity, but contrary to a widespread belief, this is not essential for success – the low-growing Pacific hybrids actually fare better in a slightly acid soil, although this, too, is not essential. *I. foetidissima* will thrive in very dry conditions. The rhizomes of bearded irises must be planted very carefully at the surface, so that the lateral roots are buried and anchored but the fleshy rhizomes themselves protrude. Other rhizomatous irises should be planted between 2 and 6in./5 and 15cm. deep, depending on their size. The bulbs of the Xiphium irises (which include the so-called Spanish and English irises) should be planted with their bases at a depth of $2\frac{1}{2}$ times their average diameter.

SITUATION Full sun, except for *I. foetidissima*, which tolerates moderate or even deep shade. Hardiness varies; many Zones 4–8.

WATERING AND FEEDING Mulch lightly in spring and early fall, taking care not to bury the rhizomes of bearded varieties completely. Top dress with bonemeal or a proprietary bulb fertilizer in early spring, and, if possible, give a liquid feed two or three times after blooming and while still in full leaf.

MANAGEMENT Irises should not require staking. Cut down the dead flower stem to the base and cut away any dead foliage as it appears during the summer. On bearded irises, cut back the fan of leaves in late fall to about 8in./20cm. above the base, and divide clumps every three or four years; dwarf Pacific hybrids, which, in my experience, take a long time to establish, should be left for six or seven years provided they are not showing signs of deterioration. Cut back the foliage of Xiphium irises as soon as it discolors – the new leaves arise very soon afterward. Divide them every five or six years. The evergreen *I. foetidissima* is best when simply tidied up in early spring and dead leaves cut away; it too should be divided every five or six years.

COMMON PROBLEMS On bearded irises, fungal rhizome rots; viruses; slugs; leaf spots. Other types are more or less trouble free.

SIZE This varies considerably. The dwarf bearded irises range from about 4 × 4in./10 × 10cm. up to 2 × 1ft./60 × 30cm. after three years. Medium-size irises range from about 1ft × 6in./30 × 15cm. to 2½ft. × 8in./80 × 20cm. Tall forms range upwards from about 3–4ft. × 8–12in./90–120 × 20–30cm. The Pacific hybrids reach about 10 × 6in./25 × 15cm. after three or four years. *I. foetidissima* reaches 2ft. × 6in./60 × 15cm. in the same time; the Xiphium irises; and Siberian irises about 2½–3ft. × 10in./80–90 × 25cm.

Iris Californian hybrid

Leucojum SNOWFLAKE

A quite superb small genus of plants that should be represented in every garden, especially by the cultivar called *L. aestivum* 'Gravetye Giant'. Usually called snowflakes and they flower when their similar, but much smaller, relatives the snowdrops fade.

SOIL AND PLANTING Tolerates most but performs best in moist, free draining, but rich soil; tolerant of moderate acidity and alkalinity. Bulbs should be planted with their bases at a depth equal to about 2½–3 times their average diameter.

SITUATION Tolerates full sun but performs best in light to moderate shade. Zones 4–10.

WATERING AND FEEDING Mulch in spring and early fall. Top dress with bonemeal or a proprietary bulb fertilizer in early spring; if possible, give a liquid feed two or three times after blooming and while still in full leaf.

MANAGEMENT Do not cut back foliage until at least six weeks after the flowers have faded, when it will still be fairly lush. The bulbs should not be lifted annually. Divide the clumps every four or five years if the clumps seem crowded.

COMMON PROBLEMS None.

SIZE The summer snowflake, as *L. aestivum* is called, reaches about 12in./30cm., but the taller 'Gravetye Giant' grows to about 18in./45cm. The spring snowflake, *L. vernum*, is earlier-blooming usually beginning as snowdrops (Galanthus spp.) finish. Its height is only about 5–6in./12–15cm.

Leucojum aestivum 'Gravetye Giant'

Lilium 'Citronella'

Lilium   LILY

Lilies need no introduction beyond dispelling their reputation for being difficult to grow. Many of the older varieties were certainly prone to deterioration through virus and other disease, but modern hybrids have few such vices; and there remain many hybrids that form magnificent garden plants, although in my experience they are best grown in pots – even if these are stood among the borders for the flowering period.

SOIL AND PLANTING The soil must be deep, rich, and free draining without ever drying out. In pots, use a mixture of good, potting or garden soil mixed with well-rotted compost, leaf mold, or Jiffy Mix. They will tolerate moderate acidity and alkalinity. Bulbs should be planted with their bases at a depth equal to 3 times their average diameter, except *L. candidum*, which should be planted just below the surface. Bulbs are sold in spring and fall.

SITUATION Full sun to moderate shade, depending on the variety, so check information carefully when buying. Some shelter from strong winds is desirable for tall lilies, but most modern hybrids are comparatively short. Zones 4–8.

WATERING AND FEEDING Mulch in spring and early fall with well-rotted leaf mold or compost to which bonemeal has been added; liquid feed two or three times after blooming and before the foliage yellows.

MANAGEMENT Do not cut back the stems until at least six weeks after the flowers have faded. The bulbs should not be lifted annually and in the open ground they may be left for seven or more years before the clumps are divided. In pots, divide every four years. Tall lilies require staking, either with wrap-around, interlocking metal stakes, or with individual slender canes.

COMMON PROBLEMS Virus; lily beetle; botrytis gray mold; mice.

SIZE This differs according to the lily; the lower-growing lilies, such as many of the modern hybrids, will reach about 3 × 1ft./1m. × 30cm. after two years' growth; others, such as *L. henryi*, can be as much as 10 × 1ft./3m. × 30cm. in favorable conditions after the same time, so check label information carefully.

Muscari   GRAPE HYACINTH

Small, pretty, and decidedly invasive, most muscaris are not trustworthy plants for confined spaces. They are exceptionally easy to grow, however, and, if you need a plant to fill paving cracks over a wide area, then this is it.

SOIL AND PLANTING Will tolerate all. The bulbs should ideally be planted at a depth equal to $2\frac{1}{2}$ times their average diameter, but in practice you can simply drop them and they will establish.

SITUATION Full sun to light shade. Zones 2–10.

WATERING AND FEEDING Scarcely necessary, but if you want particularly lush plants of selected cultivars mulch in spring and early fall; top dress with bonemeal or a proprietary bulb fertilizer in early spring; and, if possible, give a liquid feed two or three times after blooming.

Muscari latifolium

MANAGEMENT None necessary, apart from pulling out all the unwanted seedlings.

COMMON PROBLEMS None.

SIZE All of the common species, including *M. neglectum*, which is the really invasive one, will attain 6 × 4in./15 × 10cm. after three years, but bear in mind that they self-seed prolifically and each seedling will have the same growth potential.

Narcissus

By far the most important genus of garden bulbs, embracing a huge number of hybrids that are popularly divided into the long-trumpeted and the long- and short-cupped daffodils – although experts recognize ten more divisions. Most are easy to grow and undemanding and most will also naturalize well, although some hybrids raised for the show bench are fickle things. In general, the more costly the individual cultivar, the more likely it is to fail as a garden plant; although conversely, cheap or job-lot mixtures will probably be of the right variety but of poor quality.

SOIL AND PLANTING Tolerant of most, even very wet soil provided it drains freely in the summer. Tolerant of moderate acidity or alkalinity. In containers, use garden soil, or half soil and half Jiffy Mix. Plant the bulbs with their bases at a depth equal to $2\frac{1}{2}$ times their average diameter.

SITUATION Full sun to light shade; tolerant of strong winds. Zones 4–10 for most.

WATERING AND FEEDING Mulch in spring and early fall. Top dress with bonemeal or a proprietary bulb fertilizer in early spring. When planting new bulbs, mix bonemeal in the soil.

MANAGEMENT Do not cut back the stems until at least six weeks after the flowers have faded, and never tie the leaves in knots. The bulbs may be lifted, dried, and stored for replanting in the fall, but such a work-intensive effort is hardly necessary except with container-grown plants. They may also be left to naturalize with no disturbance at all; if necessary divide large clumps every five or six years in the fall.

Narcissus bulbocodium

Narcissus – Sisyrinchium

Nerine bowdenii

COMMON PROBLEMS Blindness, caused by too-shallow planting, not feeding, shade, overcrowding, or attack by narcissus fly.
SIZE Most of the large trumpet daffodils will reach 12–15 × 8in./30–40 × 20cm. after three years, but there are also some charming dwarf species and cultivars like 'Tete-A-Tete', 6in./15cm. tall.

Nerine

Close relatives of narcissi but needing much gentler conditions and careful planting. *N. bowdenii* is the species most likely to succeed in gardens, but all species make good summer pot plants.
SOIL AND PLANTING Light, free draining but fairly rich; they will not succeed in impoverished conditions. The bulbs must be planted shallowly with their tips just protruding.
SITUATION Full sun; not successful in shade or when exposed to cold winds. Zones 8–10 for *N. bowdenii*; most others 9–10.
WATERING AND FEEDING Mulch lightly in spring and early fall, taking care not to cover the bulbs deeply. Top dress with bonemeal or a proprietary bulb fertilizer in early spring; liquid feed two or three times after blooming and while still in full leaf.
MANAGEMENT Do not cut back the foliage until six weeks after the flowers have faded, and leave the bulbs undisturbed for as long as possible. In cold climates, overwinter potted plants in a cool but frost-free room. Water until leaves fade.
COMMON PROBLEMS None.
SIZE Will reach about 1½ft. × 6in./50 × 15cm. after three years.

Ornithogalum   STAR OF BETHLEHEM

Most ornithogalums are useful little white-flowered bulbs for filling in odd corners. Never plant the species *O. umbellatum* (Zones 4–10), as it will very soon become an ineradicable weed.
SOIL AND PLANTING Almost any, although least successful in very heavy, wet conditions. Bulbs should be planted with their bases at a depth equal to 2½ times their average diameter.
SITUATION Full sun to light shade. Most species Zones 6–10.
WATERING AND FEEDING Mulch in spring and early fall. Top dress with bonemeal or bulb fertilizer in early spring; if possible, liquid feed two or three times after blooming.
MANAGEMENT None necessary; allow foliage to die down naturally and do not lift the bulbs each year.
COMMON PROBLEMS None.
SIZE Some species will reach about 8 × 4in./20 × 10cm. after two years, although there are a few taller species such as *O. saundersiae*, which reaches over 3ft./1m.; and *O. nutans*, to 2ft./60cm.

Schizostylis   KAFFIR LILY

A distinctive, relatively easy to grow, and vigorous member of the iris family, yet more closely resembling gladioli with its flower spikes and grassy leaves.
SOIL AND PLANTING Well drained, rich, moist, and preferably fairly organic; tolerant of moderate acidity and alkalinity. Plant

Ornithogalum saundersiae

the rhizomes at a depth of about 4in./10cm.

SITUATION Full sun to very light shade. Zones 8–10.

WATERING AND FEEDING Mulch in spring and early fall. Top dress with a general-purpose fertilizer in spring.

MANAGEMENT Cut down old flower heads after flowering and cut back all growth above ground to soil level in the fall. Schizostylis should not require staking, but they are vigorous and should be divided every three years in spring.

COMMON PROBLEMS None.

SIZE Will reach about 2ft. × 10–8in./60 × 25–20cm. in three years.

Scilla   SQUILL

Among the prettiest and certainly the bluest of spring bulbs, scillas are extremely easy to grow and require the minimum of attention; no garden should be without them.

SOIL AND PLANTING Well drained, preferably fairly rich, and moist; tolerant of moderate acidity and alkalinity. Bulbs should be planted with their bases at a depth equal to $2\frac{1}{2}$ times their average diameter.

SITUATION Full sun to very light shade. Zones 2–9 for most.

WATERING AND FEEDING Mulch in spring and early fall. Top dress with bonemeal or a proprietary bulb fertilizer in early spring; if possible, give a liquid feed two or three times after blooming. Do not lift annually but divide the clumps every five or six years after flowering.

MANAGEMENT None necessary; allow the foliage to die down naturally and do not lift the bulbs each year.

COMMON PROBLEMS None.

SIZE They will reach about 6 × 2in./15 × 5cm. after four years.

Sisyrinchium   BLUE-EYED GRASS

These are barely bulbous in the strict sense, having very short or non-existent rhizomes, but as members of the iris family they are most conveniently dealt with here. *Sisyrinchium* is a large genus with relatively few garden representatives: the majority of these are small plants with grass-like leaves. The native *S. angustifolium* is sometimes offered in wildflower and bulb catalogues.

SOIL AND PLANTING Well drained, gritty, moderately rich; tolerant of moderate acidity and alkalinity. Plant rhizomes or roots with their tops at a depth of about 2–3in./5–8cm., depending on their size.

SITUATION Full sun to light or even moderate shade. Zones 7–8.

WATERING AND FEEDING Mulch in spring and early fall. Top dress with bonemeal or a proprietary bulb fertilizer in early spring; if possible, give a liquid feed two or three times after the bulbs have finished blooming.

MANAGEMENT None necessary; allow the foliage to die down naturally and do not lift the plants each year.

COMMON PROBLEMS None.

SIZE Depending on species and cultivars, ranges between 6 × 4in./ 15 × 10cm. and 2 × 1ft./60 × 30cm. in three or four years.

Schizostylis coccinea
Scilla siberica
Sisyrinchium striatum

Sternbergia lutea

Sternbergia

An important, if neglected, genus of predominantly fall-flowering bulbs, looking rather like crocuses and with mainly yellow flowers. They are not difficult to grow, although their site requirements are certainly much more demanding than those of real crocuses. *S. lutea* is most offered in USA.

SOIL AND PLANTING Sternbergias will tolerate most soils, but with the very important proviso that it must dry out thoroughly in summer. Bulbs should be planted with their bases at a depth equal to about $2\frac{1}{2}$ times their average diameter.

SITUATION Full sun with shelter from cold winds; the bulbs must be subjected to very hot and dry conditions during the summer if they are to flower satisfactorily. Zones 6–9.

WATERING AND FEEDING Mulch in spring and early fall. Top dress with bonemeal or a proprietary bulb fertilizer in early spring; if possible, give a liquid feed two or three times after the bulbs have finished blooming.

MANAGEMENT None necessary; allow the foliage to die down naturally and leave the bulbs undisturbed.

COMMON PROBLEMS None.

SIZE Depending on species and cultivar, ranges between 1 × 2in./2 × 5cm. and 3 × 4in./8 × 10cm. in three years.

Trillium WOOD LILY

Wood lilies, or Trinity flowers (so called because most of their parts occur in threes), are members of the lily family but are barely bulbous in the strict sense for they simply have a thick, stubby rhizome. They are easy to grow given the right conditions but will disappoint otherwise. They are best in woodland gardens.

SOIL AND PLANTING Moist, well drained, organic, and preferably rich in leaf mold; tolerant of moderate acidity or alkalinity. Rhizomes should be planted approximately 2in./5cm. deep.

SITUATION Light to fairly deep shade with shelter from winds; the plants are called wood lilies for good reason.

WATERING AND FEEDING Mulch in spring and early fall. Top dress with bonemeal or a proprietary bulb fertilizer in early spring; if possible, liquid feed two or three times after blooming.

MANAGEMENT None necessary; allow the foliage to die down naturally and leave the bulbs undisturbed.

COMMON PROBLEMS None.

SIZE The most common species, *T. grandiflorum*, white wake robin, will reach 1 × 1ft./30 × 30cm. after three or four years.

Trillium grandiflorum

Tulipa TULIP

After daffodils, these are the major spring-flowering bulbs. Although there are 15 tulip classes, as far as culture is concerned, they can be divided into two major groups: the dwarf species and hybrids; and the generally taller hybrid varieties – of which the Darwin hybrids are the best known. They can all, however, be grown in more or less the same soil and site conditions.

SOIL AND PLANTING Tolerant of most except those that are very heavy, clayey, cold, or water-logged; tolerant of moderate acidity or alkalinity. In containers, use garden or potting soil, or half soil and half Jiffy Mix. Bulbs should be planted with their bases at a depth equal to $2\frac{1}{2}$ times their average diameter.

SITUATION Full sun to light shade. The low-growing species are tolerant of strong winds but the hybrids, especially the very tall ones, benefit from some shelter. Zones 3–7.

WATERING AND FEEDING Mulch in spring and early fall. Top dress with bonemeal or bulb fertilizer in early spring; liquid feed two or three times after blooming and while in full leaf. When planting bulbs, mix bonemeal in the soil.

MANAGEMENT Do not cut back the foliage until at least six weeks after the flowers have faded. The species are best left in the ground to naturalize (so should be planted where they may be left undisturbed), and their foliage will gradually die away and shrivel. The foliage on the taller hybrids, however, tends to die down gracelessly but this can be hidden by surrounding perennials, or when flowers fade transplant bulbs to an inconspicuous spot. When the foliage has finally died down, they should be lifted and the bulbs dried off and stored. The species tulips need no support and the tall hybrids never look attractive when staked; but if it is impossible to plant them with good wind protection, use slender, green, split canes and tie each plant to these unobtrusively.

COMMON PROBLEMS Slugs; virus; fire disease; bulb rots; mice.

SIZE This differs greatly depending on species and hybrids, so check label information carefully. Most of the species will attain about $4–12 \times 8$in./$10–30 \times 20$cm. in their first year, but some of the taller hybrids can be at least 2ft. $\times$ 10in./60×25cm.

Tulipa tarda

Zantedeschia ARUM OR CALLA LILY

A genus that could appear in a number of categories for it is sometimes grown as a border perennial and in water gardens; it is also a summer pot plant in the North. Undeniably beautiful, the plants frequently cause disappointment as their site requirements are strict.

SOIL AND PLANTING Moist but free draining border soil, or, if grown in pots, rich, organic potting soil offers the best conditions. *Z. aethiopica* will grow in water gardens in several inches of water. Tubers should be planted $4–6$in./$10–15$cm. deep.

SITUATION Full sun to light shade, with shelter from cold winds. In colder areas, the plant is best grown in pots or lifted in the fall and stored indoors over winter. Zones 8–10.

WATERING AND FEEDING Mulch in spring and early fall. Top dress with bonemeal or bulb fertilizer in early spring; liquid feed two or three times after blooming and while still in full leaf.

MANAGEMENT As these are evergreen plants, do not cut back the foliage. They should not require staking.

COMMON PROBLEMS Leaf spot; tuber rots.

SIZE Differs with species and hybrids but the more common forms will reach $1\frac{1}{2}–3 \times 1\frac{1}{2}–2\frac{1}{2}$ft./$50$cm. $–1$m. $\times 45–75$cm. after three or four years.

Zantedeschia aethiopica

167

ROCK PLANTS

Alyssum
Androsace
Arabis
Armeria
Aubrieta
Campanula
Crassula
Dianthus
Dodecatheon
Gentiana
Helianthemum
Iberis
Iris

Lewisia
Myosotis
Oxalis
Primula
Pulsatilla
Raoulia
Saponaria
Saxifraga
Sedum
Sempervivum
Silene
Viola

Principles of care

To avoid giving the impression that the plants in this chapter are subjects only for the specialist, I have chosen to define them loosely as rock plants rather than alpines. The term "alpines" covers a vast spectrum of species, almost all of them exquisite but many of them demanding in their cultivation and only really able to thrive in the protection of an alpine greenhouse. "Rock plant", on the other hand, suggests something a little more robust and easily capable of being grown in a rock garden, trough, hollow wall, or similar site outdoors. For convenience, I have also included here a few non-rock-garden species belonging to predominantly rock plant genera but have indicated where their needs differ from those of rock plants in general.

Soil and site requirements

Most rock plants come from mountainous areas (although certainly not all from the Alps), and the one feature that almost all have in common is a need for a gritty, free draining soil. They will not grow in clay, and if that is your natural garden soil then you will need to resort to containers or raised beds. For most species grown in containers use a mixture of equal parts of loamy soil, peat moss, and stone chips, with a shallow topping of coarse gravel or chips on the surface.

Most rock plants also share a need for sun, and, while a few are tolerant of light shade, certainly none will thrive in really deep shadow. Not surprising, they are tolerant of low winter temperatures and snow, but not cold, clinging dampness and may require protection in the form of cloches or glass coverings during the worst spells of cold, wet lowland weather. If you live in a particularly damp region, you will be wise to avoid growing rock plants with silvery, hairy, or woolly leaves, which are especially prone to rotting. Strong winds, in general, present no problems, although the less robust species need some shelter from winter gales.

General management

Apart from the occasional need for shelter, a very little fertilizer in fall and spring and, with a few of the more vigorous types, a light clipping after flowering, there is not a great deal to be managed. Be sure regularly to remove any dead leaves that accumulate around the plants, as these absorb moisture which in turn leads very quickly to rotting of the crown. As far as fertilizer is concerned, I would recommend using bonemeal in the fall, which slowly releases phosphate and encourages root development but also contains a little nitrogen for leaf growth. A very light dressing with an organic fertilizer such as Gardentone in spring completes the feeding routine, although care should be taken during any drought periods in summer to water regularly. Organic mulches should never be used.

Provided that damp conditions can be avoided, there should be little trouble with botrytis or other fungal molds. There are few difficulties with pests, although slugs and aphids can be troublesome. The use of coarse grit over the soil surface will help to deter the former while vigilance and a contact insecticide spray should cope with the latter.

Rock garden sites

CHOOSE a site for each plant that is appropriate to its needs: some prefer soil-filled crevices, some will tolerate the shade cast by the rocks themselves.

Alyssum

Some of the annual and perennial alyssums have changed their names in recent years, one being the popular basket-of-gold which is now *Aurinia saxatilis* – but still known as alyssum.

SOIL Light, well drained, fairly rich.

SITUATION Full sun. Zones 3–8.

WATERING AND FEEDING Lightly top dress with bonemeal in fall, and apply a very light dressing of an organic fertilizer such as Gardentone in early spring.

MANAGEMENT Perennial alyssums, including the yellow-flow-ered *A. saxatilis*, may be trimmed back fairly hard after flowering to maintain a neat appearance.

COMMON PROBLEMS None.

PROPAGATION Softwood cuttings in spring, or grow from seed (the best and most compact forms of *A. saxatilis* do not, however, come true from seed).

SIZE The compact forms of *Aurinia saxatilis* will reach 8 × 12in./ 20 × 30cm. after three years, but other perennial species, such as *Alyssum montanum*, are even more compact.

Aurinia saxatilis

Androsace   ROCK JASMINE

This genus includes some of the best-loved alpine plants, even if they need more care than many others. They will benefit from some protection in most areas.

SOIL Light, well drained, fairly rich, preferably slightly acidic.

SITUATION Sun, shelter from winds and dampness. Zones 4–8.

WATERING AND FEEDING Lightly top dress with bonemeal in fall, and apply a very light dressing of an organic fertilizer such as Gardentone in early spring.

MANAGEMENT The enemy of androsaces is clinging dampness; the best way to prevent moisture from accumulating in the leaf rosette is to protect the plants with small cloches in the coldest, wettest part of the winter.

COMMON PROBLEMS Botrytis gray mold will attack tissues damaged by moisture; aphids can also be troublesome.

PROPAGATION Softwood cuttings in late spring, or some forms from seed.

SIZE Most will reach about 2–3 × 4–6in./5–8 × 10–15cm. in three or four years, although some are more wide spreading.

Androsace carnea

Arabis   ROCK CRESS

There are several genera of attractive little rock garden plants that belong, improbably, to the cabbage family, but arabis is one of the best. The silvery *A. caucasica* is hardy in much of the North. The delightful *A. blepharophylla* is native to coastal California.

SOIL Light, well drained, moderately rich; prefers slightly alkaline.

SITUATION Full sun. Varies, Zones 6–8 for *A. caucasica*.

WATERING AND FEEDING Top dress lightly with bonemeal in fall; very lightly with an organic fertilizer such as Gardentone in early spring.

Arabis caucasica

Arabis – Dianthus

Armeria maritima

MANAGEMENT A neat appearance will be encouraged by trimming back lightly after flowering.

COMMON PROBLEMS None.

PROPAGATION Softwood cuttings in summer, or from seed.

SIZE *A. blepharophylla* is fairly typical in forming a compact mat of 4–6 × 4–6in./10–15 × 10–15cm. after about three years.

Armeria

Included in this genus are some of the easiest to grow of rock garden plants; the forms derived from the wild sea thrift, *A. maritima*, are the most common, and are particularly rewarding.

SOIL Light, free draining, intolerant of clay; armeria is tolerant of high alkalinity.

SITUATION Full sun. Zones 5–7.

WATERING AND FEEDING Lightly top dress with bonemeal in fall, and apply a very light dressing of an organic fertilizer such as Gardentone in early spring.

MANAGEMENT Immediately after flowering trim back dead flower heads with shears and lightly trim the shoot tips.

COMMON PROBLEMS None.

PROPAGATION Basal cuttings in late summer, or from seed.

SIZE Reaches about 4 × 6in./10 × 15cm. in five years.

Aubrieta

These are very familiar spring-flowering perennials, with red, mauve, and bluish flowers. They are most commonly grown as mixtures from seed.

SOIL Tolerant of most, but always best when the soil is light and free draining. Wall crevices provide exactly the right conditions.

SITUATION Full sun or very light shade. Zones 4–8.

WATERING AND FEEDING Lightly top dress with bonemeal in fall, and apply a very light dressing of an organic fertilizer such as Gardentone in early spring.

MANAGEMENT Trim back dead flower heads with shears immediately after flowering, trimming well into the plant even if the result is bare and unsightly: this will restore the rounded clump shape but the plants tend to be short-lived.

COMMON PROBLEMS Mildew; flea beetles.

PROPAGATION Basal cuttings in summer, or some from seed.

SIZE Reaches about 8 × 30cm/3 × 12in over three years.

Aubrieta 'Riverslea'

Campanula   BELLFLOWER

Campanula is a large, diverse, and distinctive genus with annuals and border perennials (see page 111) among its species. For the rock garden, there are neat, compact delights like *C. cochleariifolia*, as well as some very invasive forms, most notably *C. portenschlagiana* and *C. poscharskyana*: these can become a menace, but are lovely where they can be allowed free rein through a stone wall.

SOIL Light, well drained, moderately rich, and preferably slightly alkaline.

SITUATION Tolerates full sun but better in light shade. Zones 3–9 for many.
WATERING AND FEEDING Top dress lightly with bonemeal in fall and with an organic fertilizer in spring.
MANAGEMENT None usually necessary, but the more vigorous forms may be lightly trimmed back after flowering.
COMMON PROBLEMS None.
PROPAGATION Division in early spring, softwood cuttings in summer, or some forms from seed.
SIZE The more desirable and compact species, such as the popular *C. carpatica*, will reach about 4 × 12in./10 × 30cm. after three years, but there is a wide range in vigor among the rock garden species so check label information.

Campanula cochleariifolia

Crassula

There are many tender species of *Crassula* grown as house plants, but also a few that are well worth growing in mild areas. Do choose carefully, however, and if necessary take expert advice because I have often seen species offered for sale that will be most unlikely to survive for long outdoors.
SOIL Light, very well drained soil, preferably gritty, and slightly alkaline.
SITUATION Full sun or light shade, depending on the species; the hardiest, such as *C. sarcocaulis*, are better in full sun with shelter from cold winds and moisture. Zones 8–10.
WATERING AND FEEDING Lightly top dress with bonemeal in fall, and apply a very light dressing of an organic fertilizer such as Gardentone in early spring.
MANAGEMENT None necessary.
COMMON PROBLEMS None.
PROPAGATION Softwood cuttings in summer, or some forms from seed.
SIZE *C. sarcocaulis* is a tiny shrubby species, reaching 10–12 × 10–12in./25–30 × 25–30cm. after three or four years. *C. lactea*, a semi-shrubby species 1–2ft./30–60cm. tall, and *C. schmidtii*, a 4in./10cm. high mat are both used in West Coast rock gardens.

Dianthus   PINK

A large and important genus, including rock garden forms as well as several good plants for the front of the border (border carnations and some of the larger pinks especially). They must all have sun and rather precise soil conditions.
SOIL Light and free draining; tolerant of high alkalinity and never really successful in acid soils.
SITUATION Full sun or very light shade. Many species are suitable for rock crevices and a few, such as *D. pavonius* (*D. neglectus*) tolerant of being walked on, so make good subjects for growing between paving slabs. Hardiness varies; Zones 3–8 for many.
WATERING AND FEEDING Lightly top dress with bonemeal in fall, and apply a very light dressing of organic fertilizer such as Gardentone in early spring.

Crassula sp.

Dianthus – Iris

Dianthus deltoides

MANAGEMENT Immediately after flowering, trim back any dead flower heads, using shears on large plants. On the larger-growing forms trim an inch or so into the shoots to encourage bushiness. Many plants – especially the larger border species – soon become straggly and should be replaced with new plants every four years.

COMMON PROBLEMS Slugs; fungal leaf spots.

PROPAGATION Shoot tip cuttings or basal cuttings in summer after flowering; layering or basal cuttings in late summer; some species from seed.

SIZE Varies considerably; border carnations and some of the pinks will reach about $2\frac{1}{2} \times 1$ft./75×30cm. after three years, whereas many of the true rock garden species will barely exceed 2×2in./5×5cm. in twice that time.

Dodecatheon   SHOOTING STAR

These are exquisitely lovely and always arouse attention, but they are not widely grown, probably more because of expense than difficulty. They are rarely offered by nurseries. Like cyclamen, they are members of the primrose family.

SOIL Moist, fairly rich, but well drained.

SITUATION Full sun to light shade. Zones 5–7 for some.

WATERING AND FEEDING Lightly top dress with bonemeal in fall, and apply a very light dressing of an organic fertilizer such as Gardentone in early spring.

MANAGEMENT None needed.

COMMON PROBLEMS None.

PROPAGATION Division in early spring, or from seed.

SIZE The commonest species is *D. meadia*, which will reach about 8×6in./20×15cm. after three years, although there are smaller and more compact forms, too.

Dodecatheon meadia

Gentiana

One of the most exquisite and important rock garden genera with some easy and some extremely difficult species. The correct soil conditions are especially critical, for some are lime tolerant and some emphatically not.

SOIL Varies with species. Most require moist but fairly well-drained, organic, acid soils, preferably with a high peat content. The late summer-flowering *G. septemfida* can be successful on rather heavier and alkaline soils. *G. angustifolia* and *G. clusii* are lime tolerant. The exquisite *G. acaulis* is lime tolerant but notoriously and inexplicably reluctant to flower.

SITUATION Full sun or very light shade. As a general guide, the Asiatic gentians are better in very light shade, whereas the European and New Zealand types are best in full sun. Hardiness varies; Zones 4–9 for some.

WATERING AND FEEDING Top dress lightly with bonemeal in fall; and very lightly with an organic fertilizer such as Gardentone in early spring.

MANAGEMENT None needed, although dead flower heads may be carefully snipped off immediately after flowering.

Gentiana asclepiadea

COMMON PROBLEMS Fungal leaf spots.
PROPAGATION Basal cuttings in spring, division in spring, or some species from seed.
SIZE Varies between species; the largest, such as the willow gentian, *G. asclepiadea*, have stems that reach 2½ft./75cm. and spread to perhaps 1ft./30cm. in three or four years. The typical, mound-forming gentians become a hummock of 6–12in./15–30cm. diameter, from which flowering stems rise to about 8–12in./20–30cm.

Helianthemum 'Wisley Pink'

Helianthemum SUN ROSE

This is not the only genus with this common name but it is appropriate, for helianthemums must have dry, warm conditions to succeed. Most tend to be too vigorous for troughs, but in larger rock gardens in mild areas they are admirable. *H. nummularium* is a hardy species for the North (Zones 4–8).
SOIL Light, well drained, gritty; helianthemums are tolerant of moderate alkalinity or acidity.
SITUATION Full sun, preferably with shelter from cold winds.
WATERING AND FEEDING Top dress lightly with bonemeal in fall; very lightly with an organic fertilizer in early spring.
MANAGEMENT Trim lightly after flowering for neatness.
COMMON PROBLEMS None.
PROPAGATION Semi-ripe cuttings in early summer, or some forms from seed.
SIZE Most of the common species and cultivars will reach about 8–12 × 8–12in./20–30 × 20–30cm. after three or four years.

Iberis CANDYTUFT

A genus from the cabbage family that includes a few choice rock garden species. Most form miniature sub-shrubs.
SOIL Light, well drained, preferably slightly alkaline.
SITUATION Full sun. Zones 4–8.
WATERING AND FEEDING Top dress lightly with bonemeal in fall; very lightly with an organic fertilizer in early spring.
MANAGEMENT Larger plants may be trimmed lightly after they have finished flowering to maintain a neat appearance.
COMMON PROBLEMS None.
PROPAGATION From seed; the shrubby species from semi-ripe cuttings in spring.
SIZE The common shrubby species such as *I. sempervirens* will reach about 1 × 2ft./30 × 60cm. after three years, although more compact forms exist of this and other species.

Iris

Water-loving and bulbous forms of iris are covered on pages 158 and 186, a reflection of the size, importance and diversity of this genus. For the rock garden, the important and easiest species are the small bulbous irises, especially the bluish *I. reticulata* and *I. histrioides*, and the yellow *I. danfordiae*, although the specialist alpine gardener will wish to try other, rarer species.

Iberis sempervirens

Iris – Primula

Iris danfordiae

SOIL Well drained, moist, fairly rich; tolerant of moderate alkalinity and acidity. The bulbs should be planted with their bases at a depth equal to at least 3 times their average diameter.

SITUATION Full sun or very light shade. Zones 5–9.

WATERING AND FEEDING Top dress lightly with bonemeal in fall; very lightly with organic fertilizer in early spring.

MANAGEMENT None needed, although dead flower heads may be carefully snipped off immediately after flowering and the long grassy leaves cut back at least six weeks later. *I. danfordiae* is notoriously reluctant to bloom after the first or second season, for it forms masses of small daughter bulbs that take many years to reach maturity. The only success seems to come from planting them very deeply about 8in./20cm. deep.

COMMON PROBLEMS None.

PROPAGATION Not feasible, other than by the natural multiplication of the bulbs.

SIZE Flower stems range in height from about 4in./10cm. for *I. danfordiae* to about 8in./20cm. for some of the blue-flowered hybrids, and the flimsy, grassy leaves may be 2ft./60cm. long. All will spread to about 2in./5–6cm. after three years.

Lewisia

Almost the archetypal alpine, small with a rosette of leaves (evergreen in some species), pretty in a very individual way, and demanding, not to say odd, in the conditions it requires. Lewisias are among the most admired of rock garden plants but duplicating their mountainous Western habitats can be difficult.

SOIL Moist, but very well drained, especially after flowering; intolerant of any alkalinity.

SITUATION Full sun. Lewisias are quite intolerant of any water lying in the leaf rosette, and are best planted almost vertically in soil-filled crevices in the sides of rocks. Zones 3–8 for some.

WATERING AND FEEDING Top dress lightly with bonemeal in fall; very lightly with an organic fertilizer such as Gardentone in early spring. A collar of stone chips around plants helps.

MANAGEMENT Dead flower heads may be carefully snipped off immediately after flowering, and some protection provided by a sheet of glass during cold wet weather in winter.

COMMON PROBLEMS None.

PROPAGATION Most are best from seed, although basal cuttings taken carefully in summer may also be successful.

SIZE Varies with species, ranging from 2×2in./5×5cm. to 6×6in./15×15cm. in three years.

Lewisia cotyledon

Myosotis   FORGET-ME-NOT

There are forget-me-nots suitable for the border, some annual forms, and some aquatic species. The most choice, however, are the alpines, such as the blue-flowered European *M. alpestris*, and the white-flowered New Zealand species. The species grown in North America are mostly *M. scorpioides* and *M. sylvatica*.

SOIL Well drained, fairly gritty, tolerant of moderate acidity and

alkalinity. Non-alpine species are tolerant of wet conditions.
SITUATION Full sun or light shade. Zones 4–8.
WATERING AND FEEDING Top dress lightly with bonemeal in fall; very lightly with an organic fertilizer in early spring.
MANAGEMENT Dead flower heads may be trimmed back.
COMMON PROBLEMS Mildew.
PROPAGATION Most are best from seed although basal cuttings taken carefully in summer may also be successful.
SIZE The alpine forms reach 5–8 × 3–4in./12–20 × 8–10cm. in about three years. Non-alpine species are of a similar height but are more spreading and straggly.

Myosotis alpestris

Oxalis WOOD SORREL

Oxalis includes some very pretty and easy-to-grow alpines (and some rather larger forms suitable for borders), as well as a few of the most invasive of all garden plants. *O. adenophylla* is one of the best, and *O. latifolia* and *O. pes-caprae* are the ones to avoid.
SOIL Well drained, fairly gritty soil; is tolerant of moderate acidity and alkalinity.
SITUATION Full sun to light shade; among the more shade-tolerant alpines. Hardiness varies; Zones 7–10 for *O. adenophylla*.
WATERING AND FEEDING Lightly top dress with bonemeal in fall, and very lightly with an organic fertilizer in early spring.
MANAGEMENT None needed.
COMMON PROBLEMS None.
PROPAGATION Most are best from seed, although basal cuttings, offsets, or division in early summer are also successful. The invasive weed species spread by means of bulbils.
SIZE Varies slightly between species but *O. adenophylla* will reach about 2 × 4in./5 × 10cm. in three years.

Primula PRIMROSE

One of the loveliest and most important genera of ornamental garden plants, included in this chapter because most of the major species are small and appropriate for an alpine or rock garden.
SOIL AND SITUATION The requirements vary widely (Zones 3–8 for most hardy species):
Candelabra primulas including *P. aurantiaca*, *P. bulleyana*, *P. chungensis*, *P. helodoxa* (*P. prolifera*), *P.* 'Inverewe', *P. japonica*, *P. pulverulenta*; also *P. rosea* and *P. sikkimensis*: constantly moist soil and full sun or light shade.
Border auriculas (derived from *P. auricula*), the drumstick primula (*P. denticulata*), Gold Lace primulas, polyanthus, the common primrose (*P. vulgaris*), and the many double forms and hybrids derived from it and related species, including the popular cultivar 'Wanda', the cowslip (*P. veris*), and *P. vialii*: moist but well-drained soil in full sun or light to moderate shade. I find *P. veris* is always better in full sun and slightly drier conditions.
P. alpicola, *P. bhutanica*, the oxlip (*P. elatior*), and the bird's eye primrose (*P. farinosa*): peaty or acid, gritty soil in full sun or partial shade.

Oxalis adenophylla

Primula auricula

WATERING AND FEEDING Those species growing in well-drained soils require a light top dressing of bonemeal in fall and a very light dressing of an organic fertilizer in early spring. Those in more moist soil should be lightly mulched in fall and spring and given a balanced organic fertilizer in early spring.

MANAGEMENT Primulas are at their best when allowed to self-seed, so don't cut back the dead flower heads. Divide every three years after flowering (this is most important with primulas of the primrose and polyanthus type).

COMMON PROBLEMS Leaf-eating pests; virus.

PROPAGATION Most are best from seed, although division immediately after flowering is also successful.

SIZE Varies considerably; in general, the moisture-loving species are the largest. *P. florindae*, for example, will reach 3 × 2ft./1m. × 60cm. after three years; while many of the alpine species will barely exceed 2 × 3in./5 × 8cm. in the same time.

Pulsatilla   PASQUE FLOWER

These are like low-growing anemones (they are often classified under *Anemone*) with hairy flowers and feathery foliage. Their richly colored and spectacular flowers are among the delights of the alpine garden in spring.

SOIL Moist but free draining, fairly rich.

SITUATION Full sun. Zones 5–7.

WATERING AND FEEDING Lightly top dress with bonemeal in fall, and apply a very light dressing of organic fertilizer such as Gardentone in early spring.

MANAGEMENT None necessary; do not disturb once established.

COMMON PROBLEMS None.

PROPAGATION Best from seed; root cuttings in winter are also successful but disturbing established plants risks losing some.

SIZE Varies slightly among species but most will reach 6–12 × 8in./15–30 × 20cm. after three or four years.

Pulsatilla vulgaris

Raoulia

Uniquely appealing, forming a neat, very dense mat; some species are more like a fine green carpet than any other living plants. *R. australis* is grown in colder parts of the Pacific Coast.

SOIL Light, gritty, well drained but not dry.

SITUATION Full sun to light shade with shelter from cold winds and excessive dampness. Zones 7–9 for some.

WATERING AND FEEDING Lightly top dress with bonemeal in fall; feed lightly with an organic fertilizer in spring.

MANAGEMENT They are prone to rot in damp conditions, especially the more woolly forms such as *R. tenuicaulis*, and will benefit from a sheet of glass or similar protection over them in the worst winter weather.

COMMON PROBLEMS None.

PROPAGATION Division in spring, or some forms from seed.

SIZE Most of the common species will reach 1 × 4–12in./2.5 × 10–30cm. after three or four years, depending on the conditions.

Raoulia tenuicaulis

Saponaria   SOAPWORT

Easy and attractive, low-growing plants with small, pink, or red flowers and a long flowering season. In addition to their value in rock gardens, they are useful when allowed to tumble over stone walls or down sunny banks.

SOIL Light, fairly nutrient rich, but free draining.

SITUATION Full sun. Zones 3–8.

WATERING AND FEEDING Lightly top dress with bonemeal in fall, and with an organic fertilizer in early spring.

MANAGEMENT The plants can be lightly trimmed in early spring to maintain their shape.

COMMON PROBLEMS None.

PROPAGATION Semi-ripe cuttings in late spring, or from seed.

SIZE The commonest species, *S. ocymoides*, will reach about 3–4 × 12–15in./8–10 × 30–40cm. in three years, but some others are more compact and form tiny clumps.

Saponaria ocymoides

Saxifraga

One of the largest and most important genera of rock garden plants, the saxifrages come in an astonishing array of shapes, forms and colors. There is important variation, too, in their site requirements and hardiness so read label information carefully.

SOIL Light, fairly nutrient-rich but free draining soil will suit most types. The mossy saxifrages are the most tolerant, while the encrusted forms are the most choosy, needing very well drained, alkaline soil – the ideal places to grow them would be in pockets between limestone rocks.

SITUATION Varies considerably; the encrusted forms need full sun, others light shade. Hardiness varies; Zones 4–7 for some.

WATERING AND FEEDING Lightly top dress with bonemeal in fall, and with an organic fertilizer in early spring.

MANAGEMENT Dead leaves should be carefully pulled away. If possible, protect the buds of early-flowering forms from rain damage with a sheet of glass or a cloche.

COMMON PROBLEMS Mites on some, such as *S. stolonifera*.

PROPAGATION By offsets in early spring, or some forms can be propagated by seed.

SIZE Varies considerably. The mossy saxifrages are the most vigorous; a few forms such as *S. × urbium* will reach as much as 1ft./30cm. in height and provide good ground cover with a vigorous spread of up to 2ft./60cm. within four years. Most other forms develop neat clumps of about 4 × 6in./10 × 15cm.

Sedum   STONECROP

The sedums include some very effective and attractive rock garden plants – and one or two notoriously invasive species, too. For example, although it is still widely recommended, I would steer well clear of *S. acre*, which can be very difficult to keep in check. The popular *S. spectabile*, the ice plant, is grown as a border perennial, where it is useful for its late-summer color.

Saxifraga × urbium

Sedum – Viola

Sedum spurium

SOIL Tolerates most well drained soils, and tolerant, too, of moderate acidity and alkalinity.
SITUATION Full sun to very light shade. Zones 4–9 for many.
WATERING AND FEEDING Lightly top dress with bonemeal in fall, and with an organic fertilizer in early spring.
MANAGEMENT None necessary, although unwanted seedlings should be removed regularly.
COMMON PROBLEMS None.
PROPAGATION Offsets, division or softwood cuttings in spring; in many instances, these can be short lengths of segmented stem which easily break off the parent plant. Some forms can be propagated from seed.
SIZE Varies considerably from neat clumps that attain around 2 × 2in./5 × 5cm. after three years, to larger, more spreading plants of about 1 × 1ft./30 × 30cm., so check label information carefully. *S. spectabile* and other border forms will reach 1½ × 1½ft./45 × 45cm.

Sempervivum HOUSELEEK, HEN-AND-CHICKENS

The houseleeks are compact, rather spiky, rosette-producing plants of distinctive form. Easy to grow and at home in the rock garden, they are also very effective grown separately in a trough, where their foliage color can be appreciated.
SOIL Very well drained, gritty soil, slightly acid or alkaline; in trough gardens, use the same sort of garden soil mixed with coarse grit and some Jiffy Mix. Bear in mind that the adopted home of sempervivums is on roofs, the tops of walls and similar places where the soil is all but non-existent.
SITUATION Full sun to very light shade. Zones 5–8.
WATERING AND FEEDING Lightly top dress with bonemeal in fall, and with an organic fertilizer in early spring.
MANAGEMENT Sempervivums are very slow growing (hence their name) and will not flower for many years, although this matters little since most forms are grown for their decorative foliage. The red flowers of *S. arachnoideum* are distinctive compared to other houseleeks. Each rosette dies after flowering but perpetuates itself by offsets, which are best removed and planted separately, and the dead clump cleared away.
COMMON PROBLEMS None.
PROPAGATION By offsets, or some forms from seed.
SIZE Most rosettes will reach 4–6 × 6–12in./10–15 × 15–30cm. after about eight years.

Silene CATCHFLY

These are a mixed group including some bedding annuals and border perennials, but the most splendid and important species are the rosette-forming, rock garden perennials. They are easy, bright, and should be represented in every collection.
SOIL Tolerates most types of well drained, fairly rich soil; best in slightly alkaline conditions.
SITUATION Full sun to very light shade. Zones 5–8 for many.
WATERING AND FEEDING Lightly top dress with bonemeal in

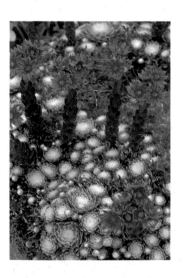
Sempervivum arachnoideum

fall, and with an organic fertilizer in early spring.

MANAGEMENT None necessary.

COMMON PROBLEMS None.

PROPAGATION Softwood cuttings or division in early spring, or some forms from seed.

SIZE The more vigorous forms will reach 4 × 8in./10 × 20cm. after three or four years, but others are smaller and more compact.

Silene schafta

Viola

This is a large and much-loved genus of plants that embraces all the invaluable pansies and violas grown as bedding or container annuals. Their deserved popularity has tended to obscure the many little perennial species that are so easily grown in the rock garden and elsewhere.

SOIL Tolerates most; some species thrive in quite heavy clays, most prefer lighter, free draining and quite poor soils.

SITUATION Full sun to light shade. Zones 4–8 for many.

WATERING AND FEEDING Top dress lightly with bonemeal in fall; very lightly with an organic fertilizer in early spring.

MANAGEMENT None needed, although some forms such as the sweet violet, *V. odorata*, self-seed very readily and it may be necessary to remove excess seedlings.

COMMON PROBLEMS None.

PROPAGATION Softwood cuttings in spring; by division; or some forms from seed.

SIZE Most of the clump-forming types, such as *V. gracilis*, will reach about 2–4 × 2–4in./5–10 × 5–10cm. after two or three years but *V. odorata* (Zones 6–9) and others can spread by seeds, runners or rhizomes, so check label information carefully.

Viola cornuta

WATER PLANTS

Principles of care

For most of us, water gardens hold a particular attraction and water plants a rather special appeal. As a group, they are less diverse than those used for more conventional plantings; there are, for instance, no really aquatic shrubs or perennials with genuine bulbs, and certainly none for garden use. Most of those that grow in or close to the water's edge are fibrous-rooted or rhizomatous herbaceous perennials (some of which are evergreen), while there are a few that fall into special categories. True water plants are rooted in the mud within the pool and have leaves and flowers that rise to the surface. Floating plants merely dangle their roots into the water, and submerged species, as their description implies, scarcely see the fresh air at all. Because of their growing habits, water plants in general make certain demands in terms of management, but perhaps the most import-ant consideration to remember is that many are invasive for small pools. It is worth pointing out that in some areas, especially in parts of the United States, the growing of some water plants is legally restricted because their aggress-ive growth can pose a threat to water courses. Hardiness must also be considered; there are both tropical and winter-hardy water lilies.

SOIL AND SITE REQUIREMENTS
With very few exceptions, water plants require full sun and there is little variation in their soil requirements. Plants grown at the water margin (so-called marginals) must be in con-stantly water-logged soil and will generally tolerate 6–8in./15–20cm. of water over their roots. True water plants, such as water lilies, which can be planted in fairly deep water, and those marginals that will grow in shallow standing water, require special treatment. The easiest way to deal with them is to plant them in purpose-made planting baskets that can be lowered into water of appropriate depth. The baskets should be filled with soil that does not have any compost, manure, or other organic matter added, and has not been treated with any fertilizer. Once the baskets are planted up, it is wise to cover the soil surface with a layer of coarse grit before lowering them into the pool; this will prevent fish from stirring up the soil and clouding the water.

Large planting baskets may also be used for vigorous marginal plants even when they are not actually growing in standing water; the baskets may restrict their growth to some extent and in any event will facilitate lifting the plants for periodic division.

GENERAL MANAGEMENT
As with other herbaceous perennials, deciduous water plants should have their dead foliage and flower stems cut back in the fall, although this is obviously not essential if they are growing some distance from the banks. In small pools, however, it is very important to remove any dead plant material promptly before it becomes water-logged, sinks, and decays to foul the water.

In my experience, water plants require no feeding since they obtain all the nutrients necessary from the soil in which they grow. Purpose-made sachets of slow-release fertilizer are available for insertion into planting baskets and may well be of benefit, but you should never use conventional garden fertilizer.

There are few pest and disease problems with water plants, although aphids can be trouble-some on some species. Very little can safely be done to discourage them, however, for insecti-cides and fungicides should never be sprayed in or close to water. (This, of course, means sprays should also not be used on normal plants growing in containers placed close to the water's edge. If you need to use a spray on them, move the containers right away.) On water plants, using a hose to wash the aphids into the water where the fish will feed on them is as much as should be attempted.

PROPAGATION
As with other perennials, water plants – unless they are growing in or close to large expanses of water, where they may be allowed freer rein – benefit from periodic division. They should always be divided in spring, just as growth is recommencing, because if they are disturbed in the fall they will be prone to damage from winter cold. Ice on a garden pool is most unlik-ely to cause harm to water plants, but it is important to use a pool heater or other device to keep a small area unfrozen, allowing oxygen to enter and foul gases to escape, for the sake of any fish. Tropical water lilies are not winter hardy above Zone 10.

Environments for water plants

POND SITES With careful construction, butyl rubber sheeting can be used to create a pond that offers a variety of environments for water plants. Grow the plants in soil held firm by rocks, or in planting baskets. From left to right: marginal plants: *Caltha* (marsh marigold), *Menyanthes* (bogbean), *Alisma* (water plantain), *Sagittaria* (arrowhead). Floating plant: *Stratiotes* (water soldier). True water plant: *Nymphaea* (water lily). Submerged plant: *Elodea* (Canadian pondweed).

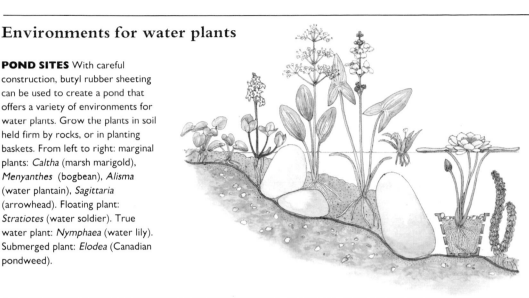

Acorus   SWEET FLAG

One of several aquatic members of the arum family, although this is not very obvious from its appearance. It is grown principally for its scented, deciduous, iris-like leaves which were once used as an aromatic floor covering. Two species, *A. calamus* and the shorter *A. gramineus*, are grown, especially the variegated forms.

PLANTING AND SITUATION Marginal/submerged, needing 4–12in./10–30cm. water depth. Full sun. Zones 4–10 for *A. calamus*, 5–9 for *A. gramineus*.

MANAGEMENT Cut back dead foliage in fall. The plants are vigorous; divide them every three or four years in small pools.

COMMON PROBLEMS None.

PROPAGATION Division in spring.

SIZE Will reach about $2\frac{1}{2} \times 2$ft./75 × 60cm. in three or four years.

Acorus calamus 'Variegatus'

Alisma   WATER PLANTAIN

For the shallow parts of large pools *A. plantago-aquatica* is a very attractive deciduous subject, with gypsophila-like, pink-white flowers, but its self-seeding invasiveness will create dreadful problems in smaller pools.

PLANTING AND SITUATION Marginal, needing 0–8in./0–20cm. water depth. Full sun. Zones 5–9.

MANAGEMENT Cut back dead flower stems and foliage in the fall. Unless the pool is very large, it will be worth cutting off the flower stems before the seed matures as it self-seeds very freely. Divide every three or four years.

COMMON PROBLEMS None.

PROPAGATION Division in spring, or from seed.

SIZE The flowers will reach $2\frac{1}{2}$–3ft./75–90cm. in height, and an individual plant spreads to about 20in./50cm. in three years; but it is the seedlings that cause the problems.

Alisma plantago-aquatica

Aponogeton – Cyperus

Aponogeton distachyus

Azolla caroliniana

Butomus umbellatus

Aponogeton   WATER HAWTHORN

One of the few aquatic plants to offer the combination of attractive foliage, flowers, and perfume but without a grossly invasive habit (although it is still not a plant for a small pool). It is fairly shade tolerant and in mild areas will be in leaf and flower for much of the year.

PLANTING AND SITUATION A true water plant, requiring 6–24in./15–60cm. water depth. Full sun to light or moderate shade. Zones 9–10.

MANAGEMENT Neaten dead foliage in the fall or as it arises and cut off the seed-heads (if within reach) if you wish to limit the spread. Divide every three or four years in spring.

COMMON PROBLEMS None.

PROPAGATION Division in spring, or from seed.

SIZE *A. distachyus* will reach 4–6in. × 3–4ft./10–15cm. × 1–1.2m. in about five years.

Azolla   FAIRY MOSS

The unique *A. caroliniana* is a tiny floating fern with minute green fronds that turn red-brown in the fall and produce overwintering "buds" that sink to the pool's bottom. It is a tempting thing but can become a problem, as once established it is all but irremovable. It is best used only in small pools, where you can easily net excess growth and remove it. Another plant that can occasionally get into ponds is the duckweed (*Lemna*). It too is irremovable and any introductions of plants or fish should be carefully examined to ensure they do not contain any fronds.

PLANTING AND SITUATION Floating; simply scatter the fronds onto the water surface. Full sun. Zones 4–10.

MANAGEMENT None required, but it can be checked, to a degree, by netting in summer.

COMMON PROBLEMS None.

PROPAGATION Not necessary; simply remove a few fronds to begin a new colony.

SIZE Will cover about 1 square yard/1 square meter after a year and increase rapidly thereafter.

Butomus   FLOWERING RUSH

A deciduous, rush-like plant with umbels of tiny pink flowers. It is attractive *en masse* in a large pool but is too large and not intrinsically pretty enough for a small one.

PLANTING AND SITUATION Marginal, needing 0–8in./0–20cm. water depth. Full sun. Zones 4–9.

MANAGEMENT Cut back dead foliage in the fall. The only species of the genus, *B. umbellatus*, is vigorous and can be divided every few years, but it is best left undisturbed to naturalize in the back of a large pool.

COMMON PROBLEMS None.

PROPAGATION Division in spring, or from seed.

SIZE Will reach 3 × 1½ft./1m. × 50cm. after three or four years.

Calla   BOG ARUM

Hardier than its larger and more showy relative *Zantedeschia*, *C. palustris*, the sole species of the genus, also grown as a water garden plant, is an obvious member of the Araceae, and perhaps best suited to smaller, more informal pools.

PLANTING AND SITUATION Marginal, needing 0–8in./0–20cm. water depth. Full sun. Zones 2–9.

MANAGEMENT In mild areas, the plant remains evergreen and requires no management other than dividing every four or five years. In colder regions, the foliage may be killed by fall frosts and should then be cut back.

COMMON PROBLEMS None.

PROPAGATION Division in spring, or from seed.

SIZE Will reach about 1 × 1ft./30 × 30cm. after two or three years.

Calla palustris

Caltha   MARSH MARIGOLD

One of the most familiar and best-loved water garden plants, suitable for informal water's edge plantings beside all except very small pools. Both golden- and white-flowered forms exist of *C. palustris*, but for more natural water garden plantings, the golden form is generally the most appropriate choice.

PLANTING AND SITUATION Marginal, needing 0–8in./0–20cm. water depth. Full sun. Zones 4–9.

MANAGEMENT The foliage tends to turn yellow and die back during the summer (often aided by mildew) and it should then be cut back.

COMMON PROBLEMS Mildew.

PROPAGATION Division in spring, or from seed, except for the very attractive, fully double form *C. palustris* 'Plena', which does not produce seed.

SIZE The single-flowered form may reach about 2 × 1½ft./60 × 50cm.; the double-flowered variant, perhaps half this.

Caltha palustris

Cyperus   UMBRELLA SEDGE

There are several cultivated species of *Cyperus* but they are only suitable for year-long pool use in mild climates. In the North, the plants must be grown in pots and carried over indoors as house plants or used around greenhouse ponds. One of the so-called umbrella or papyrus sedges, *C. papyrus* 'Nanus', is sometimes grown in water gardens, but keep in pots for removal every fall.

PLANTING AND SITUATION Marginal, needing 0–8in./0–20cm. water depth. Full sun. Zones 9–11; tolerates colder zones in summer.

MANAGEMENT The plant is evergreen so requires no more than neatening the damaged foliage in the fall. It may be divided every five or six years if space is limited, but it is better to leave it if at all possible, as it will usefully stabilize soft banks in mild climates.

COMMON PROBLEMS None.

PROPAGATION Division in spring, or from seed.

SIZE Will reach 4–5 × 1½ft./1.2–1.5m. × 50cm. in three years.

Cyperus papyrus 'Nanus'

Iris – Sagittaria

Lysichiton americanus

Iris

Irises, also described in other sections of the book, certainly make indispensable and beautiful waterside plants.

PLANTING AND SITUATION Marginal, but of three common water garden species, only *I. laevigata* and *I. pseudacorus* are truly aquatic, tolerating 0–8in./0–20cm. water depth. *I. kaempferi* will tolerate 0–4in./0–10cm. of water in summer; may rot if its rhizomes are fully submerged in winter. Full sun. Zones 5–9.

MANAGEMENT Cut back foliage to just above water level in the fall and cut flower spikes back after flowering to the point where they emerge from the leaf fan. The plants may be divided every five or six years if space is limited.

COMMON PROBLEMS Aphids.

PROPAGATION Division in spring.

SIZE Varies among cultivars but most forms will reach 2–3 × 2ft./60cm.–1m. × 60cm. in three to four years.

Lysichiton   SKUNK CABBAGE

Striking members of the arum family with vivid white or yellow spathes in spring. At this stage, they seem only moderately large, but don't be deceived as the remainder of the summer is spent producing large leaves that would completely swamp a small water garden. The true skunk cabbage, *Symplocarpus foetidus*, so common on wetlands, has attractive foliage and is very hardy.

PLANTING AND SITUATION Marginal, requiring 0–6in./0–15cm. water depth. Full sun or light shade. Zones 7–9.

MANAGEMENT Cut back dead foliage in the fall. They may be divided every five or six years in limited space but are much better left undisturbed, as they can be difficult to re-establish.

COMMON PROBLEMS None.

PROPAGATION Division in spring, or from seed.

SIZE Both of the only two species, the yellow *L. americanum* and the white *L. camtschatcensis*, will reach 3 × 2½ft./1m. × 75cm. in about three years, although *L. americanum* usually tends to be the more vigorous.

Menyanthes   BOG BEAN

Not a plant for a small pool because of its vigor but a very useful, fairly early-flowering deciduous species, *M. trifoliata*, for the margins of a larger one. The common name derives not from the flowers or fruits but from the broad-bean-like leaves.

PLANTING AND SITUATION Marginal, requiring 2–6in./5–15cm. water depth. Full sun or very light shade. Zones 4–8.

MANAGEMENT Pull away dead flower heads after flowering and dead foliage in fall before it rots. Divide every four or five years if it threatens to outgrow its space.

COMMON PROBLEMS None.

PROPAGATION By division, softwood cuttings in spring, or from seed.

SIZE Will reach about 10 × 10–12in./25 × 25–30cm. in three years.

Menyanthes trifoliata

Nymphaea   WATER LILY

The prize plants of almost everyone's pool. Water lilies are not difficult to grow provided varieties are chosen to suit the size of pool and depth of water. Perhaps more than any other type of pool plant, most are unremitting in their demand for a bright sunny position. The genus contains both hardy and tropical or annual plants.

PLANTING AND SITUATION A true water plant, requiring a depth of water of at least 6in./15cm., and up to 3ft./1m. Full sun. Hardy water lilies: (Zones 3–10); tropical kinds survive winter in frost-free zones.

MANAGEMENT Pull away dead leaves as they brown and die and also pull away dead flower heads before they become fully water-logged and sink. Both of these operations are very important in a small pool, for such large pieces of vegetation will rot rapidly and help to foul the water. Divide every four or five years.

COMMON PROBLEMS Aphids; water lily beetle; various fungal leaf spots.

PROPAGATION Division in spring.

SIZE Differs greatly with cultivar. Unless a water-garden nursery exists locally, plants must be ordered from mail-order specialists whose catalogues supply detailed information regarding cultivars. As a general guide, cultivars exist in each of the common colors (pink, red, white, and yellow) that will spread within three years to distances ranging in diameter from 1ft. to 8ft./30cm. to 2.5m.

Nymphaea 'Atropurpurea'

Pontederia   PICKEREL WEED

Beautiful for both their rich glossy foliage and their spikes of soft–blue flowers, pontederias should be along the margins of every large pool. Sadly, their invasive rhizomes are probably too much to cope with alongside smaller pools unless they are grown in large containers, sunk to their rims.

PLANTING AND SITUATION Marginal, requiring 2–8in./ 5–20cm. water depth. Full sun. Zones 3–9.

MANAGEMENT Cut away flower stems as the flowers fade – more blooms will continue to be produced throughout the summer – and cut away dead foliage in the fall.

COMMON PROBLEMS None.

PROPAGATION Division in spring, or from seed.

SIZE Will reach $2-2\frac{1}{2} \times 1\frac{1}{2}$ft./60–75 × 45cm. in three or four years.

Sagittaria   ARROW HEAD

"Arrow leaf" would be a more accurate name for this vigorous but lovely marginal species with white flowers (almost grotesquely double in some forms). Other than by a very large pool, however, it really must be restrained.

PLANTING AND SITUATION Marginal, requiring 2–6in./ 5–15cm. water depth. Full sun. Because it is so vigorous, once established, it is best put in a large container for ease of lifting. Zones 7–10.

Pontederia cordata

Sagittaria – Submerged plants

Sagittaria sagittifolia

Scirpus lacustris

Typha latifolia

MANAGEMENT Cut away dead flower heads as they fade. Divide every three or four years in spring; this is greatly facilitated if the plant is grown in a container.
COMMON PROBLEMS None.
PROPAGATION Division or offsets in spring.
SIZE The European *S. sagittifolia* will reach about $1\frac{1}{2} \times 1-1\frac{1}{2}$ft./ $45 \times 30-45$cm. within two years; the double-flowered form 'Flore Pleno' (sometimes called *S. japonica* 'Flore Pleno') is a little less vigorous.

Scirpus   CLUBRUSH

Of a number of true aquatic rushes, some of the forms of *S. lacustris*, especially the variegated 'Zebrinus', are the most attractive. They are very hardy and very easy to grow but, like so many other marginal plants, must be placed with care if they are not to swamp the habitat.
PLANTING AND SITUATION Marginal, requiring 2–6in./ 5–15cm. water depth. Full sun. Best planted in a large container to restrain its spread. Zones 5–10.
MANAGEMENT The plants tend to be evergreen, so little management is needed apart from cutting out any damaged or browned foliage. Divide every three or four years in spring; this is greatly facilitated if the plant is grown in a container.
COMMON PROBLEMS None.
PROPAGATION Division in spring.
SIZE Most of the commonly grown forms will reach about $5 \times 2\frac{1}{2}$ft./1.5m. × 75cm. in three or four years.

Typha   CAT TAIL, REEDMACE

These are the plants popularly but erroneously called bulrushes, distinguished by the brown, club-like flowering and seeding heads. They are impressive and stately plants, but even the small species tend to be invasive, so should really only be planted by a large pool.
PLANTING AND SITUATION Marginal, requiring 2–6in./ 5–15cm. water depth. Full sun. Only plant them alongside large pools and even then choose the lesser species, *T. angustifolia* and *T. minima*, in preference to the much taller *T. latifolia*.
MANAGEMENT Neaten the dead foliage in the fall, but leave the seed-heads which are the primary appeal. Divide every three or four years in spring. Unfortunately, these distinguished plants are invasive and problematic on three counts. They produce prodigious quantities of feathery seeds that blow in the wind and germinate freely where they land, they are intrinsically vigorous and invasive, and the roots have sharp points that can easily penetrate a plastic pool liner.
COMMON PROBLEMS None.
PROPAGATION Division in spring, or from seed.
SIZE *T. minima* will reach $1\frac{1}{2} \times 1$ft./45×30cm. in three years, *T. angustifolia* $6 \times 1\frac{1}{2}$ft./1.8m. × 50cm., and *T. latifolia* $8 \times 2\frac{1}{2}$ft./ 2.5m. × 75cm. in the same time.

Floating plants

There are several genera of water plants that float on or just below the surface, their roots unattached to either bed or bank. Among the most common of these are *Hottonia* (water violet), *Hydrocharis* (frogbit), *Stratiotes* (water soldier), and *Eichhornia* (water hyacinth); the latter is too tender to survive outdoors over winter, except in very mild areas.

PLANTING AND SITUATION Floating. Although these plants will float in any depth of water, they should not be grown in a pool deeper than about 3ft./1m. because their overwintering buds sink to the bottom in the fall and will not thrive in, or re-emerge from, very deep water. Full sun or very light shade. *Stratiotes*, although hardier than *Eichhornia*, is less so than the other two genera and, like *Eichhornia*, can be invasive in warmer climates; for this reason, there may be restrictions on their sale. Zones vary; 9–10 for some.

MANAGEMENT Pull out or net excess plants in the summer.

COMMON PROBLEMS None.

PROPAGATION Use a net to remove a few individual plants for transfer elsewhere. Or order new plants in the spring.

SIZE This varies with climatic conditions, but a few individual plants will usually spread to cover an area of about 1 square yard/1 square meter within two years by the redistribution of their over-wintering buds.

Stratiotes aloides

Submerged plants

Although little is seen of these plants, they play an invaluable role in oxygenating the water for the well-being of other aquatic life. They are sometimes loosely rooted in the basal mud but otherwise float just above the pool bottom. Those most commonly seen are *Myriophyllum*, *Cabomba*, and two species of *Elodea* (both of which have experienced name changes but are still usually sold under their old names). In my experience it is the first two plants which make the best oxygenators. Their whorls of tiny leaves offer a larger surface area than the broader-leaved *Elodea*, while still offering effective shelter to various forms of sub-aquatic life, and they have the advantage of being much less prone to acting as a base for the build up of algal blanket weed.

PLANTING AND SITUATION They can be submerged in any except very deep water, although they flourish best in well-lit conditions down to about 6ft./2m. depth. Although it is possible to anchor them in the mud, in shallower water, they will very soon be uprooted by fish. Grow best in full sun. Zones vary; 5–10 for most.

MANAGEMENT Pull out or net excess plants in the summer.

COMMON PROBLEMS None.

PROPAGATION Use a net to remove a few individual plants for transfer elsewhere. Or in the North order new plants in spring.

SIZE Varies with climatic conditions but a few individual plants will usually spread to furnish a water volume of about $\frac{1}{2}$ cubic yard/$\frac{1}{2}$ cubic meter within three years.

Myriophyllum aquaticum

TREES

Abies	Ilex
Acacia	Juniperus
Acer	Koelreuteria
Amelanchier	Laburnum
Araucaria	Magnolia
Betula	Malus
Catalpa	Parrotia
Cedrus	Picea
Cercidiphyllum	Pinus
Chamaecyparis	Populus
Cupressus	Prunus
×Cupressocyparis	Pyrus
Cornus	Robinia
Corylus	Salix
Crataegus	Sorbus
Davidia	Taxodium
Eucalyptus	Taxus
Fagus	Thuja
Ginkgo	Tsuga
Gleditsia	

TREE FRUIT

Apple	Nectarine
Pear	Apricot
Plum	Cherry
Peach	Fig

Principles of Care

Because of their size, trees are likely to be the most dominant plants in any garden, be it a large one with an area of woodland or a tiny one with a single tree. (As a general guideline, I call a garden small if it's under about 240 square yards/200 square meters, medium-sized if between about 240–2400 square yards/200 and 2000 square meters, and large if over about 2400 square yards/2000 square meters.) A tree's foliage, growth habit and other aesthetic qualities are all important factors to consider when choosing a tree for a particular spot, but of greater importance is to consider its ultimate height and spread. Making an unwise or hasty decision will have a lasting impact not only on your own garden and house, but on neighboring gardens too.

CHOOSING AN APPROPRIATE TREE

I hold very strongly to the view that planting a tree in a garden simply because you like the look of it, and cutting it down if it happens to grow larger than you wish, is the wrong approach. It can also lead to complications, because in many areas there are legal impediments to the felling of trees over a certain size.

I have been accused in the past of being too cautious in my general advice not to plant a tree closer to a building than a distance approximately equal to its ultimate height. I concede that this would exclude from many gardens trees that would be unlikely to cause serious damage if they fell, and I have no wish to cause alarm to the many gardeners who already have trees much closer than this to their houses (as I do myself). Nonetheless, when you are starting afresh, it is wise to be cautious, and there are a

Understanding a tree

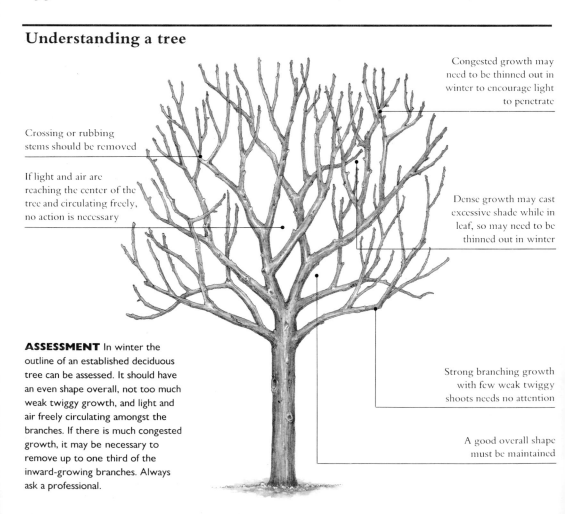

Congested growth may need to be thinned out in winter to encourage light to penetrate

Crossing or rubbing stems should be removed

If light and air are reaching the center of the tree and circulating freely, no action is necessary

Dense growth may cast excessive shade while in leaf, so may need to be thinned out in winter

ASSESSMENT In winter the outline of an established deciduous tree can be assessed. It should have an even shape overall, not too much weak twiggy growth, and light and air freely circulating amongst the branches. If there is much congested growth, it may be necessary to remove up to one third of the inward-growing branches. Always ask a professional.

Strong branching growth with few weak twiggy shoots needs no attention

A good overall shape must be maintained

Simple tree surgery

REMOVING A BRANCH Make a sloping saw cut close to (not flush with) the trunk, leaving the collar at the base of the branch intact.

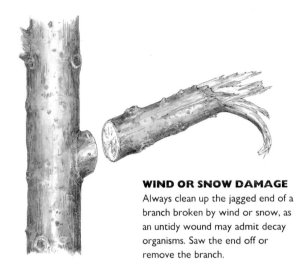

WIND OR SNOW DAMAGE Always clean up the jagged end of a branch broken by wind or snow, as an untidy wound may admit decay organisms. Saw the end off or remove the branch.

number of reasons, both practical and aesthetic, for choosing a tree proportionate to the size of your garden.

If, for instance, a potentially tall, spreading tree is planted close to a house (as happens surprisingly often) it will not only take light from the building, and from all the plants around it, it will also of course be deprived of light and nourishment itself and be unable to form a good shape. And the same is true of trees planted too close to others in a large garden: the struggle to compete will produce straggly, lopsided specimens that are unable to fulfil their potential. Trees can be the most beautiful as well as the most dominant features in a garden, but they must be well placed in order to thrive.

FEEDING AND WATERING

There is no standard guideline to distinguish shrubs from trees in terms of size, but a simple definition of a tree is a woody plant that attains a height of more than about 20ft./6m. on a single stem. There is a tendency to think of trees as self-sufficient simply on account of their size. In practice, in their early years they require as much feeding, watering (and mulching), and protection from competition with weeds as do shrubs and herbaceous perennials. It is particularly important not to allow grass or other vegetation to grow up to the stems of young trees, and a circle of turf approximately 3ft./ 1m. in diameter should be removed from

around the base of trees planted in lawns. Fertilizer and organic mulch applied to this area will quickly penetrate the soil to its intended target.

Small trees (those up to about 13–16ft./ 4–5m.) may be grown in containers of equal parts soil, peat moss, and coarse sand; a container 2½–3ft./75–100cm. in diameter will be needed. The tree will require regular watering during the summer, and varieties with a high water demand should be avoided. Trees that I consider suitable include fruit trees on dwarfing rootstocks, the smaller types of Japanese cherry, laurel, Japanese maple, hawthorn, and magnolia.

STAKING

Until their stems are strong enough to provide them with full support, trees require staking. It is impossible to give a precise age at which the stake may be dispensed with because trees grow at such differing rates, but a tree more than about 13ft./4m. tall is unlikely to require staking in most situations. In certain instances, most notably for "trees" formed artificially by training a single stem from a tall shrub, or apple trees grafted onto dwarfing rootstocks (see pages 18–19 and 225), a permanent stake will be necessary. Stakes should always be placed on the side of the stem facing the prevailing wind (so that the stem is blown away from and not toward it) and secured with purpose-made, belt-pattern tree ties. Hitherto, traditional tree

Principles of Care

Tree braces

▶ **SUPPORTING LOW BRANCHES** The branches of trees such as damsons and magnolias often dip so low to the ground around the tree that mowing is severely hindered. Prop the branches attractively with rough-hewn crutches forked at the top to cradle the limb. If necessary tie the crutches on securely to avoid the possibility of the wind blowing the branch off and perhaps breaking it.

▲ **INTERNAL WIRING**
Branches in danger of being torn away from the tree can be internally wired to the main trunk with purpose-made supports, cushioned with foam to prevent chafing.

◀ **WIRING CONIFERS** Heavy snowfalls can weigh down the branches of conifers and cause them to open outward. Rescue them by tying wires firmly and permanently around the outside, pulling all the branches in. The foliage will quickly hide the wires.

stakes have been of cylindrical, unbarked, treated timber about 2½in./6cm. in diameter, driven into the soil for about 2½ft./75cm. and protruding to a height of about 6½ft./2m. This is the type that I still prefer, although recently short stakes (only about 2½ft./75cm. tall) have gained favor, especially in England, on the principle that the tree gains the best wind tolerance when it is blown to and fro.

TROUBLESHOOTING

With the exception of fruit trees, very few trees require routine pruning, and the subject only really arises if they are large or old. In general, I believe that a tree in need of pruning on account

of its size has been planted in the wrong place, although I accept that problems may occur when buildings have been erected on old woodland or near established trees. Damaged or diseased branches can usually be removed with a fine-toothed saw, cutting neatly just above the basal collar where the branch joins the main trunk. Never use wound-sealing paints on these cut surfaces because they give no benefit and may be harmful.

Removal of a tree should really be the last resort. Even a very large specimen that is casting deep shade or otherwise creating difficulties can often be saved: crown thinning – the selective removal of some of the branches from the

Rejuvenating malnourished trees

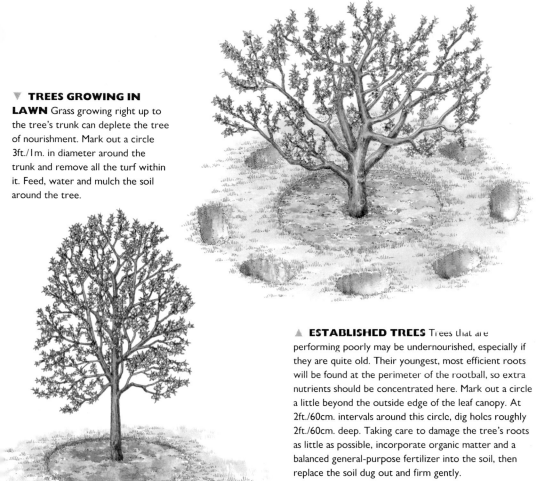

▼ **TREES GROWING IN LAWN** Grass growing right up to the tree's trunk can deplete the tree of nourishment. Mark out a circle 3ft./1m. in diameter around the trunk and remove all the turf within it. Feed, water and mulch the soil around the tree.

▲ **ESTABLISHED TREES** Trees that are performing poorly may be undernourished, especially if they are quite old. Their youngest, most efficient roots will be found at the perimeter of the rootball, so extra nutrients should be concentrated here. Mark out a circle a little beyond the outside edge of the leaf canopy. At 2ft./60cm. intervals around this circle, dig holes roughly 2ft./60cm. deep. Taking care to damage the tree's roots as little as possible, incorporate organic matter and a balanced general-purpose fertilizer into the soil, then replace the soil dug out and firm gently.

crown of the tree – is very often beneficial but must be done in such a way as to preserve the aesthetic and, most importantly, the physical balance. If an entire tree must be removed, it should generally be taken down piecemeal, one large branch at a time, again maintaining the balance in the process. Stumps should be removed if at all possible, especially those of broad leaved (non-coniferous) trees, because they may provide entry for fungus diseases. Relatively small stumps should be dug out, larger ones winched or ground out with specialist equipment. (Chemical products claimed to degrade stumps are by and large ineffective.) But do remember that the removal, or even the

pruning, of large trees is not a matter to be undertaken lightly. I cannot emphasize too strongly that major work on a large tree, or even on a small one close to buildings, should be performed by a qualified professional operator who will not only be familiar with the techniques and equipment necessary, but will also have third-party insurance.

In addition to these words of warning, it is vital to remember that felling a tree in effect means removing the equivalent of a large water pump from your garden, with the possible consequence that the soil will become saturated and begin to heave. Remember the statistic that on a warm day 1 square yard/1 square meter of

Principles of Care

Root pruning a tree

FALL Trees that have outgrown their allotted space may need the drastic measure of root pruning to stop them from growing any bigger. Never root prune plums or other species of *Prunus, Rhus typhina*, willows or poplars, as root damage to these trees will encourage the production of suckers.

Begin by marking out a circle around the tree to a radius equal to 5in./12cm. for every ½in./1cm. of trunk diameter. Dig a trench along this line, about 1½ft./45cm. deep, to reveal the tree's roots. With loppers or a small saw, cut the thick main roots right through, leaving the fibrous roots intact. Refill the trench.

Trench dug out just beyond far perimeter of leaf canopy

Fibrous roots: leave alone

Main root: cut through

leaf cover will lose over 1 gallon/5 liters of water. Even the severing of major roots without actual removal of the tree can give rise to soil swelling on some sites.

Something that often gives rise to concern is the development of suckers (shoots that arise from the roots, often at some distance from the main plant). This is most likely to occur when the plant has been grafted onto a rootstock of different type and vigor, but plants growing on their own roots are also quite capable of forming suckers. Usually it happens when the roots have been damaged in some way, perhaps by being severed with a spade or even attacked unseen, by some soil-inhabiting pest. The most notorious producers of suckers are *Prunus* species, including plums, and the stagshorn sumac, *Rhus typhina*, so special care should be taken not to damage or disturb the roots of these trees. Suckers are best pulled rather than cut away to discourage others from growing in their place. On lawns they may be mown off. Using weedkillers is unsatisfactory; contact weedkillers

simply leave a dead sucker to remove later, while systemic weedkillers may damage the main plant.

The appearance of fungal fruiting bodies on tree branches indicate decay of the wood within, and if such growths arise on the main trunk it is likely that the decay is extensive. Expert advice should be sought, as gales could tear off branches or blow the tree over.

Surface rooting is sometimes a problem with established trees and can make lawn mowing difficult or cause paths to lift. Little can be done to remedy this: heaping more soil or other material over the raised area will merely create awkward humps and can only serve as a temporary expedient until the roots grow upward again. Simply allowing the mower to slice the top off surface roots in a lawn will do the tree no harm and is probably the only solution.

Like shrubs, trees can sometimes be moved. The success of this depends rather less on the type of tree than on its size and the nature of the soil and general growing conditions, which in turn affect the spread of the root system. In most areas, I would not hesitate to transplant a broad leaved tree up to about 13ft./4m. in height (rather less for a conifer), following the procedure for moving shrubs (see page 22).

COPING WITH ESTABLISHED TREES

One of the most beautiful features of a mature garden is often its ancient trees; without them its whole aspect would be changed, and we naturally value highly any that we are lucky enough to inherit. Though every species has a character of its own, with specific requirements and susceptibilities, they hold in common the fact that great age and height tend to make them vulnerable to damage, and I am frequently asked for advice on their management. I have selected five species here to represent the problems most frequently encountered with old, established trees.

Fraxinus The European ash, which reaches a height of 80ft./27m., is better suited to the wild than to gardens as it tends to become gaunt and untidy (and prone to wood decay fungi) in later life. However, it recovers well after surgery if damaged branches are cut back to the basal collar. The popular weeping variety, *F. excelsior* 'Pendula', whose attraction lies largely in its habit – it forms a giant umbrella with a spread of up to 33ft./10m. – loses so much of its appeal after surgery that overgrown or damaged trees are generally best removed.

Juglans Fully mature walnut trees are large (up to 100ft./30m. high), wide spreading and, in the right place, magnificent – including the hardy nut-bearing butternut, and black walnut. When sheltered from strong wind, they suffer few problems, and broken branches, once cleaned up, don't usually make the tree unsightly; but if a *Juglans* must be felled, remember that walnut timber is highly prized.

Pseudotsuga A coniferous tree for very large gardens, the Douglas fir may reach a height of over 80ft./27m. Mature specimens can have broken branches cut back to just above the basal collar or leading shoots cut back to healthy wood, but a young tree disfigured by storm damage is probably beyond salvation.

Quercus Big old oaks are tough trees, and although they may lose branches (occasionally through fungal decay), they rarely become unstable; unlike beeches, and many other large species, they are deeply and securely rooted. Torn limbs should be cut clean to just above the basal collar, but the tree itself should be allowed to stand as long as it retains its natural dignity.

Ulmus Once common throughout the Northeast, the American elm is now mostly of the past. I include it here because where it survives it can be a cause of problems. Its habit of shedding large branches without warning has always made it a potential hazard, and damaged limbs should be cut back to above the basal collar. Dead trees must be felled promptly as they are a breeding ground for the bark beetle vector of the Dutch elm disease fungus.

Abies FIR, SILVER FIR

Among the less well-known garden conifers but, given plenty of space, the silver firs make fine specimens. Very few species are suitable for small gardens, although there are a few mutant dwarf forms (see page 79). Fir cones are borne upright on the branches, but usually near to the top and out of sight.

SOIL Deep, preferably well drained; most are fairly intolerant of alkaline conditions.

SITUATION Open situation to allow room to grow; intolerant of smoky industrial atmosphere. More hardy species, Zones 3–6.

WATERING AND FEEDING Normally only necessary until well established: mulch in fall and spring, and feed with a balanced general fertilizer in mid-spring.

PRUNING None; cannot be trimmed to form a hedge.

COMMON PROBLEMS Adelgids (aphid-like insects); frost, particularly late frost, may cause damage or death.

PROPAGATION Not feasible.

Abies koreana 'Lutea'

Abies – Amelanchier

Acacia dealbata

TROUBLESHOOTING Not necessary; large trees badly damaged by storms are best removed because they will never recover their appealing pyramidal shape.

SIZE Many species will reach around 16ft./5m. after ten years and 100ft./30m. or more ultimately. A notable exception is *A. koreana*, which may eventually attain 50ft./15m. but is very slow growing in the early years and bears bluish cones when only 3ft./1m. tall.

Acacia   SILVER WATTLE, MIMOSA

The evergreen mimosa, *A. dealbata*, is always greatly admired, but in the North must be grown in a greenhouse.

SOIL Light, free draining; intolerant of high alkalinity.

SITUATION Shelter is essential and they will never reach much more than shrub size unless there is little likelihood of frost. Small specimens can be grown in large containers and moved under cover in winter. Zones 9–10.

WATERING AND FEEDING Mulch in fall and spring. Feed with a balanced rose or similar potash-rich fertilizer in mid-spring, and again around midsummer.

PRUNING None except for frost damage.

COMMON PROBLEMS None.

PROPAGATION Semi-ripe cuttings in summer.

TROUBLESHOOTING Plants damaged by winter cold will re-generate if cut back at least 1ft./30cm. into undamaged wood. Frost-damaged plants usually shoot again from soil level.

SIZE Fast growing, capable of attaining at least 26ft./8m. in five years, but rarely reaching much more than 33ft./10m. ultimately except in frost-free climates. Plants are generally short-lived.

Acer   MAPLE

This is a large and quite invaluable group of small, medium-sized and, in a few instances, large trees. There is a maple appropriate for almost any size of garden, but the smallest tend to be the most expensive and also the most difficult to grow.

SOIL Tolerates most, but the smaller, shrub-sized species need a free draining soil and are best in slightly acid conditions.

SITUATION The large maples will grow almost anywhere, and the sycamore maple (not a plant I recommend for any garden) is tolerant of the worst that the climate can throw at it. The small Japanese species are quite intolerant of exposure to cold winds and hot summer sun but many are ideal for small gardens and some can be grown in large containers. Zones 4–8.

WATERING AND FEEDING With large species, normally only necessary until well established, but with small forms must be continued throughout their lives: mulch in fall and spring, and feed with a balanced general fertilizer in mid-spring.

PRUNING See opposite above.

COMMON PROBLEMS Aphids; borers; leaf spot; leaf scorch.

PROPAGATION Hardwood cuttings in winter for the large species; the small ornamental types are almost all grafted or grown from half-ripened greenwood cuttings, or from seeds.

Acer palmatum 'Senkaki'

TROUBLESHOOTING On large trees, cut back damaged or broken branches with a clean saw cut just above the basal collar. On small species, cut out cold-damaged or diseased shoots at least 4in./10cm. into healthy wood. It may be necessary to trim some healthy shoots also to restore an attractively balanced shape. Very often, unsatisfactory growth of the small ornamental maples is the result of planting them in poor, heavy, or water-logged soil. By moving them to a more suitable position, or even into a container with a proprietary soil-based compost, recovery can be remarkably successful.

SIZE Varies enormously, so check label information. As a guide, the commonest of the really large ornamental species, *A. platanoides* 'Crimson King', will reach about 16 × 13ft./5 × 4m. after five years and an ultimate height of around 26 × 16ft./8 × 5m. after twenty-five or more years. The popular medium-sized trees such as the paper-barked *A. griseum*; the snake barks, like *A. grosseri hersii*; and the Japanese maple, *A. palmatum*, will all reach about 6½ × 3ft./2 × 1m. after five years and around 33 × 13ft./10 × 4m. after twenty-five years. The shrubby Japanese maples and other species, most notably the staggeringly lovely and popular fern-leaved *A. palmatum* 'Dissectum' types, generally grow very slowly to reach perhaps 5 × 5ft./1.5 × 1.5m. after twenty years.

Amelanchier SNOWY MESPILUS, SHADBLOW

The deciduous amelanchier remains, after many years, my favorite small garden tree. It has aesthetic appeal at almost all times of the year: white spring blossoms, dainty summer leaves, delightful fall colors, and a delicate tracery of twigs through the winter. There are several species and a few cultivars available.

Amelanchier lamarckii

Amelanchier – Catalpa

Araucaria araucana

Soil Any, including heavy clay.

Situation Almost any; tolerant of full sun and moderate shade, and unharmed by strong winds. Zones 4–8.

Watering and feeding Until the tree is very well established mulch in fall and spring, and feed with a balanced general fertilizer in mid-spring.

Pruning To maintain a treelike appearance, cut away suckers that arise from the stem base at least once a year; otherwise, the plant will grow as a multi-stemmed shrub.

Common problems None.

Propagation Very difficult from cuttings; the best method is carefully to remove a rooted sucker.

Troubleshooting Should not be necessary, but cut back any branches accidentally damaged to just above the basal collar.

Size Trained as a tree on a single stem, will attain 10 × 5ft./3 × 1.5m. after five years and 26 × 10ft./8 × 3m. after twenty-five.

Araucaria MONKEY PUZZLE

The coniferous tree *A. araucaria* is too well known to describe, beyond saying that its spiky appearance is unique. It was extensively planted in the nineteenth century and many people with old gardens have inherited large specimens.

Soil Any, provided it is sufficiently deep.

Situation Almost any; tolerant of full sun and moderate shade but always grows the best in moist, milder areas. Zone 7.

Watering and feeding Until the tree is well established mulch in fall and spring, and feed with a balanced general fertilizer in mid-spring.

Pruning The lower branches tend to brown and die back unattractively; they should then be pruned to within a few inches of the main stem. There is no justification, however, for regularly cutting off healthy lower branches to produce a long, bare bole as is sometimes done in public parks.

Common problems None.

Propagation Impossible from cuttings.

Troubleshooting Old trees in urban areas often have a ragged appearance, having shed many limbs, a characteristic to which they are prone when affected by atmospheric pollution. Isolated trees may also be damaged by gales. As the tree will not satisfactorily regenerate a new leading shoot or side branch to replace those lost, a decision must be taken on whether the amount of pruning necessary to tidy it up will result in an even worse mess. A really badly damaged tree is better felled.

Size About 10ft × 6½ft./3 × 2m. after ten years but up to 100ft./30m. after about thirty years.

Betula BIRCH

Birches can be wonderful trees, given room. But their delicate tracery of twigs, fall leaf colors, and often beautiful bark are so alluring that they are often planted in small gardens where they soon out-grow their allotted space.

Soil Almost any, although usually best in acid conditions and generally intolerant of water-logging. *B. nigra* 'Heritage', the river birch, and *B. papyrifera*, the native canoe birch, are suited to most growing conditions.

Situation Almost any; tolerant of full sun and moderate shade. Zones 4–9.

Watering and feeding Until the tree is well established mulch in fall and spring, and feed with a balanced general fertilizer in mid-spring.

Pruning None. On the species with white bark, it is important to rub out any buds that appear low down on the stem, or at least trim off any twigs that appear; the longer these are left, the greater the disfiguring scar will be.

Common problems Some species, most notably *B. pendula*, are prone to heavy aphid infestation, which results in an almost constant drip of honeydew onto anything underneath. This species, *B. pubescens*, and others are also prone to attack by wood-decaying fungi and, except for river birch, borers. Most forms of birch are prone to attack by leafminers.

Propagation Almost impossible from cuttings.

Troubleshooting Some birches, especially *B. pendula* and *B. pubescens*, are not very long-lived and succumb to fungal attack. The white-barked Asian and American types seem less prone to this. Once bracket-like fungal growths are seen on the trunk, the tree's future life will be relatively short, and a careful watch should be kept for signs of instability. Fell severely attacked trees. On healthy trees, storm-damaged branches should be removed cleanly just above the basal collar, but the exposure of woody tissue will increase the likelihood of fungal attack.

Size Up to 20 × 5ft./6 × 1.5m. after about five years, and about 65–82 × 16ft./20–25 × 5m. after twenty-five to thirty years.

Betula jacquemontii

Catalpa INDIAN BEAN TREE

C. bignonioides is one of the easiest of the more exotic ornamental deciduous trees for medium-sized gardens. The huge leaves and runner-bean-like pods are eye-catching, and it also has the great merit of being surprisingly drought tolerant, provided site requirements can be satisfied.

Soil Deep, rich, and preferably moist loam; *Catalpa* is not tolerant of high alkalinity.

Situation Full sun to light shade. Zones 5–8.

Watering and feeding Until the tree is well established mulch in fall and spring, and feed with a rose or similar potash-rich fertilizer in mid-spring.

Pruning See below.

Common problems None.

Propagation Semi-ripe cuttings in late summer.

Troubleshooting Unlikely to be necessary, although damaged trees will regenerate fairly well if cut back into wood up to five or six years old.

Size About 13 × 10ft./4 × 3m. after five years, 26 × 16ft./8 × 5m. after ten years, and an ultimate height of about 50ft./15m.

Catalpa bignonioides

Cedrus deodara 'Pendula'

Cercidiphyllum japonicum

Cedrus CEDAR

There are three species of true cedar commonly seen in gardens: the cedar of Lebanon (*C. libani*), the deodar cedar (*C. deodara*), and the Atlas cedar (*C. atlantica*), usually in its blue-foliaged form. All are quite magnificent trees, hardy, and tolerant of a wide range of conditions; but in most gardens, they are also totally inappropriate. These are plants for very large gardens or for parkland.

SOIL Almost any, although best in deep, rich, moist, acid loams.
SITUATION Almost any; tolerant of full sun and moderate shade, although being so large they cast shade. Zones 7–9.
WATERING AND FEEDING Until the tree is well established mulch in fall and spring, and feed with a balanced general fertilizer in mid-spring.
PRUNING None.
COMMON PROBLEMS None.
PROPAGATION Almost impossible from cuttings.
TROUBLESHOOTING Cedars have fairly brittle wood, so gales and heavy falls of snow can easily snap off the top or break branches. Commonly a broken branch tears away a cup-shaped portion of wood from the main trunk, leaving a wound almost impossible to clean up, therefore prone to invasion by wood-decaying fungi. Nonetheless, any jagged branches must be sawn clean, either just above the basal collar if the damage is extensive, or just above the point of emergence of a side branch if less severe.
SIZE Cedars will reach up to 26 × 10ft./8 × 3m. after ten years, 40 × 13ft./12 × 4m. after twenty years and, note this carefully, 115 × 20ft./35 × 6m. ultimately.

Cercidiphyllum KATSURA TREE

An infrequently grown deciduous tree that in some seasons produces spectacular fall colors. In good soil will attain a large size, and should really only be planted where it has room to achieve its full potential.

SOIL Tolerates most, but is best on moist, rich, deep, well-drained loams, preferably slightly acidic.
SITUATION Light shade, which in practice probably means a woodland situation with even taller trees close by. In some areas, shelter from late frosts to avoid shoot tip damage. Zones 4–8.
WATERING AND FEEDING Until the tree is well established mulch in fall and spring, and feed with a balanced rose or similar potash-rich fertilizer in mid-spring.
PRUNING None needed. The plant is naturally multi-stemmed, but if a single-stemmed tree is desired all the other stems can be cut back to soil level.
COMMON PROBLEMS None.
PROPAGATION By layering, seeds and cuttings.
TROUBLESHOOTING Should not be necessary; if serious damage occurs to one stem of a multi-stemmed plant, that stem should be cut back to soil level.
SIZE Will reach about 26 × 20ft./8 × 6m. after ten years and multi-stemmed trees up to 40 × 33ft./12 × 10m. after thirty years.

Chamaecyparis, Cupressus, × Cupressocyparis

These are the three genera of important coniferous garden trees popularly called cypresses, × *Cupressocyparis* being an intergeneric hybrid between the other two and containing one particularly important tree known as Leyland cypress. Although some cypress plants are useful as ornamental specimens, many grow far too large and can lose their attractive shape as they age. They all tend to be used more as hedging plants, although here too there are important considerations of size and vigor.

SOIL Almost any, although best in fairly deep, moist loams.

SITUATION Tolerant of a wide range of situations but unsuccessful when exposed to very icy or salt-laden winds, so therefore inappropriate for coastal planting. *Chamaecyparis* species and cultivars mostly Zones 5–8; × *Cupressocyparis leylandii*, Zones 6–10; *Cupressus* spp. Zones 6–9 and 9–10 according to species.

WATERING AND FEEDING Until well established mulch in fall and spring; feed with a general fertilizer in mid-spring.

PRUNING None. When grown as a hedge, clip twice, first around midsummer and again in early fall; or clip once only in late summer, although this will look neat for a shorter time.

COMMON PROBLEMS Browning from wind damage, red spider mite, and fungal root decay (including honey fungus).

PROPAGATION Not feasible: cuttings need a misting facility.

TROUBLESHOOTING Once cypresses have grown more than about 6½–10ft./2–3m. above their desired height, they will almost inevitably remain misshapen after cutting back, because they do not regenerate sufficiently well from old wood. For the same reason, moderately large trees broken by storms or broken or bent by heavy falls of snow are aesthetically usually beyond salvation and should be felled. The commonest problems arise with the upright, columnar or pyramidal cultivars of Lawson cypress (*Chamaecyparis lawsoniana*), such as 'Ellwoodii' or 'Ellwood's Pillar'. These tend to open out naturally as they mature and are very prone to spreading outward, like peeled bananas, after snowfalls. They can sometimes be rescued by wiring (see page 194) but, because this opening out is such a frequent occurrence, I think it is sensible to wire all of these varieties anyway as a precaution.

SIZE Varies enormously, so read label information. Unfortunately, there is still a tendency for some nurseries to sell as "dwarf conifers" *Chamaecyparis* cultivars that will become rather tall trees, and while there are some fairly slow-growing cultivars, such as 'Ellwoodii', that will only attain about 16ft./5m. after twenty years, there are also some almost unstoppable monsters. Leyland cypress certainly has its value in producing rapid shelter, but if it isn't regularly and enthusiastically restrained, it can become a major problem. As the hybrid has only existed since the turn of the century, its full growth potential can only be guessed at, but it easily grows 3ft./1m. per year for a considerable time, and 115–130ft./35–40m. ultimately is not improbable. One way to thwart growth, especially of *Chamaecyparis obtusa*, is to keep its dwarf cultivars in clay pots sunk in the ground.

Chamaecyparis nootkatensis 'Pendula'

Cornus – Crataegus

Cornus kousa chinensis

Brutting hazel

LATE SUMMER Break the strongest side-shoots about half way along their length, but leave them hanging. This concentrates the plant's energies into producing a better crop.

Cornus DOGWOOD

In addition to the shrubby cornuses grown chiefly in the garden for their brightly colored winter bark (see page 33), there are tree-sized species known for their mostly showy white bracts in spring. These tree dogwoods are very popular in the East and Southeast, and sections of the West Coast and Pacific Northwest, and include *C. florida* and its many cultivars, some with pink and red bracts, *C. kousa chinensis*, and *C. nuttallii* (Zone 9), a native of northern California and the Northwest. Other dogwood trees include *C. alternifolia* and *C. controversa* with tiers of small white bractless flowers and *C. mas* with small yellow flowers on bare twigs in early spring.

Soil Tolerates most, although best on moist, rich, acid loams.

Situation Full sun to light shade. Zones 4–8.

Watering and feeding Until well established mulch in fall and spring; feed with a balanced rose or similar potash-rich fertilizer in mid-spring, and again around midsummer.

Pruning None needed, although to maintain the effect of the tiered species it is wise to cut out any intermediate branches.

Common problems None.

Propagation Semi-ripe cuttings in summer, or by layering.

Troubleshooting Should not be necessary, and although regeneration will usually occur when old branches are cut out, the shape of the tiered forms will be lost.

Size *C. kousa* will reach about $6\frac{1}{2} \times 6\frac{1}{2}$ft./$2 \times 2$m. after ten years and $10–13 \times 10–13$ft./$3–4 \times 3–4$m. after about twenty years; *C. mas* is slow-growing, but eventually may reach 20ft./6m.

Corylus HAZEL

The hardy, deciduous hazels are often underappreciated as trees for larger gardens, although they are perhaps better described as large shrubs for they seldom develop naturally on a single stem. Rather untidy in habit, there are varieties offering attractive foliage, curiously twisted stems, and a crop of edible nuts.

Soil Any.

Situation Most, from full sun to deep shade. Zones 4–7.

Watering and feeding Until the tree is well established mulch in fall and spring, and feed with a balanced general fertilizer in mid-spring. Trees grown for nuts will crop better if a potash-rich fertilizer is used instead of a general blend.

Pruning Varies, depending on the use to which the plants are put. The ornamental purples and golden-leaved cultivars need no pruning, but leaf size and color are improved by cutting back the oldest third of the shoots to soil level each spring. In smaller gardens or restricted spaces, cut these forms back to soil level every four or five years.

The cultivar of *C. avellana* called 'Contorta', with twisted stems, is slow growing and less vigorous than the other forms, and is best left unpruned.

Hazels grown for their filberts, or hazelnuts will produce some crops if left unpruned but careful pruning is needed to yield good-quality nuts. The tree should be trained initially much as an open-centered bush apple (see page 224). Once the plant has reached about 6½ft./2m. in height, all leading shoots should be pruned back by half in early winter, but the pruning of the side-shoots is best left until the flowers are evident in spring. By mid-spring, the male catkins and reddish female flower tufts will be visible and then the more slender side-shoots bearing catkins and flowers are retained, although they may be cut back to a point just above the flower or catkin itself. Stronger side-shoots with no flowers are cut back to two buds above their bases. Any misplaced or weak, flowerless side-shoots should be cut out completely.

A process called brutting (see below left) will also help the fruiting process, by encouraging better ripening of the wood at the base of the strongest side-shoots. Brutting consists of breaking (not cutting) these longest, strongest side-shoots in late summer – about half way along their length – and then leaving them hanging, to be cut back to two buds from their bases in winter, at the same time as the winter pruning of leading shoots.

C. avellana can be grown with other shrubs to form a tall, mixed, rural-style hedge, and in this case the pruning needs to keep the plant reasonably neat and within bounds, at the expense of fruit. Clip the plant over in mid-spring, leaving on a few catkins for effect.

COMMON PROBLEMS On ornamental cultivars, none; on fruiting cultivars, squirrels and nut weevil.

PROPAGATION By layering or suckers.

TROUBLESHOOTING Old, overgrown, or otherwise misshapen trees can be rejuvenated by cutting them back to soil level. This process of coppicing was once an important commercial operation for producing fencing poles.

SIZE Pruned as described, nut trees will attain a height of about 8ft./2.5m. Unpruned, they will reach about 13 × 6½ft./4 × 2m. after ten years and twice this after twenty-five years.

Crataegus HAWTHORN

Hawthorns are good for country places or large suburban lots as ornamental flowering trees.

SOIL Any, except where very dry.

SITUATION Full sun to moderate shade. Mostly Zones 5–7.

WATERING AND FEEDING Until the tree is well established mulch in fall and spring, and feed with a balanced rose or other potash-rich fertilizer in mid-spring.

PRUNING None necessary. When grown as a hedge, clip several times starting just after the time when the last frost is likely to occur, and stop at the first frost in the fall.

COMMON PROBLEMS Fireblight.

PROPAGATION Impossible from cuttings.

TROUBLESHOOTING Old or damaged trees will regenerate well, although slowly, if cut back hard into old wood.

SIZE Attains about 13 × 5ft./4 × 1.5m. after five years, 20 × 13ft./6 × 4m. after twenty-five years, and eventually, and very rarely, perhaps 40 × 20ft./12 × 6m.

Crataegus laevigata

Davidia involucrata

Davidia DOVE TREE

Once described as the finest deciduous tree to grow in a temperate climate, *D. involucrata* is definitely one for milder areas and patient gardeners, for the fabulous white-bracted flowers that inspired the common name usually only appear after twenty years or more.

SOIL Tolerates most, although best on moist, deep, rich, well-drained loams; tolerant of moderate acidity and alkalinity.

SITUATION Full sun to light shade, with shelter from cold winds. Zones 6–8.

WATERING AND FEEDING Until the tree is well established mulch in fall and spring, and feed with a balanced rose or similar potash-rich fertilizer in mid-spring.

PRUNING None needed, although some shoot death usually occurs in winter and should be cut out in spring.

COMMON PROBLEMS None.

PROPAGATION By layers.

TROUBLESHOOTING Should not be necessary; damaged branches should be cut back neatly to just above the basal collar.

SIZE The dove tree will reach about 20 × 10ft./6 × 3m. after ten years and in good growing conditions may attain about 50 × 26ft./15 × 8m. or more after twenty-five years.

Eucalyptus

The species of *Eucalyptus*, the gum trees of Australia, are not hardy in northern climates, and even those that will survive never attain the huge size reached in warmer areas such as southern California. They are attractive and useful for their steely-blue and often appealingly shaped leaves. In the North, they can be grown in containers and summered outdoors.

SOIL Will tolerate most, but least successful in water-logged conditions; best in free draining, rich loams.

SITUATION Full sun, but tolerate light shade and require some shelter from cold winds. Zones 8–10.

WATERING AND FEEDING Until well established mulch in fall and spring; feed with general fertilizer in mid-spring.

PRUNING None necessary, but hard pruning is desirable because large plants almost invariably suffer sooner or later from wind or cold damage, and also because the rounded juvenile foliage, so beloved of flower arrangers, is only produced on young shoots. The tree is best pruned every other year: cut back half of the shoots to about 6in./15cm. above soil level, or to the junction with the permanent main stem.

COMMON PROBLEMS Aphids.

PROPAGATION Impossible from cuttings; almost always raised from seed.

TROUBLESHOOTING Old or damaged trees will be rejuvenated by cutting them hard back, to soil level if necessary.

SIZE Pruned as described, the hardiest species, *E. gunnii*, attains about 10 × 3ft./3 × 1m. in two years and will remain at about this size; unpruned, it might achieve 65 × 16ft./20 × 5m. after twenty years and 100ft./30m. in height eventually.

Eucalyptus gunnii

Fagus BEECH

One of the loveliest and most typical of hardy, deciduous, British native trees, the beech, even in its colored-leaved variants, is sadly a plant only for large gardens as a freestanding specimen. The American native beech is similar. It does, however, make a superb hedge in appropriate conditions. Hornbeam (*Carpinus betulus*) is a comparable (although unrelated) hedging plant, and may be treated similarly.

Soil Most, but much the best growth is on rich, acid, free-draining soils; tolerant of alkaline conditions.

Situation Full sun or light shade; when in leaf, casts a deep shade. Zones 4–7 for *F. sylvatica*, European beech.

Watering and feeding Until well established mulch in fall and spring; feed with a general fertilizer in mid-spring.

Pruning None necessary but can be clipped very satisfactorily as a hedge: clip twice, the first time two or three weeks after midsummer, the second in early fall; or clip once only in late summer, although this will give a neat appearance for a shorter time. Frost- or wind-damaged shoots may soon be attacked by leaf spot diseases so they should be cut out promptly.

Common problems Aphids (especially as a hedge); beech bark disease (as a specimen tree); leaf spot; wood-decaying fungi.

Propagation Impossible from cuttings.

Troubleshooting Overgrown hedges will rejuvenate well if cut back into the old wood. The job is best done in early spring, after the danger of the hardest frost has passed. Mature beech trees are very prone to damage from storms, largely because they suffer from a number of wood-decaying fungi which render them unstable; and, no matter how carefully the damage is cleaned up with saw cuts, the very existence of the wounds will admit further decay organisms. While cutting back to sound tissue just above the basal collar is worthwhile, the plant is likely to become increasingly unstable. Beech are shallow rooted, and large trees growing close to buildings and exposed to the prevailing winds should be examined by an expert.

Size Attains about 16 × 16ft./5 × 5m. after five years, 50 × 40ft./15 × 12m. after twenty years, and eventually 130ft./40m.

Fagus sylvatica

Ginkgo MAIDENHAIR TREE

Part of the appeal of this strange deciduous relative of the conifers lies in its extraordinary history as the sole surviving member of a group of plants extinct millions of years ago. It is also a quite superb specimen plant for a large garden, being extremely hardy and with a fascinating leaf shape and fine yellow colors in fall. For more confined spaces the rarer upright forms, such as *G. biloba* 'Fastigiata', are well worth hunting for.

Soil Tolerates most, but always best on rich, deep loams.

Situation Full sun to light shade. Zones 4–9.

Watering and feeding Until the tree is well established mulch in fall and spring, and feed with a balanced general fertilizer in mid-spring.

Ginkgo

Ginkgo – Koelreuteria

Gleditsia triacanthos 'Sunburst'

PRUNING None necessary, although on upright forms cut off any shoots that show a tendency to spread.
COMMON PROBLEMS None.
PROPAGATION Impossible from cuttings.
TROUBLESHOOTING Rarely necessary, but damaged branches may be cut back to the basal collar and new shoots will regenerate, much as with broad-leaved trees and quite unlike true conifers.
SIZE Up to 10×3ft./3×1m. after five years; 16×10ft./5×3m. after ten years and 100×40ft./30×12m. eventually, although 'Fastigiata' should never exceed about 8ft./2.5m. in spread.

Gleditsia HONEY LOCUST

The deciduous honey locust has become one of the more popular ornamental trees of recent years, although its brittle twigs and intolerance of exposure are significant drawbacks.
SOIL Tolerates most, but best on rich, deep loams.
SITUATION Full sun to light shade; must be sheltered from winds because the twigs are brittle and very easily broken, resulting in a misshapen and unattractive plant. Zones 4–9.
WATERING AND FEEDING Until the tree is well established mulch in fall and spring, and feed with a balanced general fertilizer in mid-spring.
PRUNING None necessary.
COMMON PROBLEMS None.
PROPAGATION Almost impossible from cuttings.
TROUBLESHOOTING Damaged branches may be cut back to the basal collar and new shoots will regenerate fairly well, but the shape will never recover satisfactorily.
SIZE The selected forms grown in gardens, such as the golden-foliaged *G. triacanthos* 'Sunburst', are slower and lower growing than the true species and will reach 10×3ft./3×1m. after five years and about 26×16ft./8×5m. after twenty years.

Ilex HOLLY

As a group, the hollies are valuable garden evergreens. They are very hardy, slow growing and appealing both in their foliage and berries. Among the numerous foliage variants are some with more or less spineless leaves, and these are particularly valuable in smaller gardens.
SOIL Tolerates most, but moist, acid preferred.
SITUATION Full sun to moderate shade. Zones vary according to species, but many are hardy in Zones 4–7.
WATERING AND FEEDING Until well established mulch in fall and spring, and feed with a balanced general fertilizer in mid-spring, although on fruiting forms (hollies have the sexes on separate plants), use a potash-rich feed or Hollytone.
PRUNING None necessary. When grown as a hedge, clip twice, the first time two or three weeks after midsummer, the second in early fall; or clip once only in late summer, although this will give a neat appearance for a shorter time.
COMMON PROBLEMS Leaf miner, especially on *Ilex opaca*.

Ilex aquifolium

PROPAGATION Softwood or hardwood cuttings, seeds, grafting.
TROUBLESHOOTING Damaged branches may be cut back to the basal collar and new shoots will regenerate fairly well, but as growth is so slow, the attractive shape of the undamaged plant will seldom return satisfactorily.
SIZE Varies greatly, so check label information carefully. Some species and varieties remain as little more than dwarf shrubs, while the commonly grown *I. aquifolium* attains 10–13 × 3ft./ 3–4 × 1m. after five years, 33–40 × 13ft./10–12 × 4m. after twenty, and eventually up to 50–65ft./15–20m. in height.

Juniperus JUNIPER

Although relatively few conifers should find a place in gardens other than as dwarf forms or hedging plants, junipers are among the exceptions; such cultivars as *J. scopulorum* 'Skyrocket' contribute a useful conical or spire-like effect among other plants.
SOIL Tolerates most, including fairly dry soils, although best on moist, rich loams; tolerant of moderate acidity and alkalinity.
SITUATION Full sun to light shade, with shelter from cold winds. Zones vary according to species, the native *J. virginiana* grows in Zones 2–9; *J. scopulorum* 'Skyrocket' in Zones 3–7.
WATERING AND FEEDING Until well established mulch in fall and spring; feed with a general purpose fertilizer in spring.
PRUNING None needed; although junipers may be trimmed lightly, they do not regenerate well when cut back into old wood.
COMMON PROBLEMS Red spider mite; blight.
PROPAGATION Semi-ripe cuttings in summer, or hardwood cuttings in winter; it is often very difficult to induce rooting without a misting facility.

Juniperus scopulorum 'Skyrocket'

TROUBLESHOOTING Difficult because of the juniper's inability to regenerate from old wood. Broken or diseased branches should be cut back neatly to the basal collar, but it is important not to cut away any more growth than is absolutely necessary.
SIZE Varies greatly between species and cultivars, and as there are so many it is impossible to generalize. Suppliers regularly underestimate the sizes of conifers, whether sold as "dwarf" or "tall" selections; check the ultimate height of your chosen plant in at least two reference sources.

Koelreuteria GOLDEN-RAIN TREE

A hardy, deciduous flowering tree that could be more widely grown as a shade or lawn tree. Its golden-yellow flowers and bladder-like fruits are produced in midsummer. Leaves turn yellow in fall.
SOIL Will tolerate most, although best on moist, deep, rich, well-drained loams; tolerant of moderate acidity and alkalinity.
SITUATION Grows best in full sun, with shelter from cold winds. Zones 5–9.
WATERING AND FEEDING Until well established mulch in fall and spring, and feed with a balanced rose or similar potash-rich fertilizer in mid-spring, and again around midsummer.

Koelreuteria – Malus

Koelreuteria paniculata

PRUNING None needed.

COMMON PROBLEMS None.

PROPAGATION Root cuttings in winter, or from seed.

TROUBLESHOOTING Unlikely to be necessary; although damaged branches should be cut back to the basal collar, there will be little regeneration from old wood. *K. paniculata* often succumbs to disease and decay after about thirty years.

SIZE The normal species will attain about $16 \times 6\frac{1}{2}$ft./5×2m. after five years and perhaps 40×23ft./12×7m. after about 25 years.

Laburnum GOLDEN-CHAIN TREE

Laburnums are very hardy and in the best selected forms very beautiful, but they age rather gracelessly and old trees are invariably misshapen. The seeds are also poisonous; it is perhaps not wise to plant a laburnum in a garden with very young children.

SOIL Will tolerate most, but especially successful in well drained alkaline or slightly acid conditions.

SITUATION Full sun to light shade. Zones 5–7.

WATERING AND FEEDING Until the tree is well established mulch in fall and spring, and feed with a rose or similar potash-rich fertilizer in mid-spring.

PRUNING None.

COMMON PROBLEMS None.

PROPAGATION Very difficult, but hardwood cuttings in winter may be successful. Also seeds; grafting.

TROUBLESHOOTING Damaged branches may be cut back to the basal collar but regeneration is poor or nonexistent and the tree will almost inevitably look disfigured. Laburnums are not long-lived and tend to succumb to fungal decay and lose their attractive appearance after 30 to 40 years. They have shallow root systems and need staking throughout most of their lives.

SIZE The hybrid to grow is the long-flowered Voss's laburnum, *L.* × *watereri* 'Vossii', which will reach 13×5ft./4×1.5m. after five years, 23×13ft./7×4m. after twenty years and, if you are lucky and it lives long enough, perhaps 33ft./10m. tall eventually.

Magnolia

Although some magnolias are barely more than shrubs in many gardens, this quite magnificent genus of mainly deciduous plants does include some superb tree-sized species. In general, the larger the species, the more tender it tends to be, and the finest and biggest specimens are in mild, moist areas.

SOIL Tolerates most and, contrary to widely held belief, will thrive in moderately alkaline conditions – although it is also true that the best plants tend to be on deep, rich, rather acid loams.

SITUATION Full sun to light or moderate shade. The evergreen *M. grandiflora* (Zones 7–9) is often grown by a wall but while it thrives in this situation, it only really needs shelter in colder, more exposed gardens and can be grown successfully as a good free-standing specimen. Zones vary: Zones 5–9 for *M. soulangiana*; Zones 5–9 for *M. stellata*.

Laburnum × *watereri* 'Vossii'

Watering and feeding Until the tree is well established mulch in fall and spring, and feed with a rose or similar potash-rich fertilizer in mid-spring.

Pruning See below.

Common problems None.

Propagation Tip cuttings in spring, seeds, layers, grafts.

Troubleshooting Damaged branches or misplaced branches may be removed, but any pruning should be kept to a minimum because magnolias tend to produce masses of small twigs from the position of any cuts. *M. grandiflora* is prone to damage from heavy snowfalls, and broken branches should be cut clean and, if necessary, the plant supported with wires and stakes to aid the recovery of shape. Wall-trained plants of *M. grandiflora* should be regularly checked for the tightness of ties and retied. A common problem with the multi-stemmed *M. × soulangiana* is that the branches bend down to ground level and therefore impede lawn mowing when, as often, the plant is grown in grass. It may be worth using wires to hold the branches up (see page 194).

Size Varies greatly, so check label descriptions. As a guideline, *M. grandiflora* and *M. × soulangiana* will reach about 10 × 6½ft./3 × 2m. after five years and 26–30 × 13–16ft./8–9 × 4–5m. after twenty or more years, but others, such as *M. stellata*, seldom exceed 13ft./4m. in height.

Malus ORNAMENTAL APPLE, CRAB APPLE

The genus *Malus* plays its most important role in gardens by including the apple-producing species, but there are several valuable ornamental blossoming species, too, generally grouped as flowering crab apples. Many are much prettier than the more popular flowering cherries, but they tend to suffer from the same pests and diseases as true apples.

Soil Almost any, although least successful on very heavy, cold, wet clays.

Situation Full sun to very light shade. Most, Zones 4–8.

Watering and feeding Until the tree is well established, mulch in fall and spring, and feed with a rose or similar potash-rich fertilizer in mid-spring.

Pruning None necessary on varieties grown solely for their blossoms, but cut out diseased or crossing branches in winter. Cultivars such as 'John Downie' or 'Golden Hornet', grown equally for their fruit, may either be left unpruned or treated in the same way as bush apples (see page 224).

Common problems Scab; canker; mildew; aphids.

Propagation Not feasible by cuttings.

Troubleshooting Damaged or overgrown trees may be treated in the same way as apples (see page 227), but much of the appeal of old garden trees comes from their distorted shape. They respond to hard pruning by producing masses of new shoot growth which will itself require pruning.

Size Most ornamental *Malus* species and cultivars may be obtained grafted onto the same rootstocks used for apples, and the rootstock may dictate the overall size of the tree (see page 223).

Magnolia × soulangiana

Malus 'Golden Hornet'

Parrotia PERSIAN IRONWOOD

A deciduous tree or large shrub with coarse leaves, grown principally for its glorious fall color. Its drawbacks are a relatively dull appearance in summer, rather exacting soil requirements and fairly vigorous growth.

SOIL Moderately acidic, organic soil gives the best results and growth will never be as satisfactory in alkaline conditions.

SITUATION Full sun to light shade. Zones 4–8.

WATERING AND FEEDING Until the tree is well established mulch in fall and spring, and feed with a balanced general fertilizer in mid-spring.

PRUNING None necessary, but may be trimmed in spring if grown against a wall or in other restricted space.

COMMON PROBLEMS None.

PROPAGATION Not feasible by cuttings but may be layered.

Parrotia persica

TROUBLESHOOTING Unlikely to be necessary, but will regenerate fairly well if cut back in spring into moderately old wood.

SIZE Attains about $8 \times 6\frac{1}{2}$ft./2.5×2m. in five years and continues approximately to double every five years until reaching around 33ft./10m. tall with a spread of 26ft./8m.

Picea SPRUCE

The coniferous genus *Picea* is most familiar in the shape of *P. abies*, the Norway spruce or Christmas tree, and this is the one most likely to be seen as a garden plant. By and large, this is a genus of forest trees, although a few mutant dwarf forms are both useful and attractive (see page 79).

SOIL Intolerant of poor, alkaline, or dry soils.
SITUATION Open situation to allow room to grow; intolerant of more than light shade. Most, Zones 3–6.
WATERING AND FEEDING Until well established mulch in fall and spring; feed with general fertilizer in mid-spring.
PRUNING None; cannot be trimmed to form a hedge.
COMMON PROBLEMS Adelgids (aphid-like insects), some of which produce small, pineapple-shaped galls.
PROPAGATION Not feasible; cuttings need a misting facility for successful propagation.
TROUBLESHOOTING Not necessary. Remove storm-damaged trees, for they will never recover their appealing pyramidal shape.
SIZE Few gardeners plant Norway spruce as a specimen tree, for it grows very rapidly, especially in the early stages, attaining $13 \times 6\frac{1}{2}$ft./4×2m. after five years. Ultimately, it becomes very tall – perhaps 100ft./30m.

Picea pungens 'Koster'

Pinus PINE

A famous tree nursery once described the pines as the conifers with the most class and, undoubtedly, their long needles (very long in some instances) confer a distinction lacking in other genera. Two species distinctive enough to grow as specimens are the lacebark pine, *P. bungeana*, and *P. cembra*, the Swiss stone pine, but few species are small enough to be considered other than for fairly large gardens; although there are some dwarf forms (see page 79).
SOIL Free-draining; preferably – but not essentially – acidic.
SITUATION Open situation to allow room to grow; intolerant of more than light shade. The most attractive ornamental species are the long-needled pines: some are tender so shelter from cold winds and late frosts. Varies; many forms are Zones 4–8.
WATERING AND FEEDING Until well established mulch in fall and spring; feed with a general fertilizer in mid-spring.
PRUNING A white pine (*Pinus strobus*) hedge can be pruned in spring by cutting out the central buds or 'candles' after they start growing.
COMMON PROBLEMS Pine sawfly; pine needle scale; pine web worm.
PROPAGATION Not feasible; cuttings need a misting facility.
TROUBLESHOOTING Not normally necessary. Trees badly damaged by storms are best removed for they will never recover their appealing shape. Trees with more limited damage may be tidied by having broken branches cut back to just above the basal collar, but there will be no regeneration of new shoots.
SIZE Varies considerably, so check label information. Two species for larger gardens are *P. peuce* (Zone 5) and *P. leucodermis* (Zone 6), both with fine shapes and, in the latter case, beautiful blue cones when mature (both 13×3ft./4×1m. after ten years, 33×10ft./10×3m. after twenty years). Another species, *P. monte-zumae* (Zones 7–9), with its long, almost shaggy needles, attains $20 \times 6\frac{1}{2}$ft./6×2m. after ten years, 40×16ft./12×5m. after twenty years.

Pinus montezumae

Populus candicans 'Aurora'

Populus POPLAR

As garden plants, poplars have a fondness for water and grow much larger than their owners expect, although they do have the advantage of thriving in soils that few other trees will tolerate. There are, however, a few useful ornamental varieties.

SOIL Almost any, but especially successful in very wet soils.

SITUATION Full sun to moderate shade. Zones 2–8.

WATERING AND FEEDING Until well established mulch in fall and spring, and apply a general fertilizer in mid-spring.

PRUNING None necessary, although a denser, bushier plant will result from cutting it back hard every five or six years in the spring. Some gardeners regularly pollard poplars by cutting new growth back each spring to the main trunk (see page 196).

COMMON PROBLEMS Canker; rust; leaf-attacking insects.

PROPAGATION Hardwood cuttings in winter.

TROUBLESHOOTING Will regenerate very well if cut back hard to remove broken or misshapen branches, and this usually results in a more attractive plant.

SIZE Varies slightly between species and cultivars, so check label information. Among screening species, the Lombardy poplar will reach 16×3ft./5×1m. after five years, $33 \times 6\frac{1}{2}$ft./10×2m. after ten years and up to 115×26ft./35×8m. eventually. Other species spread much more widely, and even the popular ornamental *P. balsamifera* 'Aurora' becomes a very big tree, attaining perhaps 65×26ft./20×8m. over twenty-five or thirty years.

Prunus

The genus *Prunus* includes all of the garden pit fruits – plums, damsons, cherries, peaches, nectarines and apricots – and these are covered in detail on pages 226–34. But it also embraces the vast tribe of so-called flowering cherries, both the Japanese cultivars, overplanted almost everywhere, and a number of choice species. They are fairly undemanding in their soil and site requirements, but in my view, their flowers and foliage aren't always beautiful enough to compensate for their tendency to disease and their habit of surface rooting and suckering.

SOIL Almost any, although least successful on cold, wet clays.

SITUATION Full sun to very light shade. Varies, but mostly Zones 5–8.

WATERING AND FEEDING Until the tree is well established mulch in fall and spring, and feed with rose or similar potash-rich fertilizer in mid-spring.

PRUNING None necessary on trees grown solely for their blooms, although diseased or crossing branches should be cut out in winter. The winter cherry, in particular, is prone to a great deal of twig death and it pays to cut out the worst of this in the cause of neatness. If any pruning is necessary, delay until summer to reduce the risk of leaf infection.

COMMON PROBLEMS Bacterial canker; various dying back conditions – the cultivar 'Kwanzan' is especially prone to one from which the tree seldom recovers; aphids; various leaf diseases.

Prunus × subhirtella 'Autumnalis'

PROPAGATION Cuttings under glass; budding on seedling stock.
TROUBLESHOOTING Mature ornamental cherries are troublesome trees because they are prone to several diseases of the bark
and wood that cause die-back. The temptation is to cut out the
damaged branches but this invariably compounds the problem,
rendering the tree even more unsightly and possibly allowing
further infection by fungi and bacteria. Damaged or diseased ornamental cherries seldom recover and should be removed.

Most are grafted onto *P. avium* rootstock, which is very prone
to surface rooting. This causes problems in lawns, where the roots
foul mower blades, and also under paths and driveways. Little can
be done about this, as mounding soil over the top or cutting the
roots off is only a temporary measure; more roots surface, and the
damage often throws up suckers.

SIZE Varies considerably. Most of the popular double-flowered
cherries reach about 10–13 × 6½–10ft./3–4 × 2–3m. after five years
and perhaps 33 × 23ft./10 × 7m. after 25 years, after which they
begin to decline. The narrowly upright 'Amanogawa' reaches a
similar height, but remains at 3ft./1m. in width until it reaches the
age of fifteen to twenty years, when it tends to open out most
unattractively. The height of the weeping 'Kiku-shidare-sakura' is
largely determined by the height of its graft onto the *P. avium*
rootstock, but whatever the initial size, the rootstock will itself
grow to produce a plant perhaps 13ft./4m. tall in twenty years.
The winter-flowering cherry, *P. subhirtella* 'Autumnalis', is a useful tree but often planted in far too small a space; it may reach
26 × 20ft./8 × 6m. in 20 to 25 years. Ornamental flowering or
foliage forms of plum and peach will attain a similar size, but tend
to be lower growing if grafted onto the rootstock 'Pixy'. The
beautifully barked Tibetan cherry, *P. serrula*, reaches about 10 ×
6½ft./3 × 2m. after five years and ultimately 33 × 16ft./10 × 5m..

Pyrus   ORNAMENTAL PEAR

The best known *Pyrus* is the pear tree, but there are a few orna-
mental garden species, too, most notably the weeping, silvery,
willow-leaved pear, *P. salicifolia* 'Pendula', which has the appeal of
genuine weeping willows and fewer drawbacks. *P. calleryana*
'Capitol' has early white flowers and a narrow habit.
SOIL Tolerates almost any, but the richer the better.
SITUATION Full sun. *P. calleryana*, Zones 4–8; *P. salicifolia*,
Zones 5–8.
WATERING AND FEEDING Until well established mulch in fall
and spring, and apply a general fertilizer in mid-spring.
PRUNING None, but plants must be staked.
COMMON PROBLEMS Scab; fireblight.
PROPAGATION Not feasible by cuttings.
TROUBLESHOOTING As the tree ages, the branches tend to
become a congested mass; thin them out by removing whole
branches every few years, in winter. Any damaged by scab or
other problems should be cut out at the same time.
SIZE About 8 × 6½ft./2.5 × 2m. after five years; 20–26 × 16–20ft./
6–8 × 5–6m. after twenty or more years.

Pyrus salicifolia 'Pendula'

Robinia – Taxodium

Robinia pseudoacacia

Robinia

There are several species of fairly hardy deciduous robinias, often called the hardy or false acacias, grown for their pink and white flowers or, in one particular instance, for golden foliage (*R. pseudoacacia* 'Frisia'). Like their relatives the true acacias, they often fail because the site is not appropriate.

SOIL Tolerates most, but best on free draining fertile sites and least successful on heavy, water-logged soils.

SITUATION Full sun to very light shade, but must have shelter from winds, which damage the foliage of some varieties and can break the brittle twigs. Zones 3–8.

WATERING AND FEEDING Until the tree is well established mulch in fall and spring, and feed with a rose or similar potash-rich fertilizer in mid-spring.

PRUNING See below.

COMMON PROBLEMS None.

PROPAGATION Not feasible by cuttings.

TROUBLESHOOTING Problems are only likely to arise when plants have been damaged by wind. They will regenerate if cut back a short way into sound wood in spring, but the problem will recur while the plant remains in an exposed site.

SIZE 10 × 8ft./3 × 2.5m. after five years, up to 50 × 26ft./15 × 8m. after twenty or more years, although the pink-flowered *R. hispida* is smaller, reaching barely half this size and growth rate.

Salix WILLOW

I believe that the best of the garden willows are the shrub-sized species, but there are a few tree species that are useful for their ability to grow in otherwise difficult sites: the plants usually called *S. matsudana* 'Tortuosa', *S. alba argentea*, and *S. a. vitellina*.

SOIL Tolerates most, particularly wet or water-logged soils.

SITUATION Full sun to moderate shade. Because all large willows have water-seeking and invasive roots, they should not be planted where they may damage drains or the foundations of buildings. It is inadvisable to plant any tree-sized willows closer to a building than a distance equal to twice their ultimate spread. *S. alba*, Zones 2–8; *S* × *chrysocoma* and *S. matsudana*, Zones 6–8.

WATERING AND FEEDING Until well established mulch in fall and spring; feed with general fertilizer in mid-spring.

PRUNING None necessary, but as many of the species are grown for their colored shoots, pruning to stimulate some new growth each year is desirable. No matter how hard willows are cut back, they will regenerate. They are among the few trees for which regular pollarding to a crown may look attractive (see page 214).

COMMON PROBLEMS Many species suffer from leaf-attacking insects and fungal leaf spots, which may cause some disfigurement as summer progresses. The commonest so-called weeping willow, (usually called *S. babylonica*, but more accurately *S.* × *chrysocoma*) suffers from anthracnose disease, which causes leaf spots and shoot die-back. It is one further reason why this most invasive of willows should not be planted in gardens.

Salix alba

PROPAGATION Hardwood cuttings in winter, layers or suckers; willows root extremely readily from cuttings.

TROUBLESHOOTING Old willows almost invariably suffer from broken and damaged branches, but often look the better for it. They regenerate and heal so successfully that cutting out of damaged parts may be as hard or light as aesthetics dictate. If a large tree must be felled, especially if close to a building, take expert advice first because willows draw more water from the soil than almost any other tree and the removal of such a natural water pump can lead to water-logging and consequent problems.

SIZE All big willows grow quickly. *S. × chrysocoma* reaches 16 × 16ft./5 × 5m. in five years and up to 65 × 65ft./20 × 20m. in twenty years. The other tree species, including the popular twisted *S. matsudana* 'Tortuosa', are unlikely to achieve half this size and growth rate.

Sorbus

This is a most useful genus of medium-sized and hardy, deciduous trees, grown principally for their attractively colored berries but with good flowers and, in many instances, spring or fall foliage appeal also.

SOIL Almost any, including strongly alkaline soils.

SITUATION Full sun to moderate shade; most are tolerant of wind. Varies according to species, mostly Zones 2–8.

WATERING AND FEEDING Until the tree is well established mulch in fall and spring, and feed with a rose or similar potash-rich fertilizer in mid-spring.

PRUNING None; as many varieties are grafted suckers may arise, which should be promptly cut away.

COMMON PROBLEMS None, although some species may be attacked by leaf-spotting fungi and insects.

PROPAGATION Not successful from cuttings. Layerings.

TROUBLESHOOTING Should not be necessary, although will regenerate fairly well if cut back lightly into old wood in spring.

SIZE Varies slightly among cultivars of the main species, which are usually grouped into the mountain ashes or rowans and the whitebeams. Most, however, attain about 8 × 5ft./2.5 × 1.5m. after five years, double this after ten years and 40–50 × 16–26ft./ 12–15 × 5–8m. eventually.

Sorbus 'Joseph Rock'

Taxodium SWAMP CYPRESS

A strange but lovely tree, *T. distichum* is one of the few deciduous conifers. Its common name is misleading for it will grow in a variety of soils, but although many gardeners are attracted by young specimens, it will grow too large for most gardens.

SOIL Tolerates most except very dry conditions, and has the advantage of tolerating, although not requiring, very heavy, wet, or even water-logged clays.

SITUATION Full sun with shelter from cold winds; the key to success with this tree is not to plant it in a swamp but to grow it somewhere with warm summers. Zones 4–8.

Taxodium distichum

Taxodium – Tsuga

WATERING AND FEEDING Until the tree is well established mulch in fall and spring; and feed with a balanced, general fertilizer in mid-spring.

PRUNING None needed.

COMMON PROBLEMS None.

PROPAGATION Hardwood cuttings in winter, or from seed.

TROUBLESHOOTING If a plant threatens to outgrow its space it may be cut to about 6½ft./2m. above soil level; it will look unsightly for a time but should produce new shoots from the old wood. Dead or damaged branches may also be cut back in the expectation that they will regenerate.

SIZE Will attain 16 × 6½ft./5 × 2m. after ten years and perhaps 100 × 33ft./30 × 10m. after thirty years.

Taxus ENGLISH YEW

A uniquely special tree, living to a phenomenal age and possessed of a peculiar majesty, although best known in gardens for producing the densest and most beautiful of hedges. While the wild form is unlikely to be planted in gardens, there are a few selected form and color variants that are most attractive, if slow growing. Yew is exceedingly poisonous and its various parts should not be eaten by animals or people, but it will not poison the soil nor harm other plants; it is simply a very effective competitor because of the dense shade it casts.

SOIL Almost any, but best on deep, rich loams; excellent in strongly alkaline conditions.

SITUATION Full sun to fairly deep shade; tolerant of fairly exposed conditions, but stunted by severe winters. Zones 6–8.

WATERING AND FEEDING Until well established mulch in fall and spring, and feed with a general fertilizer in mid-spring.

PRUNING None. When grown as a hedge, clip twice, the first time around midsummer, the second in early fall; or clip once only in late summer, although this will give a neat appearance for a shorter time.

COMMON PROBLEMS None.

PROPAGATION Hardwood cuttings in winter.

TROUBLESHOOTING Should not be necessary on freestanding trees, although a yew will regenerate very well if cut back hard into old wood in spring – and thus old and overgrown hedges may be rejuvenated very successfully. It is worth remembering however, that much of the appeal of ancient yew trees is their wizened, gnarled appearance.

SIZE Both of these features of the yew, together with its great age potential, have aroused considerable and often erroneous speculation. Although the selected forms such as the fastigiate Irish yew and the golden-foliaged cultivars are slow growing, *T. baccata* when used for hedging will, after the first year, put on 6–8in./15–20cm. each season and attain a height of 6½ft./2m. to full hedge width after about ten years. A freestanding tree of the normal species will reach about 6½ × 3–5ft./2 × 1–1.5m. after ten years, 13 × 8–10ft./4 × 2.5–3m. after twenty years, and perhaps 100 × 65ft./30 × 20m. after anything from 200 to 1,000 years.

Taxus baccata

Thuja FALSE CEDAR, ARBORVITAE

These are perhaps the important garden conifers least known by the majority of gardeners, both as specimens for the large garden and as hedging plants, I find them superior. *T. occidentalis*, American arborvitae, is fairly slow growing and very hardy.

SOIL Always best on deep, moist soils, but tolerant of most.

SITUATION Full sun to light shade; *Thuja* is more tolerant of wind exposure than cypresses, but will be browned by salt spray. *T. occidentalis*, Zones 2–7; *T. plicata*, Zones 5–7.

WATERING AND FEEDING Until well established mulch in fall and spring, and feed with a general fertilizer in mid-spring.

PRUNING None. When grown as a hedge, clip twice, the first time around midsummer, the second in early fall; or clip once only in late summer, although this will give a neat appearance for a shorter time. Some gardeners are allergic to the foliage of *Thuja*, which can produce a slight skin rash when handled. It is therefore wise to wear gloves when clipping hedges.

COMMON PROBLEMS None.

PROPAGATION Hardwood cuttings in winter.

TROUBLESHOOTING Should not be necessary. Damaged trees will regenerate slowly if only cut back into wood younger than about eight years old.

SIZE A popular species in England, especially for hedges, is *T. plicata*, which will reach 13×5ft./4×1.5m. in five years and ultimately a height of up to 130ft./40m. *T. occidentalis* may eventually reach 40ft./12m. or more.

Thuja plicata 'Aurea'

Tsuga HEMLOCK

Although the full-grown western hemlock, *T. heterophylla*, makes a stately specimen coniferous tree with a characteristically drooping main shoot, it is a big and uncommon plant. I include it here because it makes a superb and very dense hedge. More widely grown in North America is the Canadian hemlock, *T. canadensis*, and its many attractive often dwarf cultivars.

SOIL Most, but usually best on free draining, moist, acidic soils.

SITUATION Full sun to moderate shade; *Tsuga* is very tolerant of wind exposure. *T. canadensis*, Zones 3–7; *T. heterophylla*, Zones 6–8.

WATERING AND FEEDING Until well established mulch in fall and spring, and apply a general fertilizer in mid-spring.

PRUNING None. When grown as a hedge, clip in late spring, and in midsummer if needed.

COMMON PROBLEMS Hemlock woolly adelgids in the Northeast.

PROPAGATION Not feasible from cuttings.

TROUBLESHOOTING Should not be necessary, although trees damaged for any reason will regenerate slowly if cut back into moderately old wood.

SIZE Freestanding trees will attain 13×5ft./4×1.5m. in five years, $26–30 \times 13$ft./$8–9 \times 4$m. in ten years, and ultimately a height of up to 130ft./40m. in favorable sites.

Tsuga heterophylla

TREE FRUIT

One of the commonest criticisms leveled at the authors of gardening textbooks is, "My tree doesn't look like the one in your pictures", for every tree is an individual and will branch and produce its buds slightly differently from its neighbors. Pruning diagrams always show idealized trees, but I have tried in the plant entries to cover individual variations in position of buds and so forth. Adhere as closely as you can to my advice, but if your tree is more or less vigorous or has some other growth quirk, don't worry; a few inches variation in the position of a pruning cut will not make the difference between success and failure.

While there are general similarities between the cultivation of fruit trees and ornamental trees, there are also a number of differences. These can perhaps be summed up by saying that fruit trees need considerably more care and attention in the early years and a little more throughout their lives, but the better you look after them when they are young the simpler they will be to care for later on.

Although it is possible to obtain a fruit crop of sorts from a wide range of soil types, the best will always come from deep, well-manured, and fertile loams. Very acid, very alkaline, and very cold, wet soils are those least likely to give satisfactory results. But I must stress the importance of feeding fruit trees, of not forcing them to compete with surrounding grass or other vegetation, especially in their early years, and of paying careful attention to watering and mulching. The greater bulk of any fruit is, in fact, water, and only by ensuring that the soil remains moist through mulching will your trees, young trees especially, be able to obtain enough water to swell the fruit and prevent premature drop.

Like many ornamental trees, most fruit trees that you buy have been grafted: a fruiting variety, carefully bred or selected over the years for its cropping qualities, has been grafted onto another, the rootstock variety, bred for its rooting efficiency. With most tree fruit, there is little choice in rootstock variety but apples are a notable exception. Here, the rootstock exerts an influence on the overall size of the tree, irrespective of the fruiting variety. It is possible, therefore, to grow apple trees appropriate to the size of your garden, but it is not always appreciated that the more dwarfing the influence of the rootstock, the better must be the growing conditions. The most dwarfing of all apple rootstocks, known as M.27, while very useful in allowing a small apple tree to be grown in a container, must be planted in a high quality, soil-based potting mixture and fed annually throughout its life. Dwarfing rootstocks also require permanent staking and are too weakly anchored for exposed sites.

With certain exceptions, fruit trees will crop better (some will otherwise not do so at all) when grown in combination with others of a compatible variety. The reason for this is simply that most apples, pears, and to a lesser extent plums, cannot be fertilized by their own pollen. The choice of the best pollinating cultivar may vary from district to district, so take advice from the nurseryman from whom you buy your plants. The problem does not arise with sour cherries, the most popular modern sweet cherry ('Stella'), peaches, nectarines, apricots, or figs, all of which are self-fertilizing.

The need for a pollinator variety of apple or pear may create difficulties for gardeners with limited space. But there are ways around the problem. The first is to grow your trees as cordons (single stems producing fruiting spurs), which take up very little room, or to choose a genetic dwarf or compact spur-type tree. Both require less pruning, the compact spur trees often bearing earlier and more fruits than semi-dwarf trees. The quality of fruit equals that on standard or other dwarf trees. Another possibility is to grow a single, family tree. This is a plant in which more than one fruiting variety has been grafted onto a single rootstock: giving a range of eating and cooking apples over a period of several months.

PRUNING AND TRAINING

The most important difference of all between fruit and ornamental trees is that fruit trees will not crop to their full potential unless they are trained or pruned in an appropriate manner. Training is essentially the shaping of a tree so that it conforms to the space around it and, in the case of a fruit tree, so that its crop may be picked with ease. Pruning falls into two categories: formative, which is the pruning carried out during the first few years in order to train a young tree, and maintenance, which is the

How a tree produces fruit

▶ **SPUR-BEARING VARIETIES** Most apples and pears produce their fruit on short branches called spurs. The spurs form naturally, but part of the aim of pruning is to encourage the tree to produce a greater number. Clearly evident in early spring are the fat blossom buds in clusters on the spurs, and the flat growth buds that will break to form non-flowering leafy shoots.

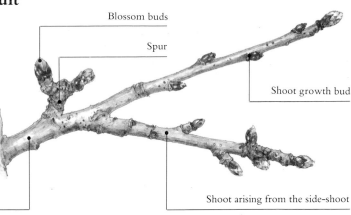

Blossom buds

Spur

Shoot growth bud

Side-shoot from main trunk

Shoot arising from the side-shoot

◀ **FLOWERING TIME** Flowers and then fruit are borne in clusters at the bases of the side-shoots or spurs. Much pruning of apples and pears involves cutting back to a prescribed point relative to this basal cluster, which encourages the spur to branch and so produce more buds the following year, while restricting the amount of leaf growth the tree makes relative to the fruit produced.

▶ **TIP-BEARING VARIETIES** Some types of apple and pear produce fruit at the tips of the branches. 'Rome Beauty', 'Granny Smith', 'Cortland', and 'Tydeman's Red' are tip-bearers but also are spur-bearers. On these forms, prune half the branches in alternate years.

annual pruning of a trained tree to maintain its cropping efficiency. Techniques of both formative (some nurseries prepare their plants) and maintenance pruning vary according to the type of fruit tree in question.

There are, however, a number of more general points that are best discussed here. First, to grasp the principles of pruning, it helps to understand the means by which fruit trees bear their fruit. Generally, the bud that develops at the base of a leaf in any given year will do one of two things. Either it grows out to form a long leafy shoot or it forms a short shoot or spur bearing a blossom bud (or fruit

bud as it is called). Sometimes the bud at the leaf base remains dormant for one or more years and sometimes it forms a blossom bud straightaway, without undergoing a second season's growth. If a tree is growing vigorously, most of the buds grow into leafy shoots; if it is growing more weakly, most tend to become plump blossom-bearing spurs. Pruning tends to encourage shoot growth and so hard pruning will reduce cropping; yet without pruning the whole plant will soon become a tangled, unkempt mass of branches. Very hard or very light pruning should therefore be avoided for the best results. The aim is to

Tree Fruit

Fans: plums, apricots, peaches, nectarines, cherries, figs

Fans can be grown trained against horizontal wires arranged free-standing in fence style, but it is very much better for them to be grown with the support and shelter of a wall. Shown here is the basic method for establishing a fan, with variations for peaches, and nectarines. The pruning of each tree is described under the individual entries.

Arrange a series of horizontal wires spaced 2ft./60cm. apart. Plant the young tree or one-year whip in suitably prepared soil in early spring, or fall in milder zones.

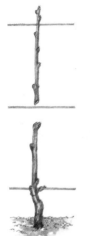
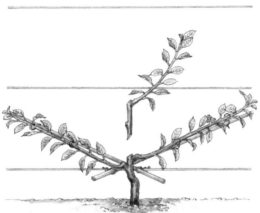

▲ **I THE SPRING AFTER PLANTING** Cut the main stem just above a bud positioned about 2ft./60cm. above soil level, choosing one that has at least two other buds below it, one facing left and one facing right. (If the plant is a one-year-old tree with side-shoots, likewise cut above two oppositely facing side-shoots.)

▲ **2 THE FOLLOWING SUMMER** Tie in the side-shoots to the wires at an angle of 45°, using canes to give added support (these side-shoots will form the lowest ribs of the fan), and cut the main stem back to the point immediately above where the uppermost side-shoot emerges.

▲ **Peach/nectarine** Treat as described left, but in addition cut all side-shoots emerging from the ribs at a point just above one leaf from their bases.

▶ **3 SPRING, 2ND YEAR** Cut back the two ribs to just above a bud about 15in./40cm. from the base of each rib, leaving the rib with at least four buds on it.

balance shoot growth and blossom bud development.

For tip-bearing apples, see previous page. Plums bear all of their fruit on one- and two-year-old shoots, and should be pruned as little as possible because they respond very vigorously, producing masses of leafy shoots. Among other pit fruit, peaches and nectarines fruit mainly on one-year-old wood, whereas sweet cherries fruit only on two-year-old shoots. Their pruning methods should therefore be adjusted. Trees that are growing too vigorously and producing too much leafy growth in proportion to fruit can be slowed down not only by pruning but also by tying down some of the branches to below the horizontal; this will limit sap flow and often induce fruit buds to form instead of leaves. With apples, although free-standing trees are normally pruned in the winter, summer pruning (as is usual with cordons, page

Tree Fruit

▲ 4 SUMMER, 2ND YEAR

Choose three side-shoots emerging from each rib – one from below, and two, spaced about 4–6in./10–15cm. apart, from above. Cut back any other shoots to one leaf. Tie the selected shoots to the support wires so they radiate outward in a fan.

▲ 5 SPRING, 3RD YEAR You

will now have eight ribs to your fan, and in this spring cut each back to a point above an upward-facing bud, leaving about 2½ft./75cm. of the previous season's growth.

◀ 6 THE FAN IN SUMMER

Tie in the extension growth on these ribs to the support wires and also tie in new shoots systematically to fill in the spaces between the ribs. Follow further training and pruning methods as described under the entries for each tree.

226) will also restrict growth by removing a proportion of the foliage and so limiting the supply of nutrients to the roots.

PROBLEMS AND DISEASES

A common problem with fruit trees is a tendency to biennial bearing, in which a crop is produced only every other year or even less frequently in very cold regions, such as Zones 2–3. A few cultivars are inherently prone to uneven bearing but in others it may be induced by stress. If a tree that has hitherto cropped annually begins to do so biennially, it can sometimes be restored to its previous habit by careful feeding and watering and by pruning only lightly. For regional advice in the USA on fruit training, pruning and cultivars, consult County Extension Specialists.

Fruit trees are subject to rather more than their fair share of pests and diseases and often little can be done to prevent attacks. Tar oil should be sprayed on the dormant plants as a regular routine in winter to kill eggs and adults of pests overwintering on the bark and, of course, damaged or dead branches should be cut away promptly. Damaged fruit within reach should be removed before the inevitable decay fungi become established on them. But, while I believe that young trees should be given protection from aphids, mildew, scab, and other problems, old-established trees can by and large be left to their own devices. Even canker, the most serious disease on most types of tree, can be tolerated in moderation.

Tree Fruit

Bushes: apples, pears, plums

Plant the young tree or one-year plant in suitably prepared soil in spring, or fall in milder areas.

▲ **I THE SPRING AFTER PLANTING** Cut the main stem just above a bud. The height of this bud depends on the type of tree being planted, and more information is given under the individual entries. The chosen bud should have three or four other buds or side-shoots below it on the stem; these will develop into the main branches.

▲ **ONE-YEAR-OLD TREE** If the plant already has side-shoots, in the spring after planting, cut the main stem at a point above three or four principal side-shoots. Cut these back by about half for an **apple** or **pear**, two thirds for a **plum**, to a point just above an upward-facing bud. Cut off all other side-shoots flush with the main stem.

▲ **2 NEWLY PRUNED** The new tree will look like this. Some nurseries send prepared trees.

◀ **4 APPLES AND PEARS** In subsequent winters, cut the previous season's extension growth on the main branches back by half, and cut side-shoots to just above four buds from their bases. Remove any shoots emerging from the main stem.

▶ **3 THE NEXT WINTER** Cut back the most vigorous of the shoots by half to two thirds of the previous season's growth, just above an upward-facing bud. Cut inward-pointing shoots hard back to very short lengths. Remove new shoots emerging from the main stem. For a **plum**, pruning and training is now complete.

◀ **5 AFTER ANNUAL PRUNING** The tree will look quite sparse, with very short side-shoots.

Apple

The most popular garden tree fruit, the easiest to grow, available in the greatest number of varieties, and with the widest range of size, form, and pruning options. There are libraries of books on apple culture, so I have restricted myself to those aspects that I believe to be of relevance to the majority of gardeners.

SOIL Most, but least successful in very heavy, cold, and wet clays, and in extremes of acidity or alkalinity.

SITUATION Full sun to light shade, although the best – and best-ripened crops will always be in full sun. Very windy sites, hilly and low-lying areas that trap frosts in spring should be avoided. Most gardens today have room for only a few tree fruits, which can receive shelter from surrounding dwellings. Zones 4–7.

WATERING AND FEEDING Modern trees on restricted rootstocks should be fed and mulched at least until well established, and preferably permanently. In early spring, apply a balanced rose or other potash-rich fertilizer and a mulch. Old and long-established trees should be self-sufficient, if cropping satisfactorily.

PRUNING Old trees producing adequate crops should be pruned as little as possible, because any cutting back will stimulate masses of twiggy growth which will itself then require pruning. The occasional cutting out of damaged and crossing branches in winter should be all that is required on old trees. Even cankered branches may be left, unless there are young and unaffected trees nearby, or if old trees are very seriously diseased, for many old varieties are highly canker prone and yet still crop satisfactorily.

Pruning is very important, however, on young trees and varies considerably depending on the growing system employed. There are three main training and pruning methods widely applicable in gardens: the restricted systems of cordon and espalier, and the free-standing bush. Once a restricted form is established, the tree will need regular annual pruning to maintain its shape; this pruning is described here under cordons, but applies to other restricted forms, too. In general, it is better to be a little late rather than early with the regular pruning, as there may be considerable further growth which will itself need pruning in early fall.

BUSHES Follow the steps opposite, noting that in step 1 the height of the first cut varies with the rootstock used: trees grafted on the dwarfing rootstocks M.27 or M.9 should be cut above a bud about 2ft./60cm. above soil level; those grafted on rootstocks M.26 or MM.106 should be cut above a bud about 2½ft./75cm. above soil level. The pruning regime for trees trained as bushes is less precise than for the restricted forms; in general, the shoots on very vigorously growing trees should be pruned by slightly less than half, those on weakly growing ones by slightly more.

CORDONS Follow the steps illustrated overleaf. When the main stem has reached about 6in./15cm. above the limit of its allotted space, cut off the tip in early summer just above a conveniently placed bud. Thereafter prune it annually in late summer to leave about 1cm/½in. of the current season's extension growth.

As well as cordons, there is also available a type of upright apple tree that may be confused with them, the spur-type tree and its

Espaliered apple

Apple

Cordons: apples

Establish a system of horizontal support wires spaced 2ft./60cm. apart. Plant the tree in prepared soil in early spring, or fall in milder areas.

▶ **I NEWLY PLANTED**
Immediately after planting, tie the main stem at an angle of 45°, and prune all side-shoots longer than 4in./10cm. to a point just above the third bud from their bases.

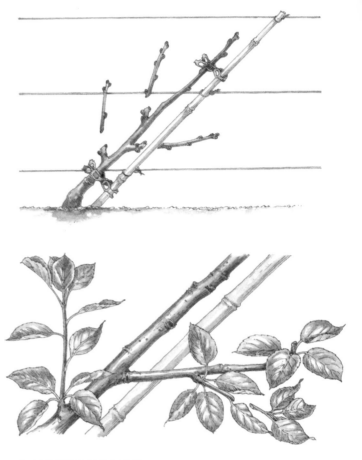

▲ **2 REGULAR PRUNING**
Thereafter every year in late summer prune the side-shoots as follows. Cut side-shoots longer than 8–10in./20–25cm. and growing directly from the main stem at a point just above the third leaf above the basal cluster.

▲ **3 AT THE SAME TIME,** cut shoots arising from the side-shoots at a point just above the first leaf beyond the basal cluster.

variants. These trees have been developed from naturally short-branched mutants; they form more compact branches, begin to bear early and require less pruning.

ESPALIERS Follow the steps opposite, repeating the stages to train further pairs of arms until the required height is reached. Once it is reached, prune the tip of the main stem as described for that of a cordon. At the same time (late summer), prune all the side-shoots on the espalier arms exactly as described for pruning cordons (steps 2 and 3).

Some nurseries offer apples trained as "step-over" trees for growing alongside paths or to edge vegetable patches. These are, in effect, single-arm espaliers and should be pruned as for cordons (steps 2 and 3).

COMMON PROBLEMS Scab; mildew; canker; fruit rots; honey fungus; bitter pit; aphids; apple sawfly; codling moth; borers.

Espaliers: apples

Establish a system of horizontal support wires spaced 2ft./60cm. apart. Plant the tree in prepared soil in spring, or fall in milder areas.

▶ **I NEWLY PLANTED**
Immediately after planting, cut the main stem: the place for the cut should be slightly higher than the first wire to come both just above a bud, and also a short distance above where two other buds, positioned facing left and right, occur close together.

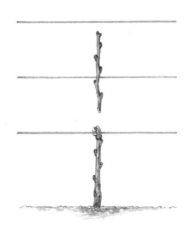

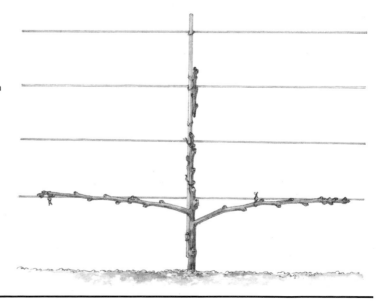

◀ **2 THE NEXT SUMMER** Tie the shoot that arises from the top bud vertically. Tie the shoots arising from the two other buds at angles of 45° (not at this stage horizontally). Cut all side-shoots to a point just above six leaves from their bases.

▶ **3 THE FOLLOWING WINTER** Untie the first pair of "arms" and pull them down to retie them horizontally along the lowest wire. Repeat step 1, cutting the main stem to form a second pair of arms in the same way. Cut all side-shoots pruned the previous summer to a point just above three buds from their bases. Once the espalier is formed, prune the side-shoots as described for cordons opposite (steps 2 and 3). Prune the tip as described for the tips of cordons (page 225).

Apple – Pear

PROPAGATION Impossible from cuttings.

TROUBLESHOOTING Old apple trees are best left to their own devices, if possible. If branches must be removed through disease or storm damage, make clean cuts to just above the basal collar to aid the healing process, for apples are particularly prone to invasion by wood rotting fungi. They are also very prone to honey fungus attack and when a tree is felled, the stump should be removed or ground out if feasible.

Trees that are cropping inadequately may be affected by a variety of factors. If blossoms are produced freely, poor pollination is the explanation and this may be because of the lack of a suitable pollinator variety nearby (or perhaps one has recently been removed); or because the site is very windy and exposed, and the pollen and pollinating insects are being blown away. Provision of some shelter may help. If blossoming is also poor, then some pruning may help. The best plan is, in summer, to cut out entire branches rather than trim away pieces from the periphery, and then gradually establish a suitable pruning regime.

Trees growing in lawns may be suffering from competition with the grass; remedy this by cutting out a circular area approximately 3ft./1m. in diameter, and then apply a rose or other potash-rich fertilizer and a mulch in early spring. Conversely, an overvigorous tree – especially one producing abundant foliage but little fruit – may be suppressed by grassing up to the base of its trunk. (Mulch may attract mice.)

RATE OF GROWTH AND ULTIMATE SIZE While old trees are likely to be growing on their own roots and to attain various, largely unpredictable sizes, modern trees are all grafted on selected rootstocks which dictate their ultimate height regardless of variety. The commonest rootstocks and the approximate sizes the trees will attain are: M.27 6ft./2m.; M.9 8–10ft./2.5–3m.; M.26 10–11½ft./3–3.5m.; MM.106 16ft./5m. In general, the more dwarfing the rootstock, the better the soil and growing conditions it requires, the longer it will require staking, and the earlier it will reach its maximum height. Rootstocks M.27 and M.9 require permanent stakes.

Pear

With some justification, pears are generally thought to be more difficult to grow than apples, and take longer to come into full cropping. As trees, they are certainly more tender but growing them as cordons or espaliers offers them wall protection, and they are very responsive to these forms. And while there are no rootstocks as dwarfing as those of apples, the modern pear tree is much more manageable than its forebears and quicker to mature.

SOIL Most, but least successful in very dry or water-logged soils, and in extremes of acidity or alkalinity.

SITUATION Full sun to light shade, although the best – and best-ripened – crops will always be in full sun. In cold and windy gardens, especially at altitudes of above about 330ft./100m., some shelter will be needed and it may be more convenient to grow the trees as cordons or espaliers. Zones 5–7; also parts of 4.

Pear 'Conference'

WATERING AND FEEDING Modern trees should be fed and mulched at least until well established and preferably permanently. Apply a balanced rose or other potash-rich fertilizer and a mulch in early spring. Old and long-established trees should be self-sufficient if cropping satisfactorily.

PRUNING Pears are pruned in the same ways as apples.

COMMON PROBLEMS Scab; mildew; canker; fruit rots; aphids; leaf blister mite; pear midge; fireblight.

TROUBLESHOOTING See Apples. When attempting to solve the problems of poor pollination, it is often overlooked that the English pear variety 'Conference', although self-fertile, will crop very much more satisfactorily if a pollinator variety is also present.

RATE OF GROWTH AND ULTIMATE SIZE While old trees are likely to be growing on their own roots and may attain a very large size (up to 50ft./15m. tall), modern trees are usually grafted on the rootstock 'Quince C'; although on poor soils, the slightly more vigorous 'Quince A' should be chosen. These will each give plants approximately 13–20ft./4–6m. tall. A Pacific NW rootstock OH × F513 produces a tree 13ft./4m. tall.

Plum 'Victoria'

Plum

Plums are not difficult to grow, provided you can offer them a sunny situation and good soil. Some of the European varieties are self-fertile, so only one tree is required; against that must be set the fact that no truly dwarfing rootstock is available. Japanese plums generally require another tree for cross-pollination.

SOIL Most, but least successful in very dry soils; tolerant of fairly heavy soils, provided there is no tendency to water-logging.

SITUATION Full sun to very light shade; warmth is essential for good ripening, so training the trees as fans against a warm wall is an ideal method of culture. Zones 5–7 and parts of 4.

WATERING AND FEEDING Modern trees should be fed and mulched at least until well established and preferably permanently. Apply a balanced rose or other potash-rich fertilizer and a mulch in early spring; give only a very light dressing for wall-trained plants. Old and long-established trees should generally be self-sufficient, if cropping satisfactorily.

PRUNING All pruning of plums must be performed in spring, not in the fall and winter when pruning wounds are liable to be invaded by the fungus causing perennial canker. In general, established plums need very little pruning because they simply respond by producing masses of dense twiggy growth. The occasional cutting out of damaged and crossing branches in spring should be all that is required on old trees. Pruning young trees is very important, however, for a few years. Several training methods are possible; the bush (vase shape, central or modified leader), and fan. On all types of tree, cut out any suckers that may arise.

BUSHES Follow steps 1–3 on page 224. In step 1, cut the main stem above a bud about 3ft./1m. above soil level. By step 4 the shape is established, and the side-shoots will become the main branches. From then on little pruning should be done other than occasionally thinning out the tree in spring if necessary.

Plum

Fans: plums, apricots, sweet cherries

Ensure shoots are evenly spaced by removing some side-shoots at pruning time

Fill gaps in the structure by leaving some side-shoots unpruned at pruning time

THE ESTABLISHED FAN A good plum, apricot or sweet cherry fan should have well spaced side-shoots with no big gaps. Once it is established (see pages 222–3), prune annually in spring and after cropping. Remove or prune side-shoots as described under the plum entry.

Fruiting shoot, pruned in spring and again after picking the fruit

FANS Follow the steps on page 222. Once the fan is established, annual pruning is as follows, and takes place in spring. Cut out any shoots facing directly toward or directly away from the wall. Cut out excess side-shoots to leave spaces of about 4in./10cm. between each one. Cut the side-shoots remaining at a point just above six leaves from their bases (unless there are significant gaps in the fan structure, when these side-shoots may be allowed to elongate to form more ribs).

After picking the fruit in late summer, cut back further those side-shoots already shortened, to three leaves from their bases. Tie in any unsupported shoots.

COMMON PROBLEMS Silver leaf; fruit rots; rust; bacterial canker; aphids; plum fruit moth; perennial canker; borers; leaf curl.

PROPAGATION Impossible from cuttings.

TROUBLESHOOTING No matter how old and gnarled, mature plum trees should be pruned as little as possible. Simply remove any dead or severely damaged branches by cutting them back to their bases in spring. As with apples, over-vigorous trees may be induced to produce less foliage and more fruit by grassing up to the base of the trunk. The wood of plums is brittle and readily breaks with the weight of fruit, so it is sensible to support wide-spreading branches of old trees with wooden props. Trees showing signs of silver leaf disease should be left for at least two seasons, for they often recover. If the disease is spreading, however, and especially if its effects appear on suckers, the tree should be felled and destroyed. For other problems, see Apple.

RATE OF GROWTH AND ULTIMATE SIZE While old trees are likely to be growing on their own roots and of unpredictable size, modern garden trees are almost invariably grafted on one of two selected rootstocks, 'St Julien A' or 'Pixy', which will produce trees 20–23ft./6–7m. or 13ft./4m. tall respectively.

Peach, Nectarine, Apricot

These three relatives of plums all have a reputation for being tender, the apricot especially so because of its early flowering and consequent exposure to late frost. I am convinced, however, that these trees – although benefiting from shelter – are much tougher than generally reckoned and worth trying in many gardens.

SOIL Most, but best in moist, deep, rich loams – preferably slightly alkaline for apricots, slightly acid for peaches and nectarines.

SITUATION Full sun to very light shade; warmth is essential for good ripening, so training the trees as fans against a warm wall is an ideal method of culture. Zones 5–7.

WATERING AND FEEDING Modern trees should be fed and mulched at least until well established and preferably permanently. Apply a balanced rose or other potash-rich fertilizer and a mulch in early spring; give only a very light dressing of fertilizer for wall-trained plants. Old and long-established trees should be self-sufficient, if cropping satisfactorily.

PRUNING All pruning must be performed in spring, because in fall and winter the pruning wounds are liable to be invaded by the fungus causing perennial canker disease.

PEACHES, NECTARINES AND APRICOTS, BUSHES Train the plant as described on page 224. Thereafter, each spring, cut out any overcrowded or crossing branches and up to one quarter of the two- and three-year-old wood, cutting in each case back to the point of emergence of a young, vigorous shoot. This ensures a supply of healthy new shoots on which the fruit will be borne.

PEACHES AND NECTARINES, FANS Follow the steps on pages 222–3, noting that in step 2 all side-shoots emerging from the ribs should be cut to a point just above one leaf. Once step 6 is reached, continue as follows. During that summer, side-shoots will arise from the ribs. Select one shoot for about every 4in./10cm. of rib, and leave this unpruned until it reaches about 1½ft./45cm.; then pinch out the tip. All other side-shoots should be cut back to one leaf. The framework of the fan is now established, and regular annual pruning is as described overleaf.

As fruits form during the summer, pinch out some of them every year to leave one for approximately every 8in./20cm. of shoot length. If possible, peg back the foliage to allow the ripening fruits maximum exposure to the sun.

APRICOTS, FANS Train as for peaches, following the steps on pages 222–3 and the notes above. Once the fan is established, prune annually in spring as for a Plum.

COMMON PROBLEMS Perennial canker; fruit rots; aphids; borers.

TROUBLESHOOTING See Plums.

RATE OF GROWTH AND ULTIMATE SIZE See Plums.

Peach 'Peregrine'

Peach, Nectarine

Pruning fans: peaches, nectarines

▶ **I SPRING** Identify the shoots to be pruned. These will be shoots made the previous year, and at pruning time they will be bearing flowers. If you are confident of what you are doing, leave the leading shoots unpruned (although they will also be bearing flowers); if not, prune all shoots bearing flowers.

Shoot to be pruned

Leading shoot

Main rib

Growth bud left at base of shoot

Shoot to be pruned (as shown below), flowering

Main rib

Flower buds

Growth bud left in center of shoot

◀ **PINCH OUT GROWTH BUDS** Ignore the flower buds, but pinch out the *growth* buds (clusters of young leaves) on these shoots to leave one at the tip, one at the base, and one in the center. Once side-shoots have developed from the growth buds, pinch them out to a point just above six leaves from their bases. This restriction of new growth concentrates the plant's energy into producing a crop of fruit.

Growth bud left at tip of shoot

▶ **2 LATE SUMMER** After picking the fruit, cut back each fruited shoot to just above its lowest side-shoot: this will then form the replacement fruiting shoot for next year's crop.

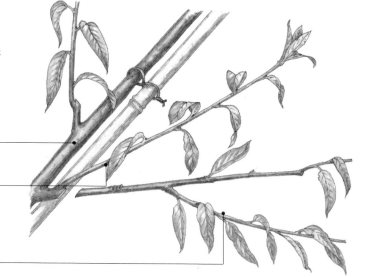

Main rib

Shoot to be pruned the next spring, as described above

Elongated shoot from growth bud, now fruited

Cherry

There are two main groups of garden cherries. The warmth-requiring sweet cherries need protection from birds, and are now very much easier to grow than formerly with the introduction of self-fertile varieties (most notably 'Stella', and 'Lapins' and the two dwarfs, 'Meteor' and 'North Star', whose fruits are good fresh or cooked). The hardier acid or sour cherries should survive in Zones 4–5.

SOIL Most, but least successful in very dry soils; tolerant of fairly heavy soils, provided there is no tendency to water-logging.

SITUATION SWEET CHERRIES Full sun to very light shade; warmth is essential for good ripening so training the trees as fans against a warm wall is an ideal method of culture. Zones 6–7.

SOUR CHERRIES Full sun to moderate shade, ideally trained against a north-facing wall if available. Zones 4–7.

WATERING AND FEEDING Modern trees should be fed and mulched at least until well established and preferably permanently. Apply a balanced rose or other potash-rich fertilizer and a mulch in early spring; give only a very light dressing for wall-trained plants. Old and long-established trees should generally be self-sufficient, if cropping satisfactorily.

PRUNING As with plums, all pruning of cherries must be performed in spring and summer, not in fall and winter when the pruning wounds are liable to be invaded by the fungus causing perennial canker. Cut out any suckers arising from rootstocks.

SWEET CHERRIES, BUSHES Train and prune as for Plums.

SWEET CHERRIES, FANS Train the tree as for a Peach, following the steps on pages 222–3 and the additional notes under the Peach entry; then prune it as for a fan-trained Plum (see pages 229–30).

ACID CHERRIES, FANS Train the tree as for a Peach, following the steps on pages 222–3 and the additional notes under the Peach

Cherry 'Morello'

Pruning fans: acid cherries

LATE SUMMER After cropping, cut back the fruited shoots to just above a new side-shoot close to its base. Tie this side-shoot to the support wires; this will form a replacement shoot to bear the next year's crop.

Side-shoot on which next year's fruit will be borne

Fruited shoot

Cherry – Fig

entry. Once the fan is established, prune as follows. In spring, cut out any shoots growing directly towards or away from the wall. Remove shoots to leave one for every 8–10cm/3–4in of rib, and tie the shoots remaining to the wires. Fruit will form on these shoots during the summer, and side-shoots will develop. After cropping, cut back each fruited shoot to just above a side-shoot close to its base. Tie in this side-shoot; it will form a replacement shoot to bear the next year's crop.

COMMON PROBLEMS Silver leaf; bacterial canker; aphids; birds.

PROPAGATION Impossible from cuttings.

TROUBLESHOOTING See Plum.

RATE OF GROWTH AND ULTIMATE SIZE Old trees are likely to be growing on a rootstock such as 'F12/1', a selection of the wild *Prunus avium*, which is perfectly capable of producing a tree 40–50ft./12–15m. tall. On the rootstock 'Colt', a bush tree rarely exceeds about 20ft./6m. 'GM 61' produces a tree about 13ft./4m. Consult catalogues for new genetic dwarf introductions.

Fig

Although there are other, tender species of *Ficus*, it is the moderately hardy, deciduous, fruiting fig that is commonly grown.

SOIL Most, but for a good crop a poor soil is needed and the plant is best confined within a bottomless cube. Line a 3ft./1m. square pit with paving slabs and fill this with a mixture of half and half by volume garden soil and limy rubble. Or grow in a tub.

SITUATION Full sun or very light shade. Figs benefit from wall protection in most areas. In the North, figs are regularly wrapped in burlap in fall, but in milder areas of Zone 7, may survive winter uncovered. Zones 7–10.

WATERING AND FEEDING Mulch in fall and spring. Feed with a very light dressing of balanced rose or other potash-rich fertilizer in mid-spring. Water copiously during the summer.

Figs

WINTER In northern climates figs will not ripen within a single season, but overwinter as tiny embryo fruits borne at the tips of the shoots. In the autumn some of the half-formed fruits shrivel and drop off, but by midwinter many more are evident on the plant, and will mature the following summer. Pruning in mid-spring has to be a balance between removing enough shoots to encourage new growth, yet not cutting off too many of the growing figs.

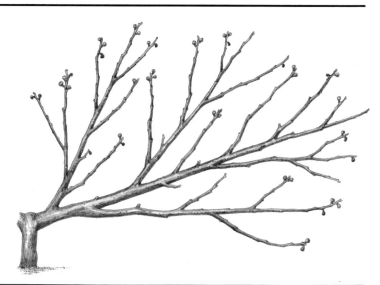

Fig

PRUNING Freestanding plants do not require any pruning other than the removal in spring of damaged shoots and the occasional cutting out of diseased or overcrowded branches. Wall trained plants do need pruning annually, in spring and early summer.

There are two principles behind the pruning of fan-trained figs. The first is that, unlike the other fruits discussed where a main framework provides a permanent structure, the fig's ribs need to be renewed gradually, ideally over a five- to six-year cycle. The plant will produce strong new main stems either from its base or from the main trunk, and a proportion of these should be retained each year and the oldest removed. The aim is a fan of five to eight main stems per plant.

The second principle of pruning is that in northern climates figs will not ripen within a single season, so those that mature in one summer passed the previous winter as tiny embryo fruits borne towards the shoot tips (see below left). Pruning is done to maintain the fan shape, encouraging new shoots to arise, without cutting off too many embryo fruits.

Train the fan initially as for a Peach, following the steps on page 222–3 and the additional notes on page 231. Once established, prune the fan in mid-spring: cut damaged side-shoots and any growing directly toward or away from the wall back to one bud above their bases. Then cut alternate side-shoots back to one bud from their bases, selecting those with the fewest embryo fruits as the shoots to remove. Tie in the remainder to the support wires, leaving a spacing of at least 6in./15cm. between adjacent side-shoots to allow for the growth of the very large leaves.

In early summer, shorten the newest side-shoots (with no fruits yet) to five or six leaves from their bases. This will stimulate the production of more, potentially fruit-bearing, side-shoots. At the same time, tie in one or two strong new main stems arising from the base or main trunk, to make a maximum of five to eight.

On plants mature enough to have their full quota of main stems, each year in mid-spring cut back one or two of the oldest main stems to the main trunk or the base of the plant. Also remove up to one quarter of the oldest side-shoots, cutting them back to their bases. Prune alternate side-shoots as before. It may be necessary to retie several of the main stems and older side-shoots to ensure that both old and new are spaced as equidistantly as possible, and that all contribute to the structure of the fan. Prune and train the plant in early summer as before.

COMMON PROBLEMS Coral spot.

PROPAGATION Semi-ripe cuttings in summer.

TROUBLESHOOTING Old and misshapen freestanding plants will regenerate very satisfactorily if cut back to the base in spring, although if the entire plant requires renewal, the work should be spread over two years. Neglected fan-trained plants may have eight or more stems arising from the base. One or two should be removed and the plant progressively renewed.

SIZE A freestanding fig tree not seriously cut back by frost will reach about $10 \times 6\frac{1}{2}$–10ft./3×2–3m. after five years, and perhaps 16×16ft./5×5m. after twenty. Wall-trained plants are pruned within these limits according to the space available.

Fig trained against a wall

ACKNOWLEDGEMENTS

The publisher thanks the following photographers and organizations for their kind permission to reproduce the photographs in this book:

Eric Crichton: 5, 28, 34 above, 36 above, 38, 39, 44 below, 47, 49 below, 50, 55, 58, 61, 70 above, 77 below, 85, 87, 91, 98, 104, 105, 110, 119 above, 123, 125, 126 above, 129, 130, 132, 140, 142–3, 146 above, 150, 153 above, 154, 172, 176 below, 180–181, 186, 187 below, 197, 199, 208, 212–5, 219, 225.

Derek Gould: 29 above, 124.

Andrew Lawson: 27, 31, 32, 41, 49 above, 54, 60, 66, 72 below, 74, 92, 107, 111, 115, 117, 121 above and center, 126 below, 131, 135, 137 above, 138, 155, 157, 159, 163 below, 164, 169, 171, 174, 176 above, 178, 184, 203, 206, 216–7, 233, 235.

S & O Mathews: 2–3, 4–5, 12–13, 29 below, 34 below, 36 below, 42, 43, 46, 57, 59 below, 72 above, 80–1, 95, 100–1, 109, 112, 121 below, 127–8, 133, 147, 156, 161, 166–7, 173, 179, 187 above, 190–1, 211.

Tania Midgley: 75.

Philippe Perdereau: 46 below, 51, 77 above, 146 below, 198, 201.

Photos Horticultural: 26, 33, 37, 67, 69, 70 below, 71, 108, 118, 119 below, 134, 137 below, 149, 153 below, 162, 163 above, 170, 175, 177, 185, 188, 210, 228–231.

Harry Smith Collection: 53.

The publishers would like to thank Valerie Buckingham, Wendy Dallas and Margaret Daykin for editorial help; Sally Powell for design assistance; Judith Harte for proofreading; Capel Manor Horticultural and Environmental Centre for help providing reference for the illustrations.

Index compiled by Indexing Specialists, Hove, East Sussex BN3 2DJ